Learning from Museums

Learning from Museums

Visitor Experiences and the Making of Meaning

JOHN H. FALK AND LYNN D. DIERKING

ALTAMIRA
PRESS

ALTAMIRA PRESS

A Division of
ROWMAN & LITTLEFIELD PUBLISHERS, INC.
Lanham • Boulder • New York • Toronto • Plymouth, UK

ALTAMIRA PRESS
A division of Rowman & Littlefield Publishers, Inc.
4501 Forbes Boulevard, Suite 200
Lanham, MD 20706

Estover Road
Plymouth PL6 7PY
United Kingdon

British Library Cataloguing in Publication Information Available

Library of Congress Cataloging-in-Publication Data
Falk, John H. (John Howard), 1948–
    Learning from museums : visitor experiences and the making of meaning / John H.
Falk and Lynn D. Dierking
        p.   cm. — (American Association for State and Local History book series)
        Includes bibliographical references and index.
        ISBN 0-7425-0294-5 (cl : alk. paper) — ISBN 0-7425-0295-3 (pbk : alk. paper)
    1. Museums—Educational aspects.   2. Museum attendance.   3. Museum exhibits.
4. Experiential learning.   5. Active learning.   6. Non-formal education.   I. Dierking,
Lynn D. (Lynn Diane), 1956–   II. Title.   III. Series.

AM7.F34   2000
069'.134—dc2100-021113

Printed in the United States of America

∞ ™ The paper used in this publication meets the minimum requirements of
American National Standard for Information Sciences—Permanence of Paper
for Printed Library Materials, ANSI/NISO Z39.48–1992.

Contents

Foreword

Back in the early 1960s, while I was in graduate school trying to pick up some research tools and findings that would help me develop more effective museum exhibitions, I came across Melton's pioneering 1935 monograph, *Problems of Installation in Museums of Art.* I was impressed. His research designs seemed imaginative, his results fascinating, his presentation clear. The Melton research suggested, at least to me, that a science of exhibitry might be possible. A set of general principles could be developed, and if conscientiously followed, more effective exhibitions produced. But with a few lonely exceptions, I didn't find much more museum-visitor research to feed my interest. The well seemed to run dry.

As an alternative, I turned to the fairly extensive research in instructional filmmaking that sprouted in the armed services during the Second World War to see if I could find a deeper spring of analogous examples and inspiration. It became clear from these studies that the hope of developing general principles—if you will, a science of educational filmmaking—was swamped by the uncontrolled variables of the art of the filmmaker. Few significant results were reported in this literature.

Even in the midst of this disappointment, there was a splendid lesson to be learned: if you tried out drafts of the script and storyboards, and later rough edits of the film, on representatives of the target audience, you could rework the material and improve the effectiveness of the completed piece. So as the dream of a science of film- and exhibition-making receded, the practical notion of prototyping to improve a specific exhibition came into focus for me. There seemed to be lots of ways to make a particular exhibition better. Thus I was introduced into the not-yet-professionalized world of formative evaluation. It served me well for many years.

When it became clear over time that the visitor, in addition to the exhibitor or programmer, contributed to the construction of his or her learning out of what he or she brought to the museum, the whole notion of what it took to create effective exhibitions and programs became even more complicated. Organizing the learning experience was no longer the exclusive responsibility of the museum; it had to be shared with the visitor. And at about the same time, some of us developed a deep philosophical commitment to offering more open-ended experiences where visitors were even encouraged to make whatever meaning they wanted to out of our offerings.

But my dream of a set of explicit and universal principles that could be applied in developing exhibitions and programs still seemed a naive, or at best distant, expectation. It turns out that I may have been looking for the wrong things in the wrong places.

As John Falk and Lynn Dierking suggest in this book, rather than immediately seeking guiding principles to improve our practice, we may need instead to step back and look at the nature of learning in a broader and more holistic way, to immerse ourselves in the research literatures of psychology, anthropology, sociology, and evolutionary biology, in addition to our familiar visitor studies. From that broader perspective, they offer reassurance that creating a set of guiding principles is likely to be much easier and the principles more valid.

In *Learning from Museums,* as in their earlier book, *The Museum Experience* (1992), John and Lynn have gone to a lot of trouble to embed practical issues in these broader theoretical and research contexts. With their help, we can begin to understand more about what is really going on during the learning process in general, information that can then be applied to the specifics of museums. For once we have a better understanding of how museum visitors make sense of these experiences, we can make more informed decisions about how to create the best possible exhibitions and programs for them.

Although none of this solid book is to be missed, practitioners should find the anecdotally rich chapters 8 and 10 particularly useful. In chapter 8, the authors flesh out a Contextual Model of Learning (a more refined version of the Interactive Experience Model from their earlier book) with eight key factors that they feel influence learning and that need to be considered—as a checklist if you like—in creating and developing any exhibition or program plan. They then go on in chapter 10 to illustrate how their contextual model and influential factors can be applied "to make museum experiences better learning experiences." These chapters suggest that even if we still do not have all the answers, we have some strategies for asking good questions during the development process.

And John and Lynn are not alone. In recent work George Hein and Chandler Screven also strikingly demonstrate that we do not really have to wander about in the dark as if there were no clues to help us develop better museum exhibitions and programs, we just need to widen our lens and apply all the theoretical and practical tools now at our disposal for making sense out of the museum experience.

To offer a few examples, we now have a pretty clear idea from both a theoretical and a practical standpoint how to write text panels that communicate with most visitors. We have figured out how to preorganize a visitor's approach to an exhibition so that he or she can get more out of the experience. We have some clues about how to arrange exhibition components to capitalize on visitors' inclinations to interact with our offerings as part of a social unit. And there are dozens of other examples, as you will see in this book. So even if we have not achieved a true science of museum interpretation, we know a lot more about how to make better public museums than we did back in the 1960s.

For all these recent, substantive, and encouraging developments, there still seems to be a stubborn streak running through our profession that treats museum exhibitry and programming as a mysterious art, entirely dependent on the instincts and skills of the exhibitor and programmer, rather than being built on a growing common body of knowledge. For there is abundant evidence that few of us seem to be paying attention to what we already collectively know. Visitors are just as likely to find themselves frustrated and disappointed by an ineffective exhibition as stimulated and informed by one that really works, and the quality of educational programming seems just as uneven.

In these flawed exhibitions and programs, you can see where their creator is, inadvertently or deliberately, ignoring generally acknowledged rules of thumb or more sophisticated analytical systems like Falk and Dierking's. To return to the earlier examples, labels are too long, copy is not broken down into manageable paragraphs with helpful subheads, type is too small and low to be read by a person with bifocals, terms are obscure to a person new to the subject. The entrance to an exhibition fails to give any clue to what it is really about, what you might be expected to get out of it, how it is organized, and where a good place to start might be. An interactive unit, appealing to a family audience, does not allow room for all members of the family to gather around and participate, is structured as a solo activity, and makes few concessions to the different skills and strategies each member of the group brings to the experience. There are perfectly straightforward ways of dealing with each of these issues, abundantly supported by theoretical frameworks and accessible research findings, which this book illustrates. Yet a discouragingly large number of us seem not to be paying attention.

Especially disturbing are our colleagues who would not think of presenting information in exhibitions and programs that was not thoroughly grounded in the current research literature of their fields but who remain the most stubbornly inoculated from the influences of the learning theory and visitor studies literature. They just don't—or won't—get it.

None of this is meant to suggest that we have finally arrived at the moment when, by following a few rules, we automatically produce a great exhibition. The interpretive gifts of the exhibitor/programmer are certainly critical, and of course the visitor is probably more than 50 percent responsible for the outcomes of the experiences we try to orchestrate. But still it is becoming harder and harder, with all that we know or can easily dig up and absorb from this and Hein's and Screven's richly referenced books, to excuse the terrible gaffes we persist in making, and then fail to correct, in carrying out our public missions.

So the challenge is there. While we may never achieve the true science of museum learning I had fantasized back in the 1960s, we no longer need to wander around in the dark. We know a lot more than we did even a decade ago. As John and Lynn so clearly show us, we are beginning to have some of the insights and tools we need to make museums better learning environments. It is time we took those insights and tools seriously, incorporated them into our professional repertoire, and learned to use them consistently, thoughtfully, skillfully.

Michael Spock
Chapin Hall Center for Children
at the University of Chicago

Preface

Books are like mountaintops jutting out of the sea. Self-contained islands though they may seem, they are upthrusts of an underlying geography that is at once local and, for all that, a part of a universal pattern. And so, while they inevitably reflect a time and a place, they are part of a more general intellectual geography.
—Jerome Bruner, *Acts of Meaning*

First and foremost this is a book about learning. However, since a major point of the book is that all learning is contextual, we would argue that one cannot talk about learning except in relationship to some place and situation. We have chosen to investigate learning in that array of institutions that includes art, history, and natural history museums; science centers; historic homes; living history farms and forts; aquariums; zoos; arboretums; botanical gardens; and nature centers, collectively referred to by the generic term *museum*. Arguably much, if not most, of what we discuss here in relation to learning from museums directly relates to learning from other situations as well, but we will leave that leap to others. For the moment, we are content in our effort to try to synthesize a vast body of knowledge about how, why, and what people learn, mining research from across the social and biological sciences and considering its application to a relatively narrow slice of the world, the world of museums.

Some who read this book will no doubt have read our earlier book, *The Museum Experience,* and might wonder about the relationship of this book to the earlier volume. We consider this to be a sequel to, or at least an extension of, that earlier work. Toward the end of *The Museum Experience* we touched lightly on the issue of learning; in this book it is the major focus. In *The Museum Experience* we proposed a framework for organizing how one approached the topic of visitor learning and behavior in museums, referred to as the Interactive Experience Model. In this book we build on and extend that model, recasting it as the Contextual Model of Learning, a model that organizes our thinking regarding the complex nature of museum learning. Be forewarned, *The Museum Experience* was a general overview of a broad topic; the current book's intent is far more focused and technical owing to the complexity of what we are describing. Still, the two volumes were designed to complement one another, the first providing a broad overview of the visitor experience in museums, and this second volume focusing on one specific aspect of that experience, visitor learning and meaning-making from museums.

Throughout this book we approach learning from an evolutionary perspective. In this view, learning is the product of hundreds of millions of years of survival-oriented evolution, a continually refining capacity for humans and other animals to intelligently navigate an ever changing social, cultural, and physical world. We pay homage to the wonders of both biological and cultural evolution, which not only shape who we are as humans but also, and more importantly in terms of our topic, define the nature of learning. In this view, evolution is related to and influences not only the process of learning but also its products. In fact, one of the aspects of learning that make it so challenging to understand is that it is always a process and a product, a verb and a noun. Even that most fundamental of all learning products, memory, is actually an ephemeral, ever changing process, while at its heart it is the result of the concrete interaction of hundreds of thousands, even millions, of very real and tangible chemicals and cells within the brain. But what does this have to do with museums?

Increasingly museums can be described as public institutions for personal learning, places people seek out to satisfy their learning needs. One way to characterize the unique and special nature of the learning that occurs in museums is to emphasize the particularly free-choice nature of much, if not most, of that learning. Free-choice learning tends to be nonlinear, is personally motivated, and involves considerable choice on the part of the learner as to what to learn, as well as where and when to participate in learning. Therefore, throughout this book, we use the term *free-choice learning* to refer generically to the learning experiences that occur in and from places like museums, as well as those that occur while watching television, reading a newspaper, talking with friends, attending a play, or surfing the Internet. In our opinion, *free-choice* captures the underlying motivational and structural nature of the learning that occurs in and from such settings better than does the other frequently used term, *informal.*

Almost all museums share a commitment to providing enjoyable, public, free-choice learning opportunities through a similar array of educational media—exhibitions, programs, and presentations, augmented by print and broadcast media and, increasingly, by distance learning media such as the Internet. Almost all museums serve both the general public and organized groups such as schools, camp groups, and senior citizens. Thousands of museum professionals invest millions of hours and hundreds of millions of dollars each year to develop educational exhibitions, programs, performances, media presentations, books, catalogues, and web sites for the public. In turn, hundreds of millions of people visit museums each year, primarily to partake of these offerings, on the assumption that they will ultimately learn and find meaning. Do they?

We have been investigating learning in museums for a long time, certainly long enough to know many, if not most, of the pitfalls that can befall anyone intrepid enough to attempt to wrap his or her arms around such an elusive topic. Over the years, we have been variously quoted as saying that no one really knows whether or not anyone learns in museums, or that people only derive attitudinal benefits rather than cognitive ones, or that the primary outcomes derived from museum experiences are social. Although we might dispute these earlier interpretations, in this book we are here to say undeniably that *people do learn in museums*. They come to learn, to find meaning and connection, and they do learn, make meaning, and find connection. Historically, however, documenting this learning has proven challenging.

Elusive or not, learning in museums is now a more important topic than ever. A generation ago it was a topic of interest, but not importance, to the museum community; today it is a topic fundamental to the very essence of museum survival and success. Twenty to thirty years ago only a few took the time to ponder the challenges and rewards of investigating learning within free-choice learning settings. Today, virtually all in the museum community at least ponder, and many are investigating, the questions surrounding how people learn in museums. Why do people go to museums? In what ways do museums facilitate learning? And, in particular, what do people learn in museums?

We are not alone in this quest. Beginning with a modest base of researchers, initially joined by a few and now by many, our inquiries have been built upon, and continue to benefit from, the work of many others, both in the museum field and outside. In fact, among other things, this book is an effort to bring together the thoughts and findings of a diverse set of investigators from the fields of neuroscience; evolutionary biology; cognitive, experimental, developmental, social, and ecological psychology;

anthropology; ethology; behavioral ecology; education; communications; business; and, of course, museum studies. To the extent we have been successful in synthesizing this eclectic group of disciplines, we feel we have been successful in understanding and accurately presenting the story of museum learning. All of us have been guilty of viewing the world with too limited a lens. We feel it is time to change our lenses, to pan the camera back in time and space, and view learning as a panoramic, lifetime event, an effort to find and make meaning. Museum learning is a subset of a larger, ever evolving continuum of learning and meaning-making across the life span.

In the following pages we will attempt to describe the many facets of museum learning, using the Contextual Model of Learning as our map. We will first ground our exploration by sharing data from two museum experiences in chapter 1. Using the framework in chapters 2 through 4 we will investigate the general impact of personal experience and history, social and cultural overlays, and the effects of the physical world on what and how we learn. Throughout these chapters, we have judiciously inserted findings from the burgeoning field of neuroscience. Although focused on museums, these early chapters are the most generic in the book, laying the foundation, as it were, for understanding learning as it occurs in and from museums.

However, to really understand learning from museums requires delving into the specifics of the museum context. Therefore, in chapters 5 through 7 we explore personal context variables related to museum-going and describe the specific sociocultural and physical contexts of museums and how these contexts influence learning.

We put these ideas together in chapters 8 and 9 to address the fundamental questions of the nature of museum learning and what people learn in and from museums. In chapter 10 we present concrete recommendations on how to apply these ideas to the task of making museums better learning environments.

Throughout the book, we will argue that much of what people know is constructed through free-choice learning experiences. It is our belief that this has always been the case but that it will become ever more apparent and true as America and the rest of the world fully transition into the knowledge economy, as we truly become a Learning Society. As we move beyond a service economy to one based on experience, and ultimately transformation, free-choice learning will be at the core of what we in our society consider valuable. From this perspective, understanding free-choice learning is a fundamental foundation for the new Learning Society, and savvy museum professionals need to recognize that museum learning does not occur merely within the limited temporal and physical envelope of the museum. Therefore, in chapter 11 we extend the limits of our inquiry beyond the boundaries of the physical museum and explore learning from museums within the larger leisure and learning context of the greater society. Finally, in chapter 12, we apply what we have learned about learning from museums to argue how museums can better succeed in the coming Learning Society.

It is our hope that this book will be a useful guidepost for all those concerned with learning in America and beyond, not just those concerned with museums. This is a book about museum learning, but it is also a book about free-choice learning in a Learning Society. Both are topics of extreme importance and timeliness.

We want to thank Mitch Allen and Pam Winding of AltaMira Press for publishing this book and affording us the opportunity to share these ideas with the field. We are grateful to Scott Paris, Dennis Schatz, Marvin Pinkert, Kris Morrissey, Marilyn Hood, Michael Spock, Elizabeth Donovan, Kathy Walsh-Piper, Herbert Weingartner, Jessica Luke, Kathryn Foat, Nancy McCoy, and Wendy Pollock, who read earlier versions of this manuscript and provided important comments and suggestions, all of which have contributed to making this a better book. We would also like to acknowledge a number of individuals who suggested examples, helped track down references and organize citations, and generally contributed to the all-important detail that a book like this requires. For this we thank Dale Jones, DeAnna Banks Beane, Heather O'Mara, Marianna Adams, Leslie McKelvey Adelman, Jody Grönborg, and Mary-Beth Prokop. We also owe a special thank-you to all the staff of the Institute for Learning Innovation who over many years supported us in this effort intellectually, spiritually, and physically.

We are especially grateful to Michael Spock. He has contributed much to the museum field, and we are honored that he would grace this book with a foreword.

Finally, we want to thank all of those in the field who have supported us through their research, practice, and commitment to helping make museums wonderful communities in which to work and learn. Ultimately this is a book for all of you.

1

Learning from Museums:
An Introduction

The idea that knowledge is essentially book learning seems to be a
very modern view, probably derived from the mediaeval distinctions
between clerk and layman, with additional emphasis provided by the
literary character of the rather fantastic humanism of the sixteenth
century. The original and natural idea of knowledge is that of "cun-
ning" or the possession of wits. Odysseus is the original type of
thinker, a man of many ideas who could overcome the Cyclops and
achieve a significant triumph of mind over matter. Knowledge is thus
a capacity for overcoming the difficulties of life and achieving success
in this world.

—G. S. Brett, *Psychology Ancient and Modern*

Beware stories that dissolve all complexity.

—David Shenk, *Data Smog*

As America and the rest of the world transition from an industrial to a
knowledge-based economy, knowledge and meaning-making more than
ever before become key to social and economic well-being. Even though
the quantity of information grows exponentially all around us, our thirst
for knowledge, for meaning-making, remains unsatisfied. Much as an
individual on a life raft in the middle of the ocean says, "Water, water
everywhere, but not a drop to drink," so too do we find it difficult to
become "knowledgeable and satisfied meaning-makers" despite a glut of
information. Where can a knowledge-thirsty public turn for learning?
There are books. Despite the hype about declining literacy, the number of
books sold per year is at an all-time high.[1] There is television. Not only is

television viewing up,[2] but so too is the amount and diversity of information-oriented programming.[3] There is the staggering growth of the Internet, a fact of which we are all aware.[4] And, yes, there are museums!

Museums—art, history, natural history, and science museums; zoos and aquariums; botanical gardens and arboretums; and historical sites—are tried-and-true sources of understandable information, places one can trust to provide reliable, authentic, and comprehensible presentations of art, history, natural history, and science objects and ideas.[5] They are places that both children and adults can leisurely browse to discover the past, present, and future of humanity, the natural world, and the cosmos, where the public can seek and find meaning and connection.[6] In large part as a result of this classic convergence between ever rising popular demand (the public's desire for knowledge and meaning-making), and a reliable and trusted supplier (institutions capable of presenting ideas to the public in enjoyable and comprehensible experiential formats), museums of all types have been enjoying unprecedented popularity and growth.[7]

Let us put these changes in perspective. Thirty years ago only about one in ten Americans went to museums with any regularity. Ten to fifteen years ago that number had increased to nearly one in four. Today, depending upon which statistic you believe, somewhere between two and three out of every five Americans visit a museum at least once a year.[8] This number is likely to continue to increase so that, if not already, soon the majority of Americans will visit some kind of museum at least once a year.[9] Although museums have clearly changed what and how they present objects, ideas, and information, as well as the types of exhibitions and programs they present, the change has not been so dramatic as to totally explain this explosion in popularity. This change suggests a fundamental shift in the public's values and priorities relative to museums, a change in the public's perceptions of the role museums can play in their lives. Whereas as recently as twenty years ago museums were widely considered dusty anachronisms, today they enjoy a high level of public awareness and prestige. It was not so long ago that the vast majority of Americans would rather have been bound and gagged than visit a museum. Today museums rank along with shopping and sports as one of the most popular out-of-home leisure experiences in America.[10] Doubtless, the causes for this sudden shift in appreciation and popularity in museums are many, but we would argue that at the core there is but one thing—learning. Learning is the reason people go to museums, and learning is the primary "good" that visitors to museums derive from their experience. In large part responding to both of these realities, the museum community currently justifies and boldly promotes itself as a bedrock member of the learning community.[11] Yet many inside and outside the museum community privately, and sometimes publicly, question whether any real learning occurs in museums. Do visitors to museums learn, and if so, how do they learn and what do they learn? This book intends to answer these questions. However, as we will soon make clear, the answers are neither simple nor easily investigated. Unlike only a few short years ago, though, they are now answerable.

LOOKING AT SOME OF THE DATA

The place to start, or so it would seem, is with the museum experience itself, where the proverbial rubber meets the road: the exhibition or program. The prevailing model for understanding learning in museums runs something like the following: *Visitors come to museums, look at exhibitions, or participate in programs, and if the exhibitions or programs are good, the visitors learn what the project team intended.* This seems simple enough. You create a quality educational exhibition or experience, add visitors, and, voila, you get learning! Informed project teams have even expanded their notions of learning to include a host of previously excluded dimensions, including changes in attitudes, aesthetic appreciation, and family communication, to name a few. But is it that simple? Let's follow two visitors whom we observed as part of a research effort at the Smithsonian's National Museum of Natural History explicitly designed to test our assumptions about museum-based learning and see whether this traditional model seems to explain what is going on.[12]

Two women in their late twenties enter the Museum of Natural History on a Sunday morning in early fall. They begin by walking up to the elephant in the rotunda. After a brief pause there, they obtain a map at the information desk and head for the dinosaur and paleontology exhibitions. They quickly make their way around the dinosaur exhibitions, stopping occasionally to read a few labels here and there. For example, one of them seems particularly interested in the head of the *Triceratops*. After about ten minutes they exit again by way of the rotunda and, checking their maps, head down the escalator to a temporary exhibition on spiders. They spend about fifteen minutes in *Spiders*. Sometimes they watch other groups interacting with exhibits, and sometimes they interact with exhibits themselves. Most of the time, the two women stay together and look at the same exhibits; occasionally they drift apart and look at exhibits separately. Next they go back up the escalator and walk through the other temporary exhibition at the museum, *Ocean Planet*. This exhibition they view at about the same pace as *Spiders*; total time in the exhibition is also about fifteen minutes. Next they briskly walk through the various vertebrate exhibits on birds, mammals, and amphibians, briefly pausing at a few scattered exhibits but never for more than a few seconds. They take the elevator up to the second floor and very quickly walk through the *Geology, Gems and Minerals,* and *Insect Zoo* exhibitions. Ninety minutes after entering the museum, they are ready to leave.

Before they leave, we conduct an open-ended interview, inquiring about why they had visited, what they had discovered that was new to them, what they had found interesting, and a whole series of other questions designed to understand their personal experience within the museum. One of the women chooses to talk about the *Spiders* exhibition and the *Insect Zoo*. She says the *Insect Zoo* was her favorite exhibition area. When asked why, she says, "Just because of the way it was set up. There was a lot of interactive stuff, and I liked how the designs kind of incorporated the walls . . . and cages." The other woman says her favorite exhibit was *Ocean Planet;* however, she finds it difficult to give a specific reason other than saying, "Conserving the ocean is important." When questioned further, each is able to give one or two specific examples of new tidbits of information they learned. For example, one comments on how surprised she was at the diversity of spiders and how interesting some of their webs were. She also volunteers a comment on the dinosaur exhibition, saying she had learned about the shapes of some of the aquatic dinosaurs. When probed about the *Triceratops,* she says she really found the size of it remarkable. The other woman mentions that she enjoyed all the exhibitions and thought that the quality of the displays was quite good. Other than these few comments, neither woman has too much to report. The only mention made of any of the exhibitions seen in the last half of their visit, the period when they were "skating" through the museum, was the one woman's comments about the design quality of the *Insect Zoo*.

So, what did these women learn? If you are an optimist, you might conclude that they clearly came away with a greater appreciation of spiders, their variety and adaptability (although they didn't exactly say this, it could be inferred); at least one also seemed to have a richer sense of the size and diversity of dinosaurs. Also, one of the women seemed to have her commitment to ocean conservation reinforced. If a pessimist, you would be justified in concluding that these two women learned precious little in their ninety-minute visit.

However, this is not the end of the story. Five months later we telephoned each of these two women, and among other things, we asked them if they had thought about their trip to the National Museum of Natural History at all since their visit. We asked whether they had discussed their visit with anyone or whether any event had made them aware of something they had seen or done while at the museum. One of the women said that the part of her Washington trip she mentioned to her family was the time she spent in the museums, "because we spent most of our time there." She was bubbling over with enthusiasm about her trip, in general, and her visit to the Museum of Natural History, in particular. She mostly described the *Spiders* exhibition and the *Insect Zoo* and its impressive design. She reiterated what she had said immediately after her visit, that the *Insect Zoo* had really good displays and interactives for kids and adults and was colorful and interesting. In detail, she went on to describe several of the exhibits in both the *Spiders* and *Insect Zoo* areas, recalling what they looked like, how she interacted with them, and what she remembered about their messages. She described in much more detail than immediately after her visit ideas and facts she learned. For example, she said that since seeing the *Spiders* exhibit, she was more aware of the types of spiders that live in her community, such as the brown recluse. She said she had never realized that there were poisonous spiders living in her hometown. As she thought about it more, she said she thought she might have mentioned to someone that there are poisonous spiders in her community, but she was not sure. This latter recollection came up in conversation when she noted that she was currently working on editing a new textbook (she works as a school textbook editor) that included chapters on insects and spiders. She said that she found her natural history museum experience useful for this chapter and that it may have been in the context of that project that she mentioned what she learned to a coworker.

She also remembered telling her parents about the architecture of the building, because it was so distinctive. She was particularly struck by the size of the dome and the impressive inlays on the floor and ceiling. She also recalled telling her family that she thought the animals and dinosaurs were more interesting than the gems. She could not remember if she mentioned the Museum of Natural History specifically to anyone after her visit, just the Smithsonian museums, in general. She said she talked to people a lot about the Holocaust Museum, primarily because it was new: "It was the highlight . . . I mean, not the highlight [in terms of it being uplifting], but . . . [a highlight in terms of it having made the strongest impact on me]." She found it to be depressing, but interesting and well done.[13]

As she talked more about the National Museum of Natural History, she said she remembered the elephant at the entrance to the museum and that it reminded her of the elephants at the Field Museum of Natural History in Chicago, where she lives. She wondered whether all natural history museums have elephants in the entrance.

Then she launched into another story she felt related to her trip to the museum. She indicated that when she went to visit her parents, who had recently moved to Michigan, she had seen black squirrels there. When she saw them, she said, she remembered having seen an exhibit about albinism and melanism in squirrels at the Museum of Natural History.[14] She said she remembered wondering whether the Michigan squirrels were an example of melanism but said she was not sure that they really were.[15] She concluded by saying she had been to the museum before, so she knew it would be interesting. Since she is "into science," she wanted to see what was new at the museum since her last visit and so was particularly interested in new aspects of the museum, such as the *Spiders* and *Insect Zoo* exhibitions.

In contrast to the first, the second woman said that she had visited many museums and learned a lot, but nothing stood out in her mind several months later specifically about the Museum of Natural History. She could remember a few assorted details about the museum—for example, that she saw an exhibition on spiders, that her friend was really excited about the *Insect Zoo,* and that generally she saw lots and lots of rocks and bones.

The only exception to her general lack of recall related to a book she was reading. She said she was reminded recently of the Museum of Natural History when reading a popular novel about amphibians (Tom Robbins's *Asleep in Frog Pajamas*). She said the book reminded her of just how many different types of amphibians she had seen at the museum. She went on to say, "Having seen the Natural History Museum's habitats and reconstructed [amphibian] environments made the book easier to picture—it is about the fictional lifestyle of amphibians."[16] She said that although she is trained in art, "I enjoyed [the Museum of Natural History] anyway. . . . I liked the variety of the trip."

The second woman went on to describe how she and her friend had also visited art museums during their visit, for example, the National Gallery of Art, which she said she enjoyed more than the Museum of Natural History. She proceeded to describe a number of the paintings she had seen, discussing some of her favorite pieces of art and artists at length (e.g., Picasso, Braque, and Cézanne). She said she enjoyed the exhibitions she saw at the natural history museum because they "reinforced her knowledge." But she said that while she was not sure she learned that much new, it was wonderful to see things that made "real for her" things she already knew. She compared the museum to watching TV nature shows, which she said she does often. She said the museum's exhibitions and TV nature shows are similar in that they "look at one species in depth and allow you to put an image with an idea."

MAKING SENSE OF THE DATA

What an amazing difference! Five months later both women seemed to have constructed additional knowledge about the experience, despite initial appearances. In particular, one of the women seemed to have come away with several new insights, a number of new ideas, and an overall renewed excitement and interest in natural history. Although her friend seemed to have found less to connect with, at least at this museum—obviously her personal interests lay in art—she too came away with a few new tools for visualizing and making more comprehensible the natural world around her. All in all, not bad for a quick ninety-minute spin through the museum! But this is not all we can learn from this example.

Equally important, and perhaps most startling, is the fact that these demographically nearly identical individuals (well-educated, professional—both children's textbook editors—white women in their late twenties living in the same Chicago community) visited the same museum on the same day, saw the same exhibitions for exactly the same amount of time, even viewed and discussed with each other some of the same specific exhibit elements, and yet what they learned was totally different. How can this be? Certainly these data throw into question our initial museum learning model that posited that if visitors look at exhibitions or participate in programs, and if the exhibitions or programs are good, they will learn what the exhibition team intended. These data would suggest that the model, if not completely wrong, at the very least is seriously flawed. Understanding the content and quality of exhibitions and programs is necessary but not sufficient for understanding the complexity of museum learning.

As we look at the data gathered during the follow-up interview, we begin to see the important roles played by prior knowledge, interest, and the museum experience itself, as well as the unpredictable but important role of subsequent experiences, such as later seeing a black squirrel in Michigan. All these variables played major roles in affecting what these women were able to remember and what they ultimately learned. The truth of the matter is that if we had known beforehand that one of these women was a self-described "science person" and the other an "art person," we might have better been able to predict that they would have focused on different aspects of the experience. If we had known that one of the women was a children's science textbook editor and the other a children's art textbook editor, we would have understood why they focused on different features of the museum. If we had known that this was not the first visit for one of the women but was for the other, we might have understood why they spent their time as they did. If we had known more about how this particular museum visit fit within these two women's visit to Washington, we might have better understood why they spent such a relatively small amount of time at the museum. If we had known that one of the women was only visiting this museum in deference to her friend but that shortly the roles would be reversed when they visited the National Gallery of Art, we would have better understood the differences in time, attention, and meaning-making invested in the museum by the two. Finally, we could not have known beforehand what events would transpire after the visit, but certainly we could have predicted that events would transpire and that these events would play a powerful role in what subsequently was remembered from the experience.

In short, in order to understand what these two women learned at the National Museum of Natural History on this particular Sunday morning required knowing much more about them and their visit than merely what exhibitions they visited and for how long. To the extent that we can generalize from this one example, learning from museums involves a wide variety of variables, some of which relate to the exhibitions and programs and many that do not. Why visitors come, with whom they visit and for what reasons, what they already know, what their interests are, what their prior museum experiences are, and what subsequent reinforcing events occur in their lives play as great a role in learning—if not a greater one—as anything that happens inside the museum.

At this point it is probably important to reiterate that this is real data, albeit on just two individuals from a larger study of fifty visitors. However, we are quite certain that the results would not change dramatically if we repeated this experiment with the same individuals in a different museum (for example, if we had compared these women's learning at the National Gallery of Art or the U.S. Holocaust Memorial Museum), nor would results be different with other pairs of individuals at the same museum. In fact, we have done this experiment, as have others, directly and indirectly, with hundreds if not thousands of individuals. The same thing happens. It is not that these two individuals were oddities, it is that our traditional model of learning is flawed.

Yes, people learn in museums, but over the years providing compelling evidence for museum-based learning has proved challenging. As it turns out, this is not because the evidence did not exist but because museum learning researchers and the public alike have had the wrong search image and were using flawed tools. There are many reasons for this, but the primary reason has been the strange and fundamentally erroneous way that learning has been traditionally conceptualized. Perhaps the greatest impediment to understanding the learning that occurs in museums has been that social scientists, educators, museum professionals, and the public at large have historically thought of museum learning as being similar to traditional models of learning, such as the transmission–absorption model.[17] This line of thinking suggests that museum visitors should learn the same types of things and in the same manner as do students at school; the only major difference is that in museums people learn less. The standard museum learning paradigm described above is a good example of this; the visitors are the students and the exhibition is the lesson. Bring the students into the classroom, present them with a lesson, and they will learn it. In the case of the classroom, they will have plenty of time to absorb it all; in the case of the museum, they spend less time, so maybe they will only get the gist of the message. As we have seen, this model does not quite work in museums— and, of course, in truth, it does not quite work in schools either.

Defining learning is a tricky business. For example, learning is simultaneously a process and a product, a verb and a noun.[18] So slippery is learning as a concept that even the social scientists that study learning for a living, such as psychologists, anthropologists, and sociologists, have difficulty agreeing on a single definition.[19] Many of these professionals have avoided the dilemma by identifying numerous types of learning. For example, it has been argued that there is one type of learning that occurs when remembering sensory experiences and another type of *higher* learning that occurs under conditions of instruction such as might occur in a school classroom.[20] Although one could find merit in such taxonomies for some purposes, for the purposes of understanding museum learning, they certainly have little value. It is better to think more holistically, to think about learning as a series of related and overlapping processes, appreciating that such systems can be difficult to make sense of because of their complexity and ephemeral nature. By analogy, it is traditional to discuss the complex and ephemeral functioning of the human body by thinking of the circulatory, respiratory, and nervous systems as separable and discrete entities. This approach has many benefits, particularly if one does not lose sight of the fact that in a fully functioning, living human, none of these complex systems is in fact separate or discrete, nor can their individual functions be completely isolated without damaging the whole. To understand the living system, it ultimately makes more sense to talk about respiration or digestion, activities that involve many of these systems simultaneously. Similarly, there are benefits to a reductionist view of learning, as long as it is ultimately appreciated that learning in museums is a whole-body, whole-experience, whole-brain activity.

THE CONTEXTUAL MODEL OF LEARNING

To this end, eight years ago we formulated a framework for thinking about learning that tried to accommodate much of the diversity and complexity surrounding learning, a framework that we called the Interactive Experience Model.[21] Today we have built upon and refined that model, recasting it as the *Contextual Model of Learning.* The Contextual Model posits that all learning is situated within a series of contexts. In other words, learning is not some abstract experience that can be isolated in a test tube or laboratory but an organic, integrated experience that happens in the real world. We argue that learning is a product of millions of years of evolution, an adaptation that permits an ongoing dialogue between the whole individual and the physical and sociocultural world he or she inhabits. The Contextual Model was derived from observations of real people in real settings, and thus it is not surprising that other thoughtful individuals, before and since, also considered models similar to this one.[22] The Contextual Model involves three overlapping contexts: the *personal,* the *sociocultural,* and the *physical.* Learning is the process/product of the interactions between these three contexts. Intentionally, this model of learning is more descriptive than predictive. The power of the Contextual Model is not that it attempts to reduce complexity to one or two simple rules but rather that it embraces and organizes complexity into a manageable and comprehensible whole. In so doing, the Contextual Model successfully accommodates much, if not most, of what is currently known about learning.

After working with this model for nearly a decade, we believe it is still reasonable but, as initially described, incomplete. Over the intervening years we have come to appreciate that the model needs a fourth dimension—*time.* Looking at the museum experience as a snapshot in time, even a very long snapshot (e.g., the time a visitor spends in the museum), is woefully inadequate. To understand learning, any learning, requires a longer view. It is as if you need to pan the camera back in time and space so that you can see individual learners across a larger swath of their life and can view the museum within the larger context of the community and society.

A convenient, though admittedly artificial, way to think about this model is to consider learning as being constructed over time as the individual moves through his sociocultural and physical world; over time, meaning is built up, layer upon layer. However, even this model does not quite capture the true dynamism of the process, since even the layers themselves, once created, are not static or necessarily even permanent. All the layers, particularly the earliest ones, interact and directly influence the shape and form of future layers; the learner both forms and is formed by his environment. For convenience, we have distinguished three separate contexts, but it is important to keep in mind that these contexts are not really separate, or even separable.

Western science in general and psychology in particular are strongly tied to ideas of permanence—the brain is a constant, the environment is a given, memories are permanent. None of this appears to be, in fact, reality. None of the three contexts—personal, sociocultural, or physical—is ever stable or constant. Learning, as well as its constituent pieces, is ephemeral, always changing. Ultimately, then, learning can be viewed as the never-ending integration and interaction of these three contexts over time in order to make meaning. Perhaps the best way to think of it is to view the personal context as moving through time; as it travels, it is constantly shaped and reshaped as it experiences events within the physical context, all of which are mediated by and through the sociocultural context. A valiant effort at depicting this model is shown in figure 1.1. This model really should be depicted in three dimensions and animated, so that both the temporal and the interactive nature of learning could be captured. In the absence of 3D animation, we invite you to use your imagination.

DOCUMENTING LEARNING

It is essential to document the learning that results from museum experiences. We believe that educators and psychologists, as well as policymakers and the public, have historically found this a challenging task because they have approached the problem incorrectly, quite literally asking a fundamentally flawed question. In museums and schools alike, we have framed the question as, What does an individual learn as a consequence of visiting this museum, or seeing this exhibition, or attending

Figure 1.1   The Contextual Model of Learning

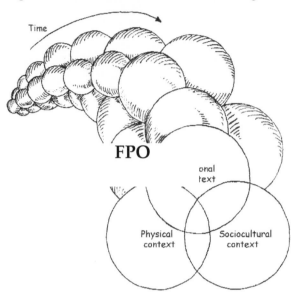

this lecture? The better, more realistic question is, How does this museum, exhibition, or lecture contribute to what someone knows, believes, feels, or is capable of doing? All learning is a cumulative, long-term process, a process of making meaning and finding connections. All educational institutions exist within a larger educational infrastructure. What we know about any particular topic is the accumulated understanding constructed from a wide variety of sources, typically including school; newspapers and magazines; books; conversations with friends, family, and knowledgeable acquaintances; television shows; films; observations in the world; and, often, museums. People do not learn things in one moment in time, but over time. Since we have framed the problem inappropriately, we have set out inappropriately to document it. And perhaps more profoundly, since we have framed the problem inappropriately, we have set out inappropriately to achieve our goals as well. Thus you can neither expect to share knowledge or beliefs or feelings or capabilities in one moment in time, nor can you expect to be able to document that knowledge, belief, feeling, or capability as if it were constructed in one moment in time. The net effect of this faulty model has been poor practice and poor documentation.

Thus, the learning model we need, the learning model we will attempt to develop in this book, is a contextual model that includes a time dimension. We will use the museum as a case study, as an example of how people learn when they freely choose to learn. Free-choice learning tends to be nonlinear, is personally motivated, and involves considerable choice on the part of the learner as to what to learn, as well as where and when to participate in learning. This type of free-choice learning is not restricted to museums, but it is in museums that we currently best understand it. To the extent we can develop a better model of learning in museums, we, as a community, can do a better job of facilitating learning in museums and other free-choice learning settings, and a better model will also enable us to do a better job of documenting the learning that results.

The questions that many museum directors, trustees, and professionals are currently asking are, Do people actually learn as a result of museum experiences? And if so, what are they learning? We would assert that the answer to the first question is an unequivocal yes. Answering the second question is much more difficult since it requires knowing something about who is visiting, why they are visiting and with whom, what they are doing before and after the visit, what they see and do in the museum, and how all these factors interact and interrelate. The place to begin this investigation is with the fundamentals of how people learn, through an inquiry into the roles of the personal, sociocultural, and physical contexts and how these contexts interact over time and space to affect learning.

KEY POINTS

- Free-choice learning occurs during visits to museums, when watching television, reading a newspaper, talking with friends, attending a play, or surfing the Internet. Free-choice learning tends to be nonlinear and personally motivated and to involve considerable choice on the part of the learner as to when, where, and what to learn.

- To understand human learning, it is important to appreciate that it is the product of hundreds of millions of years of survival-oriented evolution, an adaptation enabling people to intelligently navigate an ever changing social, cultural, and physical world.

- One of the aspects of learning that makes it so challenging to understand is that it is always both a process and a product, a verb and a noun.

- The *Contextual Model of Learning* suggests that learning is influenced by three overlapping contexts: the *personal*, the *sociocultural*, and the *physical*. Learning can be conceptualized as the integration and interaction of these three contexts.

NOTES

1. Achenbach 1999; U.S. Bureau of the Census 1996.
2. Godbey in press; U.S. Bureau of the Census 1996.
3. Gross 1997.
4. Achenbach 1999; Schwartz 1998.
5. Pitman 1999.
6. Pitman 1999.
7. Lusaka and Strand 1998.
8. Cf. Lusaka and Strand 1998; Falk 1998.
9. Falk 1998; Association of Science-Technology Centers 1998.
10. Falk 1998; Association of Science-Technology Centers 1998.
11. American Association of Museums 1992.
12. This excerpt describes the museum experience and subsequent interviews with two people who were part of a larger study of fifty visitors conducted at the National Museum of Natural History in 1994 (Falk et al. n.d.) The following methodology was employed: (1) Randomly identify individuals, either in a group or alone, as they enter the museum. (2) Conduct a brief introductory interview to know more about who the visitors are, where they come from, why they are visiting, and what they hope to see and discover. (3) After securing permission, track the visitors as unobtrusively as possible throughout their entire museum visit (including stops at the gift shop, food service, etc.), noting where they go, what they do, and, to the extent possible, what they converse about. (4) Conduct an open-ended, face-to-face postvisit interview that seeks to learn why they visited the museum, what they were interested in, and what they felt was interesting and informative during their visit. (5) Four to five months later, call individuals back and reinterview.
13. We did not pursue in any detail her memories of the Holocaust Museum or, subsequently, her friend's memories of the National Gallery of Art.
14. This exhibit is located in the mammal exhibition hall, which is currently being redesigned, one of the areas this woman zipped through in the latter half of her visit. Note: Albinism is an absence of pigmentation that causes an animal to appear white; melanism is an abundance of pigmentation that causes an animal to appear black.
15. She was correct in thinking the black squirrels she saw were an example of animal melanism.
16. The exhibit she referred to could have been located in either the vertebrate exhibition hall or the *Insect Zoo;* both of these were areas this woman zipped through in the latter half of her visit.
17. Hein 1998; Hein and Alexander 1998.
18. Falk and Dierking 1995.
19. Bransford 1979.
20. Churchland 1986.
21. Falk and Dierking 1992.
22. See, e.g., Lewin 1951; Ceci and Roazzi 1994; Mead 1934; Shweder 1990.

2

The Personal Context

The history of educational theory is marked by opposition between the idea that [learning] is development from within and that it is formation from without.

—John Dewey, *Experience and Education*

Learning is a very personal experience that depends on a number of conditions for success, some within the brain and others more a function of the external environment. This reality is well illustrated by a letter written to us in 1995 by a colleague, Edward Jay Pershey, Director of Education at the Western Reserve Historical Society, Cleveland, Ohio.

I was attending the American Association of Museums' Learning in Museums seminar in Chicago in November, 1994. During the day-long seminar the first day, a portion of the discussion centered around the idea that it is difficult to measure just what people learn while visiting the museum, since the learning is informal to begin with and may not manifest itself for some time, sometimes years. . . .

That evening I called back to my wife Monica Gordon Pershey, who is an Assistant Professor of Speech & Hearing at Cleveland State University. Her areas of interest are language and reading development in children. She started off telling me how her day went. That morning she had an appointment at a school on Cleveland's West Side. Cleveland State and our neighborhood are on the East Side. [Cleveland's East Side and West Side are divided by the Cuyahoga River, which runs through the industrial Flats and marks the west border for downtown.] When she went to go over to the West Side, she remembered that the high level bridge crossing the Cuyahoga Valley was under repair and closed, and so she chose to follow a route through the Flats that I had showed her a few weeks before. There are several smaller bridges, lift and swing bridges, at river level that she could cross.

When she got to river's edge, she found that a large ore boat was traveling down the Cuyahoga and the lift bridge was up. She waited while the boat passed and the bridge came down. While waiting she had watched the mechanism of the bridge, and proceeded to excitedly tell me that she understood the way that the counterweights and gears were making the huge mass of iron, steel, and roadway go so easily up and down. She was using terminology that I didn't realize that she knew. She recalled that she had learned all this from an exhibit on bridges at the Cleveland Children's Museum, which we had visited the YEAR BEFORE with our young grandson. She hadn't needed that information prior [to watching the bridge] and didn't know that she had really learned anything the day of the museum visit, but clearly she had and was able to apply that knowledge in a "real world" situation.

This brief but intriguing description of Monica and the bridge illustrates four important lessons that are at the heart of the context we call the personal context. These lessons are: (1) learning flows from appropriate motivational and emotional cues; (2) learning is facilitated by personal interest; (3) "new" knowledge is constructed from a foundation of prior experience and knowledge; and (4) learning is expressed within appropriate contexts. We'll begin by exploring the first lesson. Why would Monica want to learn about bridges when, according to her husband, prior to this point she had shown no interest in such topics? What motivated Monica to learn about bridges?

MOTIVATION

Humans learn many things and for many reasons. Just telling someone to learn to read, multiply fractions, or memorize the parts of a cell or a historical chronology does not mean that learning *will* happen. And the fact that someone does not have to learn something does not mean that it will *not* happen. Two hundred years ago, it was appreciated that motivation and learning seemed always to be tightly intertwined.[1] Unfortunately, the Behaviorist paradigms of the twentieth century, as well as many Cognitive ones more recently, ignored this relationship.[2]

Learning as a process evolved long before there was language or mathematics, in fact, before there were humans, primates, or other mammals at all. No matter how eloquent the learning theory or how poetic the description, ultimately learning is the process/product of a complex series of electrochemical interactions in the brain and body, processes/products that have evolved over many hundreds of millions of years (for reference, humans in any form have been on this planet for less than ten million years, modern humans for considerably less than one million years). Learning, even twenty-first-century human learning, is built upon a very ancient, whole-body, biological base. It is profoundly important to appreciate the long evolutionary history of human learning; learning is not just a recent cultural overlay unique to "modern humans."

A very important and relatively unappreciated by-product of this long evolutionary history is the feedback loops that exist between emotional and cognitive processes. In large part these feedback loops are mediated by one of the oldest parts of the brain, the area known as the limbic system. Located in the middle of the brain and made up of a number of discrete structures (e.g., the amygdala, hippocampus, and thalamus), the limbic system probably first evolved among reptiles and is well developed in all mammals. The limbic area was recognized early on as the major center in the brain for emotional and geographical memory—functions that are appropriate to its ancient lineage.[3] However, in a shift from early ideas, the brain is now appreciated to be highly integrated and only loosely specialized.[4] The limbic system structures have been found to be extensively connected in looped circuits to all parts of the brain, as well as to all of the body's organs and systems, responding to the needs and demands of various body functions and cycles.[5] The limbic system turns out not only to help regulate emotions and geography but also to be the focal point for regulating all memory.[6]

Of course, central to all learning is our perceptual system; information must somehow be perceived—seen, heard, smelled, tasted, touched, or in some way sensed. Learning requires more than perception, though; it also needs a filtering system, since in any instant far more things are perceivable than could possibly be incorporated into memory. There needs to be some way to judge what among all this welter of information is worthy of remembering. Enter the limbic system. Before any perception begins the process of being permanently stored in memory, and hence learned, it must first pass through at least two appraisal stages involving the limbic system.[7] All incoming sensory information is given an initial screening for meaningfulness and personal relevance by structures in the limbic system. It is also filtered for its relationship to our internal physical state (e.g., "I'm hungry, so I guess I'll focus on things related to food rather than Shakespeare"). This filtering and interpretation of incoming sensory information, though centered in the limbic system, involves virtually every part of the brain and the body.[8] In essence, this process both determines *what* is worth attending to and remembering (i.e., "Will this be important information in the future? Does it relate to something I already know, feel, or believe?") and *how* something is remembered (e.g., "That idea reminds me of an interesting television show I once saw" or "is associated with a beautiful painting I was viewing at the time"). Research in the last quarter-century has shown that learning cannot be separated in the Cartesian sense between rational thought and emotion nor neatly divided into cognitive (facts and concepts), affective (feelings, attitudes and emotions), and psychomotor (skills and behaviors) functions, as many psychologists and educators have attempted to do for nearly a half-century. All learning, even of the most logical topic, involves emotion, just as emotions virtually always involve cognition.[9]

By virtue of its journey through the limbic system, it seems that every memory comes with an emotional stamp attached to it.[10] The stronger the emotional value, the more likely sensory information is to pass this initial inspection and be admitted into memory; interestingly, pleasant experiences are strongly favored over unpleasant ones.[11] Evolution has thus ensured a dependence between learning and survival by making the process of acquiring and storing information both very thorough and, owing chiefly to its relationship to the limbic system, more often than not an intrinsically pleasurable and rewarding experience.[12]

Nowhere is this more evident than in children. Children find innate joy in learning. They appear to learn almost effortlessly some of humanity's most challenging tasks, such as walking, talking, getting along with others, taking care of themselves, and assimilating the basic rules of their culture. And as perhaps best evidenced by the young (and young of heart), learning is a whole-body, emotionally rich experience. Children learn exuberantly, with their eyes and ears, their hands and feet, their mouth and nose, with their "head" and with their "heart." It is only when these joyful learning experiences are reprogrammed by societal goals and expectations into the externally imposed, cognitive-focused tasks of schooling and work that "learning," for many, becomes onerous, unpleasant, and difficult.[13] However, no matter how unpleasant the thought of some types of learning might be, people never stop learning. In the appropriate context, and with the appropriate motivation, learning continues to occur naturally. As a society, we do not always acknowledge that what goes on outside of school and the workplace involves learning, but it does.

Humans are genetically programmed to learn, and learn we do all the time. Much, if not most, of what we know, we learn outside of school.[14] Most human learning is self-motivated, emotionally satisfying, and very personally rewarding. A number of investigators have found that humans are highly motivated to learn when they are in supporting environments;[15] when they are engaged in meaningful activities;[16] when they are freed from anxiety, fear, and other negative mental states;[17] when they have choices and control over their learning;[18] and when the challenges of the task meet their skills.[19] When in the right context, adults as well as children find learning fun and easy. This joy of learning manifests itself differently in different individuals. Reading an engaging book, fixing a broken machine, watching a good movie, having a stimulating conversation with a friend, playing sports, successfully preparing food with a new recipe, or solving a challenging crossword puzzle can be fun for some, boring for others. However, what all of these tasks have in common is that they require learning. They require the application of prior knowledge and experience to new circumstances and come with the expectation that that new knowledge and experience will be useful in completing similar tasks in the future. This is learning freed from the external reward system of society; it is learning for the sake of learning. Within this context, it is easy to imagine Monica Gordon Pershey readily learning about the role of gears and counterweights in the functioning of bridges as she plays with her grandchild at a children's museum. If we are to believe Edward Pershey's account, it is harder to imagine Monica learning about the mechanics of bridges in a more traditional educational setting. If this scenario is even partially true, how do we account for the rapid and, for all intents and purposes, seemingly unconscious learning Dr. Pershey accomplished?

Over forty years ago, psychologists realized that a basic dichotomy existed in learning: either people learned when they felt they wanted to or they learned because they felt they had to.[20] The outcomes of learning, it seemed, differed significantly depending upon whether the motivation was *intrinsic* or *extrinsic*.[21]

Action is extrinsically motivated when the anticipated benefits are external to the activity. Extrinsic rewards might include getting good grades or a high salary, or the "benefit" could be avoiding punishment, like not being ticketed for exceeding the posted speed limit. By contrast, intrinsic motivation means that an action is done for its own sake, even in the absence of some external reward. Participating in evening arts and crafts, exercise, and relaxation classes; visiting a museum or theater while on vacation; and playing sports and games after school are examples of intrinsically motivated activities. Except for the few professionals who derive an income from these activities, the people who engage in them receive no rewards other than the joy of the experience itself. People are intrinsically motivated when they are freely expressing themselves by doing something purely for the joy of doing it.[22]

These two types of motivation are not mutually exclusive, nor are they good or bad in and of themselves. The professional dancer or athlete can thoroughly enjoy what he or she does. Many children do enjoy school. In fact, it is not uncommon for people to strive for situations that combine both types of motivation. For example, most people try to have jobs that they enjoy doing. In that way, they can derive personal, professional, and remunerative benefit from performing a single task. Given the amount of time earning a living requires, it is clearly ideal to combine "business and pleasure," as it were. However, not all people enjoy their jobs, so they work to earn money so that they can do what interests them during their free time. For these people, there is a clear separation between extrinsically and intrinsically motivated activities. Not all intrinsically motivated activities involve learning, but a surprisingly high percentage do. When learning occurs for intrinsic reasons, it has been shown time and again to be highly effective learning.[23]

As reviewed in 1997 by psychologist Scott Paris, motivation theorists have contrasted two types of goal orientations—mastery orientation and performance orientation.[24] "Individuals who have a mastery orientation believe that effort is critical for their own success. These individuals are inclined to work hard at their goals, taking risks, exhibiting creative and effective strategies, and pursing the completion of the task for the sake of learning. This contrasts with those having performance-oriented goals. In these circumstances, individuals believe that success is defined by outperforming others. Their behavior is marked by efforts to complete the task quickly, avoiding challenges, giving up in the face of difficulties, and attributing failure to personal inadequacy.[25] Learners who are intrinsically motivated are more likely to have a mastery orientation while learners who are extrinsically motivated are more likely to have a performance orientation."[26] In schools, students who are intrinsically motivated tend to have higher achievement scores,[27] and they tend to make the most of their abilities.[28] Intrinsic enjoyment of learning appears to be associated with higher creativity as well, and under certain conditions, external rewards even appear to undermine intrinsic motivation and the individual's ability to do well.[29]

In the review cited above, Paris makes another important point, worth quoting in its entirety:

> "Motivated to learn" may not adequately characterize the actions of all [museum] visitors, though, because it suggests that learning is limited to acquiring new information. For many people who visit museums, zoos, botanical gardens, and similar places, their motivation may be to construct, elaborate, and relive their personal experiences. They may "learn" more about themselves and their experiences through reflection inspired by exhibits and moods stimulated in these settings. The construction of per-

sonal meaning may also involve reminiscing and finding comfort in recollections stimulated by exhibits because people are challenged to find and make meaning in these contexts that bring a sense of self-fulfillment. These affective reactions and restorative feelings of peacefulness may represent a neglected aspect of learning: emotional adaptation and aesthetic appreciation. They are deeply motivating because they may rekindle memories, embellish previous knowledge, and extend understanding in idiosyncratic, personal ways.[30]

Learning is not just facts and concepts; learning, particularly intrinsically motivated learning, is a rich, emotion-laden experience, encompassing much, if not most, of what we consider to be fundamentally human. At its most basic level, learning is about affirming *self*.

Among the myriad psychological constructs that psychologists have identified as influencing our perceptions of ourselves as learners and ultimately affecting what, how, and why we learn, probably one of the most important is our sense of self. Given the constructive nature of learning, having a sense of self—an awareness of personal needs, interests, and abilities—is fundamental to all learning. It is this sense of self that serves as the primary filter of experience, enabling the mind to focus on those issues and events perceived as relevant and to ignore those perceived as irrelevant. Self is the mind's gatekeeper. The roots of self go deep into our evolutionary past. At the most basic level, awareness of self appears to be an ancient, perhaps essential quality of all life,[31] and it appears to be fundamental to even the most primitive forms of learning.[32] However, *self* as we use it here in the context of learning from museums is a highly developed and uniquely adaptive human construct.

It is not clear whether infants are born with a sense of self; however, it does not take long for awareness of self to develop in the child, and once established, it quickly becomes an integral part of all social and cognitive life. In fact, the development of complex emotional responses and empathy cannot occur until a sense of self emerges. The capacity to form plans and recognize the consequences of one's own actions also requires an active, independently existing self. In addition, self-recognition is the first step toward developing a differentiated psychological self-concept, that is, a personal theory of what the self is like as an experiencing, functioning individual. Collectively, these developments represent one of the major achievements of the childhood years,[33] in their own right as amazing, profound, and important as speech or thought itself.

Psychologists have discovered that a wide range of issues surrounding self-concept influence learning, such as self-esteem, the judgments individuals make about their self-worth;[34] attribution, the common, everyday speculations about the causes of behavior;[35] and locus of control, also called fate control, individuals' sense of the control they have of their own experiences.[36] For example, self-esteem has been found to predict children's school achievement and their curiosity and motivation to engage in challenging tasks.[37] Investigations of children's achievement-related attributions have found them to be important influences on learning in a variety of learning situations.[38] And children with a strong locus of control are more likely to be successful learners than children with a weak locus of control, who tend to feel that external, environmental factors prevent them from succeeding.[39] These various dimensions of self play a significant role in learners' interests, attitudes, and choices of when, how, and what to learn.

INTEREST, AFFECT, AND FLOW

Many psychologists, and educators, treat motivation as a vague, everyday term, of which interest is a component. Psychologist Ulrich Schiefele has pointed out that motivation, in general, and interest, in particular, are complex, multidimensional states.[40] For example, even the construct of intrinsic motivation described above is usually subject or topic specific, rather than a generalized quality.[41] In other words, someone can have a strong interest in history and be attracted to history-related museums but not find art or science interesting and thus avoid those museums. Individuals find activities enjoyable when they are related to their subject-specific interests.[42] The experiences of the two women in the previous chapter illustrate this clearly. It is also important for us to clarify that when we use the term *interest* we are not just referring to what someone likes or dislikes. Rather, we refer to a psychological construct that includes attention, persistence in a task, and continued curiosity, all factors important to an understanding of what might motivate someone to learn in a museum, to become fully engaged in a museum exhibition, program, or event.[43]

People are bombarded with stimulation all the time. The human brain is designed to sift through this abundance of information to selectively determine what to attend to and what to ignore. One filter for this selection process is *interest*. If we had no interests, our senses would be deluged with information, and total mental chaos would result. This reality was appreciated more than a hundred years ago by pioneering psychologist William James:

The moment one thinks of the matter, one sees how false a notion of experience that is which would make it tantamount to the mere presence to the senses of an outward order. Millions of items in the outward order are present to my senses which never properly enter into my experience. Why? Because they have no interest for me. My experience is what I agree to attend to. Only those items which I notice shape my mind—without selective interest, experience is an utter chaos.[44]

What determines interests includes a range of variables, some of which are universal, some the result of individual experiences, and some the result of personal history. Most people have interest in food, sex, whatever gives them power and acclaim, babies, and pets.[45] Beyond these, though, interests diverge tremendously. Some people are interested in sports, some people enjoy fashion, and still others find ancient Roman history particularly fascinating. When people like something, they attribute positive feelings and values to it; the result is a high probability that they will choose to follow up on that interest with action.[46] One action that can, and for many people does, flow from interest is the decision to attend a selected museum or pay selective attention to specific exhibitions or exhibit elements once inside a museum.

Such interest, and the learning that results, can have application to real-life situations, as Monica's example suggests. Museum professional Aubrey Tulley described an encounter with a young woman he met at a reception who ascribed great significance to her learning experiences at the Science Museum in London.[47] According to the woman, she had recently visited her sister, who said that she was worried that her small children might leave the house unsupervised because the lock on the back door was broken. Upon hearing her sister's concern, the young woman borrowed a screwdriver and mended the lock. A week before this incident, she had spent time assembling the lock-and-key exhibit at the Science Museum. She asserted that without having encountered the exhibit, she would never have had the confidence to respond to her sister's problem as she did. She described this as an emotional effect on her "confidence," but clearly it was an emotional, cognitive, and psychomotor learning experience, a learning experience that was rich enough to be transferable to a new situation.

It is significant that both this learning and Monica Gordon Pershey's learning about bridges occurred not from a book or lecture but at a museum. Both learned while doing, while playing with locks, gears, and counterweights. And it is also significant that, at least in Monica's case, the learning occurred while she was actively engaged in playing with her grandson. As theorized by neuroscientist Gerald Edelman, learning is a whole-body experience, involving the emotions and the senses, the physical as well as the mental.[48] Sigmund Freud appreciated this fact over a hundred years ago when he observed that memories unattended by emotion were unrecognizable.[49]

A wide range of investigators have remarked on the presence of *affect* (feelings, attitudes, and emotions) in the learning and behavior that occur in free-choice learning settings like museums.[50] However, to suggest, as many in the museum field do, that affect is the main or primary outcome of such experiences is to minimize the significance of the learning that occurs. As it turns out, the affect and behaviors observed in museums and other engaging free-choice settings closely resemble the descriptions of learning recorded by psychologists studying intrinsically motivated learning.

During investigations, psychologist Mihalyi Csikszentmihalyi observed that people exhibit a common set of behaviors and outcomes when engaged in free-choice tasks for which extrinsic rewards are absent. This observation has been confirmed by a wide range of other investigators.[51] Chess players, rock climbers, dancers, painters, and musicians use similar explanations when describing the attraction of the activities they enjoy. They stress that what keeps them involved in these demanding activities is an inherent quality of the experience.[52] Csikszentmihalyi calls this common experiential quality the *flow experience*, because it is generally described as a state of mind that is spontaneous, almost automatic, like the flow of a strong current.[53] A general characteristic of activities that produce flow is that they have clear goals and appropriate rules. In a game of tennis or chess, one knows every second what one would like to accomplish. Playing a musical instrument, one knows what sounds one wishes to produce. In addition to clear goals, flow activities usually provide immediate and unambiguous feedback. One always knows whether one is doing well or not. Musicians find out immediately if they hit a wrong note; tennis players know if they hit the ball badly. According to Csikszentmihalyi, this constant accountability is a major reason one gets so completely immersed in a flow activity.

Another universally mentioned characteristic of flow experiences is that they tend to occur when the opportunities for action in a situation are in balance with the person's abilities. In other words, the challenges of the activity must match or be attainable by the skills of the individual or group. If the challenges are greater than the skill levels, anxiety results; if skills are greater than challenges, the result is boredom.[54] This phenomenon appears to hold across a wide array of skills, including physical, mental, artistic, and musical talents. The more one does an activity, the greater one's skill. The greater one's skill, the greater the challenges required to continue enjoying the activity and remaining in a state of flow.

Successful museum exhibitions, performances, films, programs, and web sites share this quality. A good medium of communication permits the participant to seek the level of engagement and understanding appropriate for the individual. It is often said that a good exhibition, performance, film, etc. can be understood at many different levels and from many different perspectives. By this it is meant that the learner can become engaged via many entry points and can be challenged at a variety of different skill levels. Thus engagement, a flow experience, can result because there is sufficient depth to permit appropriate levels of challenge for a wide range of users. In free-choice learning situations, learners can select the challenge they wish, rather than have it imposed upon them. This element of control emerges as another fundamental component of motivation.[55] For example, in a museum this is evidenced by the high degree of self-selection that visitors exercise over which exhibits to view or utilize. No visitor views/utilizes all exhibits in a museum, but virtually every visitor views/utilizes some.[56] Generally, the ones selected are ones that interest the visitor and provide appropriate levels of intellectual, physical, and emotional challenge. While investigating behavior in a children's museum, Paris found that when exhibits were partially completed, whether a tangram puzzle or a wall maze, children were more likely to approach the exhibit and complete the task than if the puzzle or wall maze were either totally disassembled or completed.[57] Paris speculated that "maybe there was a need for closure, maybe visitors thought that it was 'doable' because someone else had done it halfway, or maybe the task was clear and the challenge was just high enough that successful completion led to feelings of pride and satisfaction."[58]

Flow learning experiences are not just mental experiences; one characteristic of flow experiences is the total involvement of all the senses. As Csikszentmihalyi states, "When goals are clear, feedback is unambiguous, challenges and skills are well matched, then all of one's mind and body become completely involved in the activity."[59] In this state, the person becomes unaware of fatigue or the passing of time. It is truly an exhilarating experience, physically, emotionally, and cognitively. It is also extremely pleasurable. People who experience something even approaching flow experiences desire to do them over and over again. At some level, most frequent museum-goers can be characterized as having something akin to a flow experience. If they did not derive deep intrinsic rewards from going to museums, they would not keep going to them again and again.[60] But not all learning involves flow. People learn all kinds of things, sometimes even about things that they did not even know they were particularly interested in.

This is the second lesson the description of Monica's bridge experience helps to illustrate. From the description, we can assume that Monica would not describe herself as innately interested in bridges and mechanics, but two unrelated events piqued her interest—a day playing with her grandchild at a children's museum exhibit and being stuck in front of an open bridge. In this respect, interest can be seen to be "situated." Interest, it seems comes in at least two "flavors": personal and situated.[61] Personal interest develops slowly over time and tends to have long-lasting effects on a person's knowledge and values. This is the deep-seated interest meant by someone who says, "I have a passion for Greek vases." Situated interest, on the other hand, tends to be evoked more suddenly by something in the environment and may have only a short-term effect, only slightly influencing an individual's knowledge or values. Monica's bridge experience is likely an example of situated interest; the immediacy of both bridge events influenced Monica's learning. Both personal and situated interest are factors in the learning that occurs in and from museums.

THE CONSTRUCTION OF KNOWLEDGE

Now we come to the third lesson that Monica's bridge experience helps to illustrate, the lesson that a person's ability to learn is constructed from a base of prior experiences. In Monica's case, learning about how a swing bridge worked required prior knowledge gained while visiting a children's museum (and possibly other sources that we do not know about). Given that her learning was supposedly not in an area inherently interesting to her, that knowledge lay dormant, waiting for an environmental cue or necessity to evoke it. The cue for Monica was being stuck waiting at a closed bridge. With nothing better to do, she watched the bridge, which prompted her memories of the children's museum exhibit, which in turn prompted her memories of how a swing bridge worked. Without her prior experience, she might have watched the swing bridge and never thought about how it worked. In the absence of relevant memories about bridge mechanics, her thoughts would very likely have drifted to other things. However, the confluence of relevant cues provided by the real swing bridge and her prior experience resulted in additional memories, additional learning.

Monica's experience is not unique. Over the past decade, hundreds of people have shared their museum memories with us, and in virtually all cases, prior knowledge figured prominently into their recollections. A particularly striking example was offered by a fifty-four-year old salesman who recalled a boyhood trip to the Smithsonian Institution:

> The thing I remember best was seeing the *Spirit of St. Louis.* It was suspended from the ceiling. I had heard about it in school and I marveled at the history. I was really struck by the way it was designed, the fact that it had no forward windows. I had never realized that Lindbergh couldn't even see in front of him as he flew, that he was flying blind. I was also impressed by the scalloped effect of the metal. It was such a weird, special type of plane. I remember just how amazed I was by that plane.[62]

He had heard about the plane quite a bit from school and read about it in textbooks, but he had never seen it. The combination of his prior knowledge of the plane and the real object produced an indelible memory and additional learning. In a similar way, other people seemed to recall most vividly exhibitions that built upon prior knowledge, rather than those that presented totally novel objects and ideas. The experience of seeing tangible examples of previously learned verbal or pictorial material obviously plays a major role in facilitating long-term learning.

The important role that prior knowledge plays in all learning requires a theoretical shift in our thinking about learning.[63] For many years, researchers believed that learning occurred through the repetitive presentation of appropriate stimuli, the process of accumulating and absorbing information. However, it is now widely believed that although some learning can occur through such gradual accumulation and absorption, more often learning requires conceptual shifts in how an individual deals with new information, shifts that no amount of drill and practice could ever accomplish.[64] This view suggests that learning is always a cumulative transformation of mental structures, a transformation in which the individual actively makes sense of the world on the basis of prior knowledge and understanding.[65]

In a 1995 review on the subject, psychologist Jeremy Roschelle provides several examples of the importance of this concept for learning.[66] Roschelle suggests that if there is a discrepancy between a learner's current understanding of a topic and the explanation presented by an "expert," no amount of instruction on the topic will result in a changed understanding without a total reconstruction of the learner's mental models. Learning requires building upon prior knowledge with additional information and experiences. This reveals both the strengths and constraints of human learning.

Research in the neurosciences confirms the fundamentally constructive nature of learning. Quite literally, memories are built up and combined as they are created and then reconstructed and recombined.[67] The result is that numerous comparable experiences are combined into a single composite recollection, creating personal "constructs" (sometimes very accurate and sometimes not so accurate) rather than exact "reproductions."[68] Thus learning is an extraordinarily flexible process. Ideas, images, and even events can be assembled into totally new and unique configurations. Although the impermanence of memory can sometimes be a liability—for example, when trying to remember the name of an acquaintance at a party—it can also be a benefit. The constructive quality of memory enables humans to invent, theorize, and create. If memory and recall were totally rigid, like the record on a videotape or computer disk, humans would be doomed to repeating the same behaviors over and over again and would still be swinging from trees and dodging leopards. Memory enables us to respond to new events, particularly emergencies, with the wisdom of prior experience, by influencing what a person will perceive and attend to in the future.

Consistent with brain research, psychological research on prior knowledge has found that it not only affects how individuals approach and solve problems, but that it also significantly influences how people perceive an event or what part of a situation is attended to in the first place.[69] The more investigators come to learn about people's prior knowledge, the more difficult it becomes for many to explain how new knowledge could ever circumvent the hurdles imposed by prior knowledge. These studies, often referred to collectively as *misconception studies,* reveal that the construction of new knowledge is a very slow, in fact almost improbable, event.[70]

According to Roschelle, the fairly negative view of many of these misconception studies has resulted in part from inherent biases in the way psychologists and educators have interpreted the data on prior knowledge.[71] The first of these is an inherent bias in the data sets themselves. Almost all of the prior knowledge research has focused on learning failure rather than learning success. If successes were investigated, these too would have been found to be the result of prior knowledge. Prior knowledge is properly understood not as a case of failure or success but rather as the raw material that fuels learning.[72] For example, in a study of the National Museum of American History's major exhibition *American Encounters*, visitors were interviewed to determine the nature and extent of their meaning-making about Hispanic and Indian cultures.[73] Less than a third of visitors felt they had learned new information about Hispanic and American Indian peoples, information that had changed their under-standing or appreciation of how people did or currently do live in New Mexico. When probed, this group of visitors gave a wide range of exam-ples of things they learned in *American Encounters*, including details about cultural objects, history, and traditions, as well as more thematic elements relating to struggles for identity and economic survival. For this small group, the exhibition helped shift their mental constructs and resulted in what they described as "new" knowledge. However, nearly half of the visitors interviewed felt that their prior knowledge (of New Mexico, His-panic culture, and American Indian culture) was not changed but merely reaffirmed. Thus, for most of the visitors to this exhibit, learning repre-sented the gradual expansion and consolidation of previously known mental constructs.

Missing from much of the research on prior knowledge is the impor-tant role that assimilation, the reinforcement of known things, plays in learning. Swiss psychologist Jean Piaget described two processes of learn-ing, or adaptation as he called it: *assimilation* and *accommodation*. Accord-ing to Piaget, when we assimilate, we interpret the external world in terms of our current schemes or presently available ways of thinking about things, building additional understanding and reinforcing known things.[74] In accommodation, the schemes are revised to take into account newly understood properties, changing and refining structures to achieve a better adaptive fit with the experience.[75] Most of the time, for most peo-ple, learning appears to be a process of reaffirmation and assimilation; more rarely does it involve accommodation. That assimilation is an important facet of learning is strongly reinforced by recent findings in neuroscience.[76] However, historical models of learning have been predi-cated on the assumption that "real" learning is the measurable change in understanding that comes about through accommodation. This is a very important fact since virtually all research methods for assessing learning, in both museums and schools, have been based almost exclusively on measuring fairly major, fundamental changes in knowledge structure, rather than the more subtle reinforcement of preexisting known things. Thus, much, if not most, of learning, has remained effectively undocu-mented.

Also not always taken into consideration in studies of conceptual understanding has been the influence of development on thinking, par-ticularly in studies involving children. The ability to develop theoretical understanding changes over the course of intellectual development, inde-pendent of intelligence. In other words, not all twelve-year-olds are capa-ble of the same degree of conceptualization. As first described by Piaget, cognition proceeds from the *concrete* to the *abstract*.[77] Children first under-stand the immediately observable aspects of their world, such as physical appearance and overt behavior. Only later do they grasp less obvious, abstract processes such as intentions, motivations, and time.[78] In general, thinking becomes better organized and integrated with age, as children gather concepts about the world. Over time, children also revise their con-ceptions of the causes of behavior, moving from simple one-sided, single-variable explanations to complex interacting relationships that take into account multiple variables.[79] Ultimately, at about the age of adolescence, cognition moves toward what is known as *metacognition*.[80] This is the abil-ity to think about thinking, to literally step outside one's self and think about what others might think about that, or even what others might think about you. This developmental process dramatically affects the nature of both thinking and behavior, and of course it affects how some-one might respond to a question about the nature of the world.

Finally, there is a problem with the way these studies have been con-ducted. The pessimistic view of learning that results from cognitive psy-chology studies of schoolchildren is at least partially an artifact of the con-text in which the studies were conducted. Without denying the basic premise of what has been presented above—that learning often requires a reconstruction of prior knowledge, the mental accommodation of new ways of seeing, feeling, and thinking about knowledge—learning occurs best when accompanied by supportive contexts. In fact, learning can seemingly emerge out of such supportive contexts, when, for example, a fact or idea long "forgotten" suddenly pops to mind. This is the fourth important lesson to be learned from Monica Pershey's experience described at the beginning of this chapter.

THE IMPORTANCE OF CONTEXT

Monica learned about the mechanics of bridges, but she only realized her learning when a situation many months later gave her reason to apply that knowledge. This is exactly what happened to the visitor to the National Museum of Natural History whom we discussed in the first chapter when she saw a black squirrel in Michigan. Learning is always a continuous process of constructing knowledge, both literally and figura-tively. Although the total picture is yet to be understood, one theory holds that all of our memories are stored as images, but not as whole images, as pieces of images.[81] Different parts of the brain may actually store different pieces. When we attempt to reconstruct something, we reassemble the pieces as best we can. The result is usually a perceptual whole, even if some of the details are fuzzy or glossed over.[82]

Returning to Monica, it is probably safe to conjecture that she did not possess a permanent "bridge mechanics" memory as such. Instead, she possessed pieces of memory, which, when cued by a real bridge, she could reassemble into a holistic perception of the workings of a swing bridge. No doubt, pieces were drawn from many experiences and many places in her brain and constructed into a single "memory."[83] Even though the children's museum experience might have been the most salient, other bits and pieces of prior experience were undoubtedly added together also. Learning always involves such constant assembly processes. An increasing body of research leads us to appreciate that, quite literally, learning has no real beginning and no real end.[84] At the core of all learning are memories, and memories are not permanent entities but rather the creation of new patterns from preexisting patterns. This is why today's memories can be different from yesterday's and why, for example, eyewitness testimony at trials is notoriously unreliable.[85] As a consequence, if someone asks visitors as they are leaving an exhibition or a program what they "learned," the answer they give at that moment may or may not be the same as the answer they might give to the same question a month or two later. The differences are not due to some effort at obfuscation but are an artifact of the constantly changing and evolving nature of memory and learning.

This reality was documented by psychologists Maria Medved and Phillip Oatley in a systematic study of museum impact conducted at a Canadian science center.[86] Medved and Oatley studied visitors to the Science Arcade section of the Ontario Science Center, a gallery that contains interactive displays that focus on physical science concepts such as electricity, air pressure, and sound waves. Visitors were interviewed as they left the Science Arcade and by telephone a month later. There were no significant differences between the amount and type of exhibition-related conceptual understanding recorded immediately after the visit and one month later. The results were presented to a panel of independent raters, blind to whether an explanation was from the initial or the follow-up interview. The panel was asked to categorize the conceptual change statements as either "deterioration of conceptual understanding," "no change," or "improved understanding." Results of this analysis revealed that 36 percent of the responses showed deterioration of conceptual understanding over the one-month period, 36 percent showed an increase in understanding over the one-month period, and 28 percent remained the same. In other words, conceptual understanding was just as likely to improve over time as it was to deteriorate. The individuals in this study were not aware that they would be taking part in a memory test, a condition often described in terms of incidental learning and associated with poor memory.[87] However, as we have described above, when learning occurs for reasons of intrinsic motivation, it appears to be remarkably robust, requiring only an appropriate environmental context or prompt to stimulate recall.[88]

This, then, is the final lesson to be learned from Monica's experience. Not only does learning require prior knowledge, appropriate motivation, and a combination of emotional, physical, and mental action; it also requires an appropriate context within which to express itself. In the absence of contextual cues from the outside world, the patterns and associations stored within each person's head would remain dormant or meaningless.[89] Consequently, there are two constants about context. The first is that context, like so much in life, is always changing. The second is that context is always relative to the person; this is a major reason learning is such a personally constructive process. This is also the reason it is not possible to understand learning acontextually.

For the moment, though, we can ask, How do experiences become part of our personal repertoire? In other words, why do we attend to some experiences but not others, choose to learn some things but not other things? What determines the filters our brain uses to judge what to put into memory and what to exclude? Literally, how do we come to be interested in some things and not others? Of course some of what we choose to learn is determined by what we encounter in the world, and arguably a small percentage is dictated by our genes. But humans, more than most creatures, are largely shaped by neither genes nor the physical environment. As we will explore in the next chapter, humans and human learning are most fundamentally shaped by other humans—what we refer to broadly as the sociocultural context.

KEY POINTS

- Most human learning is self-motivated, emotionally satisfying, and very personally rewarding. Humans are highly motivated to learn when they are in supporting environments; when they are engaged in meaningful activities; when they are freed from anxiety, fear, and other negative mental states; when they have choices and control over their learning; and when the challenges of the task meet their skills.

- Learning is never just facts and concepts. Learning, particularly intrinsically motivated learning, is a rich, emotion-laden experience, encompassing much, if not most, of what we consider to be fundamentally human. At its most basic level, learning is about affirming self.

- New learning is always constructed from a base of prior knowledge. Prior knowledge is properly understood not as a case of failure or success but rather as the raw material that fuels learning.

- Not only does learning require prior knowledge, appropriate motivation, and a combination of emotional, physical, and mental action; it also requires an appropriate context within which to express itself. In the absence of contextual cues from the outside world, the patterns and associations stored within each person's head would remain dormant or meaningless.

NOTES

1. Herbart 1965.
2. Schiefele 1991.
3. Sylwester 1995; Calvin 1997.
4. Calvin 1997.
5. Sylwester 1995.
6. Rose 1993; Sylwester 1995; Hilts 1995.
7. Rose 1993; Sylwester 1995.
8. Aggleton 1992.
9. Damasio 1994; Piaget 1981.
10. Damasio 1994.
11. Sylwester 1995; Damasio 1994.
12. Csikszentmihalyi and Hermanson 1995.
13. Csikszentmihalyi and Hermanson 1995.
14. Albjerg Graham 1997; Csikszentmihalyi 1995.
15. Deci et al. 1981; Deci 1992; McCombs 1991.
16. Maehr 1984; McCombs 1991.
17. Diener and Dweck 1980; McCombs 1991; Baddeley 1994.
18. Pintrich and DeGroot 1990; Covington 1992; Paris and Cross 1983; Paris 1997.
19. Csikszentmihalyi 1990a, 1990b.
20. Harlow 1954.
21. Csikszentmihalyi and Nakamura 1989.
22. deCharms 1992; Deci and Ryan 1985; White 1959.
23. Dewey 1913; Gottfried 1985; McCombs 1991; Schiefele 1991.
24. Paris 1997.

25. Dweck and Leggett 1988.
26. Dweck and Leggett 1988; Heyman and Dweck 1992.
27. Hidi 1990; Lepper and Cordova 1992; Gottfried 1985.
28. Csikszentmihalyi, Rathunde, and Whalen 1993.
29. Amabile 1983, 1985; Deci 1971, 1972; Lepper and Greene 1978; McGraw 1978.
30. Paris 1997, 22–30.
31. Falk and Lynch 1981; Zimmer 1995.
32. Beck and Habicht 1991, 1996; Beck et al. 1994.
33. Epstein 1973; Harter 1983.
34. Harter 1983.
35. Kelley 1973; Weiner 1974, 1987.
36. Rowe 1974a, 1974b.
37. Harter 1981; Marsh, Smith, and Barnes 1985.
38. Dweck and Elliott 1983.
39. Harter 1983; Rosenberg 1979.
40. Schiefele 1991.
41. Schiefele 1991.
42. Schiefele 1991.
43. Hidi 1990; Dierking and Pollock 1998.
44. James [1890] 1950, 1: 237.
45. Csikszentmihalyi and Hermanson 1995.
46. Pintrich and DeGroot 1990.
47. Tulley and Lucas 1991.
48. Rosenfield 1990.
49. Freud 1959.
50. Ramey-Gassert, Walberg, and Walberg 1994.
51. Csikszentmihalyi and Hermanson 1995; Clifford 1991.
52. Csikszentmihalyi and Hermanson 1995.
53. Csikszentmihalyi 1975, 1990b.
54. Rohrkemper and Corno 1988; Csikszentmihalyi and Hermanson 1995.
55. Paris 1997.
56. Falk and Dierking 1992.
57. Henderlong and Paris 1996.
58. Paris 1997, 24.
59. Csikszentmihalyi and Hermanson 1995, 70.
60. As we will explore more fully in a subsequent book, flow experiences are part of an elaborate evolutionary feedback system for building and extending self.
61. Hidi 1990.
62. Falk 1988.
63. Roschelle 1995.
64. Strike and Posner 1985; West and Pines 1985.
65. Bruner 1990; Roschelle 1995; Hein and Alexander 1998.
66. Roschelle 1995.
67. Edelman 1987.

68. Rumelhart and McClelland 1986; Sylwester 1995; Damasio 1994; Barclay 1988; Neisser 1982.

69. Trowbridge and McDermott 1980; Anzai and Yokohama 1984; Larkin 1983; Chi, Feltovich, and Glaser 1980; Chi and Koeske 1983.

70. Roschelle 1995.

71. Roschelle 1995.

72. Roschelle 1995.

73. Falk and Holland 1994.

74. Piaget and Inhelder 1969.

75. Piaget and Inhelder 1969.

76. Calvin 1997; Sylwester 1995.

77. Piaget 1954.

78. Berk 1989.

79. Berk 1989.

80. Flavell 1981.

81. Damasio 1994.

82. Damasio 1994.

83. Rose 1993.

84. Rose 1993; Sylwester 1995.

85. Loftus 1979; Loftus and Marburger 1983.

86. Medved and Oatley in press.

87. Nickerson and Adams 1979.

88. Cf. Falk and Dierking 1997.

89. According to Edelman (1985) dreams seem so nonsensical because they are mental patterns created in the absence of meaning-making external context; see also Hobson 1989.

3

The Sociocultural Context

The central fact about our psychology is the fact of social mediation. Higher mental functions in the individual have their origins in the social life of the individual.

— L. S. Vygotsky, *Mind in Society*

A father and his six-year-old daughter enter a life science exhibition and approach an exhibit on the size and capacities of different kinds of animal hearts. The following conversation was recorded:

The girl shouts, "Oh look, look over there," as she runs towards the exhibit. "Look at all those things in jars. What are they, Daddy?" Her father responds, "Those are hearts of different kinds of animals." Reading the labels, he continues, "See, there's a heart of an elephant, a cow, a dog, a rat and a mouse."

The girl looks closely at the hearts. Then her father asks, "Honey, do you know how big your heart is?" She shrugs her shoulders. "Well, do you think it is bigger or smaller than this elephant's heart?" "Silly," the girl answers, "It's smaller." "Ok," says the father, "that's right. Is it bigger or smaller than this cow's heart?" "Smaller." "Is it bigger or smaller than this dog's heart?" "Bigger," she says, "because I'm bigger than Scamp." [Scamp is the family beagle.]

"Scamp's ok, isn't he?" she asks [a reference to Scamp's visit that morning to the vet]. "Yes, Scamp is a very healthy dog for his age." "Good," she says, "I wouldn't want Scamp to be sick. He's such a silly." "Yes he is, isn't he?" replies the father.

Dad then attempts to get her back into looking at the exhibit. "Look how tiny the mouse heart is." "Oooh, it's so tiny," she says in a tiny voice. "So," says dad, "Isn't it interesting that your heart is smaller than the cow's heart and bigger than Scamp's heart, because you are in between the size of a cow and a dog like Scamp?" "Yep," says the girl. The father then asks: "So, show me how big your heart is." The little girl then holds up her hands and says about this big, fairly accurately indicating the size of her heart, a size between that of the cow and the dog. (Conversation between a father and his six-year-old daughter in the *World of Life* exhibition at California Science Center)[1]

This conversation provides a rich window through which to begin to understand the sociocultural context of learning. Deconstructing this conversation can lead to topics as direct as the obvious social bond between father and child or to issues as indirect as the role of parents in "enculturating" their children. This episode between father and daughter provides a glimpse into the ways humans build knowledge and understanding through conversation and also demonstrates the role of family narrative in creating shared meanings between individuals. Finally, the fact that this dialogue occurred at all is reflective of the larger sociocultural function that places like museums play in fostering communities of learners, a concept that will be developed later in this chapter. Most important, this conversation is reflective of the fact that much of the way humans make sense of the world is through social interaction with others, through distributed meaning-making. For learning, particularly learning in museums, is a fundamentally social experience.

Humans are social animals, and much of what they learn is mediated through conversation, gestures, emotions, the observation of others, and the use of culturally and historically constructed tools, signs, and symbol systems, as well as the cultural and historical overlays of societal beliefs, values, and norms. All of these have a sociocultural foundation. Consequently, who we are, what we are, and how we behave are products of the sociocultural context in which we are immersed.[2]

It is no accident that learning evolved a strong sociocultural component. Understanding the social world is a fundamental building block of learning; a long evolutionary history supports the fact that humans are first and foremost social creatures. The human brain contains a rich collection of dedicated, functionally specialized, interrelated mechanisms organized to guide thought and behavior about the social world.[3] There is also fossil evidence of human social behaviors dating back several million years.[4] Social behaviors are universal and highly elaborated across all human cultures—including hunter-gatherer, agrarian, and urban cultures—as would be expected if these behaviors were an ancient and central part of human life.[5] Supporting this evidence is the fact that the nearest human relatives, the chimpanzees, also engage in certain types of sophisticated social behaviors, implying that adaptations to social inter-action were present in prehuman ancestors at least as far back as the com-mon ancestors we share with the chimpanzee, five to ten million years ago.[6]

Each human possesses both a long evolutionary history of social understanding and interaction and a long personal history. From cradle to grave we are surrounded and influenced by other humans. These social influences begin prior to birth, in utero. From the earliest moments of con-ception, humans are immersed in a rich physical and social context that envelops and nurtures the fetus. Research suggests that beyond the expected exchange of nutrients, waste products, and gases, there is also a great deal of social exchange between the fetus and the mother. In utero infants hear music and conversations, and their development is strongly influenced by the mother's emotional and social milieu.[7] An individual's influence upon others can even extend past his or her death. Memories of a loved one, a friend, a leader, or mentor often guide our behavior long after the individual has passed away.

CULTURE

The sociocultural context defines both who we perceive ourselves to be and how we perceive the world we inhabit. In a very real sense, the world in which each of us lives is socioculturally constructed. The world has meaning for us because of the shared experiences, beliefs, customs, and values of the groups that inhabit it with us. This collection of shared beliefs and customs is what we have come to call *culture.*

Culture is the fundamental concept of an entire social science disci-pline, anthropology. However, as stated by educational anthropologist John Ogbu, culture is a problematic concept both within and outside anthropology.[8] There are literally hundreds of different definitions of cul-ture within academic circles; many bear little resemblance to the common understanding of the word among the general public.[9] In the spirit of this book's effort to integrate the latest research in neuroscience, evolutionary biology, psychology, and museum studies, we have chosen to use an eco-logical approach, which defines culture as an adaptation, a social mecha-nism enabling individuals to survive. Within this context, learning can be viewed as the process by which a society "shapes the mind" of individu-als to create the kind of persons who, as adults, will "be able to meet the imperatives of the culture."[10] According to Ogbu, this approach suggests that culture is composed of five components:

1. Customary ways of behaving (e.g., of making a living, eating, expressing affection, getting married, raising children, responding to illness and death, getting ahead in society, dealing with the supernatural, going for a job interview, holding conferences, and so on).

2. Codes or assumptions, expectations, and emotions underlying those customary behaviors.

3. Artifacts, or things that members of the population make or have made that have meaning for them (e.g., airports, cars, family homes, freeways, museums, computers, restaurants, schools, supermarkets, television, wristwatches, etc.).

4. Institutions—economic, political, religious, and social—sometimes called the imperatives of culture, which form a recognizable pattern requiring knowledge, beliefs, competencies or skills, and customary behaviors in a fairly predictable manner.

5. Patterns of social relations.[11]

These five components constitute a kind of "cultural world" in which people live. People create, change, and pass their culture on to their children, who in turn may change it. But their culture also influences them. Culture can thus be seen both to persist and to evolve over time, but unlike most other defining qualities of living systems, culture is passed on nongenetically through learning.

When children are born, they do not yet possess the ideas, values, emotions, perceptions, skills, and behavior patterns that are shared by members of their society, all of which they will need to survive and achieve social competence as adults. These "cultural products" are constructed by the individuals who make up the child's society and represent its past history.[12] There is not a single set of human cultural products but, rather, numerous ones, one for every set of human populations that has ever lived. One of the wonders of human evolution is that although culture itself is not genetically transmitted, the capacity to acquire it is. Human children are born with the innate predisposition to attend to and assimilate cultural products. According to Ogbu, "as they 'develop' or reach different phases of maturation, children learn the appropriate phases and types of their society's customary behaviors and the accompanying thoughts and emotions that support these behaviors. They gain knowledge and understand the meanings of cultural artifacts or symbols and societal institutions, and they learn the practical skills that make those institutions work. They recognize patterns of social relations and behaviors with their supporting assumptions."[13] For example, in the case of the father-and-daughter experience that began this chapter, the father was sharing an important lesson with his daughter that was not related to the size of animal hearts at all. By taking her to the museum in the first place and facilitating her inquiry there, he was demonstrating to her how she could use the museum institution as a place for learning.

This learning results in societal members who can keep the society functional and a society that defines for its members what it means to be a functional human. Thus, according to ecological anthropologist Robert Shweder, psyche and culture are "seamlessly interconnected."[14] In this view, humans are at once individuals and members of a larger group or society; learning is both an individual and a group experience. What someone learns, let alone why someone learns, is inextricably bound to the cultural and historical context in which that learning occurs. Our perception, descriptions, and understanding of the world are all culturally and historically bound.

Several studies have been conducted that show that even such "basic" human perceptions as color recognition,[15] facial expressions,[16] and even emotion[17] are culturally bound. For example, English speakers distinguish between the colors "blue" and "green" and distinguish shades of gray in the "black" color range. Navajo speakers lump "blue" and "green" together and distinguish no gradations of "black."[18] The meaning of facial expressions also varies culturally. For most people in the United States, raising the eyebrows means surprise; a single raised eyebrow, doubt or questioning. For people of the Marshall Islands in the Pacific, a raised eyebrow signals an affirmative answer, while in Greece a raised eyebrow is a sign of disagreement.[19]

Even when learning seems not to be directly influenced by sociocultural interaction, there is indirect interaction. The books one reads or the television program, exhibition, or film one views alone are all cultural products; all have been created by other humans with the intention of communicating, that is, "conversing," with the reader or viewer, and all have been created within some sociocultural context of their own. As solitary individuals read and interact, they bring their own experience, emotions, and values to the fore, all mediated by their own social and cultural backgrounds. As suggested, meaningful learning results when a person is able to actively construct and find personal meaning within a situation. Virtually all such learning is either directly or indirectly socially mediated. From this perspective, all communication media represent a socially mediated form of culturally specific conversation between the producers of that medium (exhibition, film, catalogue, performance, program, book, audiotape, Internet) and the user.[20]

SOCIAL COGNITION

As suggested earlier, when children are born, they do not possess the ideas, values, emotions, perceptions, skills, or behavior patterns that will allow them to become socially competent adults. Psychologists use the term *social cognition* to describe this set of skills and knowledge of self and others that humans develop as they grow and mature. Social cognitive psychologists investigate how children and adults conceptualize themselves and others as psychological beings and how they perceive and understand relationships between people.

Historically, social development and cognitive development were studied separately, but in the last twenty years, efforts have been made to look at the disciplines more holistically. This holistic approach recognizes that children are active social thinkers who bring cognitive skills to social interactions and make meaning from these interactions that influence other areas of learning in their lives.[21] Not surprisingly, then, many of the same developmental trends we described in the previous chapter seem to apply to the development of social cognition. For example, social cognition develops from the concrete to the abstract. Social thinking also appears to become more highly organized and integrated with age, as children construct increasingly coherent socially relevant concepts, such as personalities and identities, from early observations of people's separate behaviors. Social cognition also moves toward a metacognitive level of understanding.[22] As development proceeds, children become more adept at self-regulation in the social arena. One important unique capacity that humans also develop is perspective-taking, or the capacity to imagine what another's thoughts and feelings might be.[23]

Although social cognition skills are used to navigate the social world, they are very closely tied to self, as was suggested in chapter 2. Again, the personal, sociocultural, and physical contexts of learning are not independent of one another but inextricably linked.

SOCIOCULTURAL APPROACHES

Just as the sociocultural milieu is seen to influence the development of social cognition, sociocultural approaches suggest that the most fundamental aspects of learning, including perception, processing, and meaning-making, are socioculturally constructed. Thus the study of learning should not only focus on the individual but also incorporate the investigation of the group and its sociocultural milieu. Although this view was not a main-stream perspective within psychology, philosophy, medicine, or biology for most of the twentieth century, as early as the nineteenth century, individuals such as Emil Durkheim and Auguste Comte, considered by many to be the founders of the discipline of sociology, suggested that social processes affected individual behavior.[24]

In the early part of the twentieth century, sociologist C. H. Cooley and social psychologists George Mead and Kurt Lewin in the United States and Lev Semanovich Vygotsky and his students in Russia independently argued for a nonindividualistic view of learning and behavior. Cooley and Mead felt that even the contents of our minds and our self-concepts are learned in interaction with others.[25] Lewin agreed with this view and developed a framework for thinking about the individual that included an extended self that incorporated not only other people but also objects and artifacts.[26] Vygotsky believed that individual cognition develops as a result of interactions in the social life of the individual.[27] Although, as we suggested, Mead, Lewin, and Vygotsky were ignored and largely forgotten by a generation of social scientists, today their ideas, especially Vygotsky's, are enjoying a rebirth in interest and popularity.

Vygotsky approached cognition from a biological and evolutionary perspective, feeling that the emergence and transformation of forms of mediation had benefited humans and increased their survival as a species over the course of evolutionary history. Like Mead, he felt that one could not analyze individual processes to understand social processes, suggesting it was the other way around entirely, that in order to understand the individual, one must first understand the individual's social relation-ships.[28] According to social psychologists Luis Moll and James Greenberg, one of the most interesting and important contributions of Vygotskian psychology is the proposal that human thinking must be understood in its concrete social and historical circumstances.[29] As Alexander Luria, one of Vygotsky's students, explained it, "to understand thinking one must go beyond the human organism. One must search for the origins of 'conscious activity,'" not in the "recesses of the human brain or in the depths of the spirit, but in the external conditions of life." Luria continued, "Above all, this means that one must seek these origins in the external processes of social life, in the social and historical forms of human existence."[30] In this view, all learning is built upon previous learning, not just of the individual, but of the entire society in which that individual lives.

The words and concepts we use in our daily life, as much as the concrete artifacts we use, such as automobiles, computers, and can openers, are historical legacies of our society/culture; these are the tools that we are given to build a life. These are what Ogbu referred to as "cultural products."[31]

Vygotsky researched concrete social interactions within small groups of individuals (frequently dyads), particularly adults and children. His notion of mediation was extremely rich, emphasizing meaning-making and verbal and nonverbal language. Vygotsky believed that all higher mental functions have social origins and are first expressed between individuals (on an *interpersonal* plane) before they are internalized within the individual (on an *intrapsychic* plane).[32]

Central to Vygotsky's theory of cognitive development was the notion of social mediation through language.[33] Vygotsky believed that people use language not only for social communication but also to guide, plan, and monitor their activity in a self-regulatory manner. He referred to such self-regulatory language as "private speech," feeling that people, particularly children, use this language as a tool in their thinking. In other words, the same language that mediates social interaction *between* individuals is used to mediate cognitive activity *within* individuals. Children take the language of everyday interactions, make it part of their private speech, and use this speech to organize their own independent cognitive efforts.[34]

Vygotsky stressed the central role of social communication in the development of children's thinking by conceiving of children's learning as taking place within the "zone of proximal development." He defined this zone as the distance between a child's "actual developmental level" in solving a problem independently and the higher level of "potential development" if they were to solve the problem under adult guidance or in collaboration with more capable peers.[35] Tasks within a child's zone of proximal development were ones that were too difficult to be done alone but that could be accomplished with the verbal guidance and assistance of adults or more skilled children, a social mediation process he called *scaffolding*. The scaffolding process involves the creation of processes and ideas between two or more individuals (Vygotsky referred to these as *intermental*), which are internalized by the individual and become *intramental*. Thus, another way of thinking about the zone of proximal development is as the mediation potential between *inter*mental and *intra*mental processes and ideas.

The conversation between the father and his daughter that started this chapter, overheard during research in the *World of Life* exhibition at the California Science Center, is a concrete example of the zone of proximal development. It also demonstrates the creation of private speech, with its potential for use in future problem-solving situations. In the conversation, the father provided social support, or scaffolding, for the child's investigation about the size of her heart, assisting her in developing a strategy for figuring out how large her own heart was, relating it concretely to a family pet. The father assisted her in solving a problem that she would have struggled to solve alone, helping her make the leap between her *intra*mental, vague knowledge of the relative sizes of various animal hearts and the *inter*mental knowledge constructed in the conversation with her father. This intermental knowledge provided a strategy for observing the size of the animal and inferring the size of its heart. In other words, this was her zone of proximal development for this particular situation. If internalized, the problem-solving strategy becomes a part of the child's private speech and *intra*mental memory, available in the future to solve similar problems. Vygotsky argued that examples like this are the rule rather than the exception in learning situations. He believed that humans virtually always learn through such dialogues, whether explicitly, as in this case, or implicitly, as would be the case if the child used this logical strategy in the future to help her estimate the size of another animal heart. Meaning-making is distributed.

Unfortunately, most efforts to understand learning have not permitted social exchange and hence have missed out on being able to incorporate social interaction and notions such as the zone of proximal development into the determination of what an individual does or does not know. Research has shown that two individuals ostensibly understanding the same idea about a given topic do not necessarily possess equivalent zones of proximal development; one individual may be capable of discussing the idea more fully when in the presence of a well-informed adult or peer.[36]

As Vygotsky observed, sociocultural information is transmitted through social interaction. People spend a majority of their time in conversation, asking questions, answering questions, gesturing, and the like. Adults ask children questions, children ask adults questions, children interact with one another, and adults do likewise.[37] This social interaction happens constantly, during mealtimes, during visits to museums, and in other free-choice learning settings, even while supposedly reading the newspaper alone.

As people interact, they also talk about what they know from previous experiences, discussing what they see, hear, and read in terms of these experiences and memories. As researchers have observed, these discussions provide opportunities for people to reinforce past experiences and, in the case of families, family history, such as Scamp's visit to the vet, and to develop a shared understanding among the members of the group. It is during many of these conversations that one also observes people's efforts to negotiate personal and cultural meaning, actively making sense of the interpretation presented and attempting to relate it to their own experience and worldview.[38]

It is fair to surmise that the sociocultural facilitation of learning is a typical component of most museum learning. In the real world, unlike in the classroom or a laboratory, if you do not know the answer to something you want to know about, you ask for help, read about it, or in some way seek out ways to maximize your zone of proximal development. Free-choice learning in general and museum learning in particular are commonly marked by some sort of socially facilitated learning.

COMMUNITIES OF LEARNERS

Recently psychologists have attempted to extend Vygotsky's ideas beyond the small groups of individuals he researched to larger groups. These psychologists now suggest that all learning occurs within a context they call a "community of learners" or "communities of practice."[39] According to this view, which begins with the premise that all knowledge, including the specific knowledge of any group or society, is socioculturally constructed, knowledge is not the same for all individuals in society but is shared within often delimited communities of knowers.[40] In other words, there exist myriad communities of learners, defined by the boundaries of shared knowledge and experience. The family makes up one such community. The parent(s) and children, aunts and uncles, and other members of the extended family share a set of beliefs, values, language, and customs that is similar to that of other families but is in many ways unique to that particular family. Researchers refer to the social sharing of knowledge in a household as the exchange of funds of knowledge, another way of thinking of distributed meaning-making within a family.[41] Similarly, other groups of individuals share specific knowledge and experience. For example, the groups that call themselves carpenters or physicians, as well as the group of individuals who consider themselves history museum or historic-home devotees, belong to distinct learning communities. To become a member of such a community, long periods of learning are often necessary, though the learning usually involves no external tests and little praise or blame, progress being visible to the learner and others in the process of the work itself.[42] Membership in a community of learners can be either conscious, as when a child aspires to become an astronaut and does everything possible to achieve that goal, or unconscious, as when an individual "independently" pursues an interest or avocation only to discover that there are many others who share a similar interest—for example, finding yourself part of a community of learners interested in art when you attend a special art exhibition program and see others interested in the same type of art. The father and daughter at the beginning of this chapter constitute a community of learners, and the California Science Center they chose to visit that day is a cultural institution designed to support a variety of communities of learners.

Throughout human history, the primary means of initiating newcomers into a community of knowers has been through face-to-face talk in the context of ongoing "work."[43] These types of apprenticeships were once a common feature of all enterprise, whether child-rearing, farming, hunting, or some type of trade. Today, we rarely think about apprenticeships, but they are still remarkably common and effective ways to transmit knowledge. Growing up to become an adult member of a culture, whether learning to play a musical instrument or a sport or becoming a tailor or an accountant, involves some level of apprenticeship. Apprenticeships remain the primary mechanism by which a newcomer becomes a member of a community of knowers.

All of these ideas jell as one tries to understand why people have the knowledge they do and, equally important, desire the knowledge they desire. From this perspective, knowledge—and, implicitly, learning—is always socioculturally "situated" within a larger culture and within the social setting of an event. According to Vygotsky, high-quality sociocultural teaching facilitates mediation that takes into account the zone of proximal development and thus guides intellectual and developmental pathways.[44] In our example, the father's effort to facilitate his daughter's understanding and ability to solve the problem presented was very much socioculturally mediated as he assisted her in developing a problem-solving strategy in which she was able to use prior knowledge and experience (Scamp as a frame of reference). Lave argues that learning is actually the process of becoming a member of a sustained community of practice and suggests that legitimate peripheral participation in communities of practice (her term for the process of enculturation, apprenticeships, and mentoring) is the critical driving force for learning.[45] From her perspective, if that father and daughter continue to pursue their inquiry at home, in museums, and so on as a sustained community of practice, they will learn.

Because of the diversity of sociocultural practices in different cultures, children in different communities have different developmental pathways. Vygotsky followers Roland Tharp and Ronald Gallimore report: "Boys in Micronesia, where sailing a canoe is a fundamental skill, will have a [zone of proximal development] for the skills of navigation, created in interaction with the sailing masters. A girl in the Navajo weaving community will have experiences in a zone not quite like any ever encountered by the daughters of Philadelphia."[46] As summarized by social psychologists Eugene Matusov and Barbara Rogoff, "the diversity of goals of different communities necessitates defining development in terms of progress toward more responsible participation in specific communities of practice rather than assuming that development is a generic process independent of the goals and institutions of the communities in which an individual develops. At the same time, the developing individual contributes to the further development of the practices (and goals and institutions) of the community."[47]

The sociocultural context influences both the individual and the community in which that individual lives at a variety of levels; at the micro level this context influences the number and types of social interactions in which people engage, consequently affecting perception and the processing of information. At the macro level the sociocultural context shapes the meaning that is made of the perceptions and concepts formulated by the individual and the community. Within this framework, any attempt to make sense out of learning requires an effort to understand the sociocultural context at both the micro and macro levels.

ROLE OF NARRATIVE

Accepting the fact that an important part of learning involves this sociocultural overlay, are there particular ways sociocultural "information" is shared? One important avenue seems to be through narrative or story form. Children as young as three years seem to remember familiar daily experiences in terms of scripts or stories, organized representations of event sequences that provide a general description of what occurs and when it occurs in a given situation. Scripts that are held in long-term memory can be used to predict what will happen in the future on similar occasions. With increasing age, as well as repetitions of a particular kind of experience, children's scripts become more complex.[48]

Researchers believe that scripts are the basic building blocks for people's structured knowledge, a basic means through which they organize, interpret, and predict their world. This is seen very readily when interacting with young children. For example, they rely on scripts when listening to and telling stories. They recall more events from stories based on familiar than unfamiliar event sequences, and they also use script structures for the stories they make up and act out while they play.[49]

There is also a great deal of evidence supporting the role these scripts or stories play in building mature, long-term memory stores.[50] For example, cognitive research demonstrates that, universally, people can mentally organize information effectively if it is recounted to them in a story.[51] However, these stories are a mechanism for transmitting not only the individual's cognitive heritage but also cultural/historical heritage. Through the social acts of play, performance (music and drama), and various story forms, such as myths and poetry (perhaps even a good exhibition), people transmit much of their culture, including customary ways of behaving, codes, assumptions, expectations, and emotions underlying these customary behaviors and patterns of social relations. Often these story forms utilize cultural artifacts, and sometimes the stories themselves become cultural artifacts. Stories and artifacts play a critical role in transmitting culture. Researchers also recognize that people tell themselves stories about their experiences and that these stories help to provide meaning and significance to events.[52]

Group play, both early fantasy play and later group games with defined rules and roles, serves as an avenue for children to practice social roles, learn to recognize and use symbols and signs, and socialize. Researchers who have studied children who do not engage in much pretend play and other researchers who have tried to increase the level of pretend play among toddlers have found that pretend play actually fosters cognitive and social development.[53]

MODELING

Another important way that sociocultural learning occurs is through modeling. Modeling—that is, learning through observation and imitation, also often called *social learning* or *observational learning*—has been studied in both animal behavior and human learning and is considered a powerful tool for childhood (and adult) socialization.[54] Role models turn out to be powerful mechanisms for affecting learning and behavior. Much of what we learn, many of our most fundamental and individually characteristic patterns of behavior—how we talk, how we walk, how we raise our children, what foods we eat, what we value in entertainment and lifestyle, even our political views and affiliations—are *nonverbally* learned, primarily during childhood from our parents, close relatives, and friends.[55]

An extensive line of laboratory investigations by behavioral psychologist Albert Bandura and his associates in the 1960s demonstrated that modeling is the basis for a wide variety of children's learned behaviors, such as aggression, prosocial behavior, and sex stereotyping.[56] Bandura recognized that from an early age, children acquire many of their responses simply by watching and listening to others around them, without direct rewards and punishments and without being explicitly "instructed."

Bandura was particularly interested in what would motivate children to imitate the behavior of certain models. Research by him and his followers showed that children are drawn to models who are warm and powerful and possess desirable objects and other characteristics.[57] Modeling has also been used as an effective tool to modify behavior. For example, Bandura showed that watching a peer play comfortably and pleasurably with a dog can help children who are afraid of dogs to overcome their fears.[58] Reinforcement and modeling have been used to teach social skills to those children who have few friends because they lack effective social behaviors.[59] Modeling can also affect attitude and emotions. Laboratory evidence indicates that exposure to models who behave in a helpful or generous fashion is very effective in encouraging children to act more prosocially themselves.[60] Modeling is also a frequently observed social interaction in museums and will be looked at more closely in that context in chapter 6.[61]

KEY POINTS

- Humans are at once individuals and members of a larger group or society; learning is both an individual and a group experience. What someone learns, let alone why someone learns, is inextricably bound to the cultural and historical context in which that learning occurs. At one level, learning is distributed meaning-making.

- All communication media (television, film, radio, magazines, newspapers, books, museum exhibitions or programs, the Internet, etc.) represent a socially mediated form of culturally specific conversation between the producers of that medium and the user.

- Knowledge, rather than being the same for all individuals, is shared within often delimited communities of learners. In other words, there exist myriad communities of learners, defined by the boundaries of shared knowledge and experience.

• Universally, people mentally organize information effectively if it is recounted to them in a story or narrative form.

NOTES

1. Falk and Amin 1998. Unpublished dialogue recorded in the *World of Life* exhibition at the California Science Center.
2. Falk and Dierking 1995; Schauble, Leinhardt, and Martin 1998.
3. Barkow, Cosmides, and Tooby 1992.
4. Barkow, Cosmides, and Tooby 1992.
5. Cashdan 1989; Lee and Devore 1968; Weissner 1982.
6. De Waal 1982; De Waal and Lutrell 1988; Cheney and Seyfarth 1990.
7. Gallagher 1993, Hofer 1987.
8. Ogbu 1995.
9. Ogbu 1995.
10. Cohen 1971.
11. Ogbu 1995, 79–80.
12. Hansen 1979.
13. Ogbu 1995, 80.
14. Shweder 1990, 3.
15. Berlin and Kay 1969; Heider 1972; Lucy and Shweder 1979; Garro 1986; Kay and Kempton 1984.
16. Gerber 1975, 1985; Levy 1973, 1985; Lutz 1982, 1985; Poole 1985.
17. Wierzbicka 1986; Gerber 1985; Lutz 1986.
18. Fishman 1964.
19. Taylor 1988.
20. Silverman 1990.
21. Youniss 1975.
22. Flavell 1981, 1985.
23. Hoffman 1981.
24. Comte 1855; Durkheim [1895] 1938.
25. Cooley 1902; Mead 1934.
26. Lewin 1951.
27. Vygotsky 1978.
28. Mead 1924–25, 1934; Vygotsky 1979.
29. Moll and Greenberg 1990.
30. Luria 1982, 25.
31. Ogbu 1995.
32. Vygotsky 1978; Wertsch 1986.
33. Vygotsky 1978.
34. Berk 1986; Wertsch 1985.

35. Vygotsky 1978.

36. Wertsch 1985.

37. Birney 1986; Birney 1982; Chase 1975; Dierking 1987, 1989; Draper 1984; Falk and Dierking 1992; Griffin and Symington 1997; Hilke and Balling 1985; Lakota 1975; McManus 1987; Rosenfeld 1979; Tuckey 1992; Tunnicliffe 1995; Wolins, Jensen, and Ulzheimer 1992.

38. Silverman 1990, 1995; Taylor 1986.

39. Tharp and Gallimore 1988; Newman, Griffin, and Cole 1989; Rogoff 1990; Lave and Wenger 1991; Lave 1991; Matusov and Rogoff 1995.

40. Roth and Roychoudhury 1992.

41. Greenberg 1989; Velez-Ibanez 1988.

42. Lave 1991.

43. Lave 1990; Rogoff 1990; Matusov and Rogoff 1995.

44. Vygotsky 1978.

45. Lave 1991.

46. Tharp and Gallimore 1988, 53.

47. Matusov and Rogoff 1995, 100.

48. Schank and Abelson 1977; Nelson 1986.

49. Hudson and Nelson 1983; Nelson and Gruendel 1981.

50. Nelson and Brown 1978.

51. Schauble, Leinhardt, and Martin 1998; Mandler and Goodman 1982; Mandler et al. 1980.

52. Bruner 1996; Feldman et al. 1995; Cortazzi 1993; Roberts 1997.

53. Rubin 1980; Saltz and Saltz 1986.

54. Bandura and Walters 1963; Bandura 1964, 1977; Canale 1977; Elliot and Vasta 1970; Gray and Pirot 1984.

55. Bandura and Walters 1963.

56. Bandura and Walters 1963; Bandura 1964, 1977.

57. Bandura 1977.

58. Bandura 1967.

59. Asher, Odden, and Gottman 1976.

60. Bryan and London 1970; Canale 1977; Elliot and Vasta 1970; Gray and Pirot 1984.

61. Koran et al. 1988; Dierking 1987, 1989.

4

The Physical Context

> Man's sense of space is closely related to his sense of self, which is an
> intimate transaction with his environment.
> —Edward T. Hall, *The Hidden Dimension*

We went on the bus to the Glens of Antrim at Glenarrif [sic] forest park.

Our guide was called Penny McBride. Penny took us for a walk and the
first things we saw were phesants. We saw bamboo shoots. Then we went
over a bridge and it was made of wood and log. Then we walked along the
footpath. Then we saw the Redwood tree and it had spongy bark. The tree
came from America. I[n] America the Redwood tree is 300 feet tall. The redwood tree was 130 years old.

Penny picked garlic leaves and let us smell them.

Then we walked on the footpath and we saw a dead bird. Then we saw
a squirrell going around a tree. We saw lot's of beautiful waterfuls.The
water had foam and bubbles in it. There were platis bottle[s in] the water.
We saw a wooden hut and the windows were all steamed up. We climbed
up steep steep hills and steps. Shaw dropped his money on the footpath.
There were trunks there. We had our lunch at the picnic table. We tidied up
the rubbish that was lying around.

We went to the beach in Ballygalley. We played games like chasing Miss
Armstrong a[nd] paddled in the water. We explored the rock pools. And we
had a treasure hunt. At 3 o'clock we went home and we where very tired and
happy. THE END. (Sarah Jane Minford, seven-year-old Irish schoolgirl)[1]

When people are asked to recall their museum experiences, whether a
day or two later or after twenty or thirty years, the most frequently
recalled and persistent aspects relate to the physical context—memories
of what they saw, what they did, and how they felt about those experiences.[2] Seven-year-old Sarah Jane Minford, who lives in a small village

approximately thirty miles north of Belfast, Ireland, was able to recall a considerable number of details of her daylong school field trip to an outdoor environmental preserve in Northern Ireland. Although several days had elapsed between her visit and her writing about the experience, she was able to remember quite vividly what she saw and did that day. Similarly, Stevenson found that all seventy-nine of the individuals he contacted six months after a visit to a science center could "recall in vivid detail" much of what they had seen and done during their visit.[3] The persistence of people's memory for physical details after a museum visit has been documented for history exhibitions,[4] health exhibitions,[5] science exhibitions,[6] zoo and aquarium exhibitions,[7] children's museum exhibitions,[8] sport exhibitions,[9] and art museum exhibitions.[10] This turns out to be less surprising when it is appreciated that the ability to later make sense of an experience—in fact, the ability to learn—is strongly dependent upon individuals' ability to frame prior experiences within the context of their physical setting.

BEHAVIOR SETTINGS

Over forty years ago two Midwestern psychologists shook up the psychological world when, after years of painstaking research, they announced that contrary to conventional wisdom, settings, rather than the individual characteristics of people, dictate behavior. Roger Barker and Herbert Wright chronicled entire days in the lives of children, recording all their interactions not only with people but also with places and things. After examining their data, Barker and Wright came to the startling conclusion that "the behaviors of children could be predicted more accurately from knowing the situations the children were in than from knowing individual characteristics of the children."[11] When children were in math class, they were quiet and pensive, seated facing the teacher. When children were at recess, they were loud and exuberant, running about the playground. This was true of all children, boys and girls, "bright" and "not-so-bright." Although the children in Barker and Wright's studies did show individual variability—for example, some squirmed more in their seats during class than others—they generally restricted their behavior to conform to what Barker and Wright called "behavior settings." Subsequent research by other investigators in numerous settings with both children and adults has shown that behavior settings are the rule rather the exception in human behavior.[12] According to Barker and Wright, behavior settings are culturally determined. Barker went on to study whole towns in Kansas and Yorkshire, England. The more he watched all sorts of people go about their business in shops, offices, churches, and pubs and on playing fields, the more certain he became that individuals and their inanimate surroundings together create systems of a higher order that take on a life of their own. When a person entered a behavior setting—a school, museum, hospital, or library— everything in that environment encouraged him or her to maintain the status quo. In a sense, the person was no longer an idiosyncratic individual but a teacher or student, museum professional or visitor, doctor or patient, librarian or book borrower.[13]

We unconsciously rely on behavior settings to provide much of the stability in our social institutions, indeed, in our lives. "Under its influence, we line up to buy movie tickets rather than clubbing our way to the window, stop at red lights, and lower our voices in libraries, museums and churches. Sometimes we even gang up with others to enforce a setting's rules, as when we join in shushing whisperers in theaters or giving the cold shoulder to the neighbor who doesn't keep up his yard."[14] Behavior settings serve as a physical-social glue that helps to hold societies together. But perhaps equally, if not more, important, behavior settings probably developed as a mechanism for reducing cognitive dissonance, simplifying relationships within a physical-social milieu. If people needed to relearn the "rules of behavior" every time they walked into a behavior setting, their ability to learn other things would be significantly limited. In fact, this is exactly what happens when people enter new behavior settings. Research in museums shows that first-time visitors behave, and learn, very differently than do frequent visitors.[15] Much of the first-time museum visitor's attention is absorbed in orientation, way-finding, behavior modeling, and general efforts to cope with novelty. The frequent museum visitor, by comparison, knows where he or she is going and how to behave and is able to focus more on exhibitions than is the first-time visitor. Learning to consistently associate familiar settings with a range of "acceptable behaviors" obviates the need for continuous learning. Once appropriate behavior is learned, an individual can focus attention on other aspects of the setting. The result is greater learning and a higher degree of personal security and emotional stability.

So powerful are these behavior settings that people learn to associate certain settings with learning—for example, museums and libraries—and other settings with not learning—for example, playgrounds and theme parks—despite the fact that learning can and does occur in all of these settings. The mechanics of this place-dependent aspect of learning is deeply embedded within our psyche. Because learning is context specific, contexts can facilitate or inhibit learned behaviors. Most adults find simple mathematics a reasonably rote behavior, but when placed in a situation where mathematics is not normally considered, they can find even simple math problems almost impossible to solve.[16] As stated by Wilhelmina Gallagher in her book *The Power of Place,* "Once you see that the ability to access and use your skills varies a lot with the context, you realize how discontinuous your sense of self and your abilities really are."[17]

Barker and Wright's concept of behavior settings was not limited to just the physical environment. After all, behavior settings are an amalgam of the physical and sociocultural contexts. The notion of communities of learners—what Jean Lave refers to as communities of practice, delimited communities of knowers defined by the boundaries of shared knowledge and experience—build on these early notions of Barker and Wright.[18] Humans are exceedingly social creatures, so much so that at some level, we and others have argued, all human learning is socioculturally mediated. However, unlike some sociocultural psychologists, we do feel that the physical environment plays an important mediating role in sociocultural interactions, thus in learning. Rather than finding the physical view of context "constraining," as Lave does,[19] we feel that the "action" is at the intersection of the physical, sociocultural, and personal contexts. In a sense, the sociocultural context described in the previous chapter serves as a bridge between the individual's sense of self, the personal context, and the nonself, or physical context, the individual must live within. Just as a person's sense of who he is and what he represents is defined socioculturally and historically by the people he lives with and those who have lived before, so too is nonself. This understanding develops even before birth. Until very recently, the uterus was regarded as a kind of static puddle in which the passive fetus floats, largely oblivious to what is going on around it. Delicate research shows that far from waiting inertly for birth to raise the curtain on environment, from its first cellular murmurs the fetus is profoundly attuned to the uterine world and gradually to the one beyond. From these early days on, every human's development and behavior depend as much on place as on genes.[20]

Despite the obvious importance of physical context, the history of learning research is replete with efforts to define the process of learning and to deemphasize the importance of context.[21] With only a few exceptions, the major psychological theories of cognitive development have downplayed the importance of context in cognition, preferring instead to emphasize the role of basic cognitive and biological processes.[22] This is just as true for developmental psychologists like Jean Piaget[23] as it is for information processing,[24] neurophysiological,[25] and psychometric psychologists.[26] Even cognitive and constructivist psychologists have underestimated the importance of physical context.[27] In the search for universal truths, it is disappointing to learn that a phenomenon is situationally specific. The thrust of this position was captured by psychologist Ulrich Neisser when he argued that perception and action occur in continuous dependence on the environment and therefore cannot be understood without an understanding of the environment.[28]

However in recent years there has been a growing awareness of the importance of physical context on all cognition, as outlined by neurophysiologist Gerald Edelman in his models of neural development,[29] in the area of memory research,[30] in the research on "situated cognition,"[31] and in the understanding of museum-based learning.[32] In fact, psychologists Stephen Ceci and Mark Leichtman state that:

> The crux of the current view is that memory processes cannot be adequately understood or evaluated acontextually: To think about memory without considering the contexts that lead children to remember is akin to thinking about smiles independently of the faces on which they appear. Different contexts not only evoke different strategies to aid recall, but they also differentially shape an individual's perception of the recall task itself.[33]

IMPORTANCE OF PHYSICAL CONTEXT

People live within a physical context that is not limited to the soil, plants, and animals of the natural world; homes, cars, and offices are also part of the physical context. Within the built environment, the physical context includes the architecture and *feel* of a building, as well as the objects contained in it. People select physical contexts to visit and live within. The decision to visit a museum rather than a shopping mall, let alone the choice of which museum or mall, is determined in part by an appraisal of the physical context. Distance, ease of getting there, and appeal of the architecture are all considerations people employ when deciding how and where to spend their free time. How an individual behaves in these physical spaces, what they observe, and what they remember are also strongly influenced by the physical context; much of this impact occurs subtly and/or subconsciously. For example, whether a visitor learns in a museum can be influenced by the presence or absence of carpeting and adequate seating, as well as by the variety and quality of the objects on display.[34] Author Gallagher stated, "Like those of other living things, our structure, development, and behavior rise from a genetic foundation sunk in an environmental context. Yet while we readily accept that a healthy seed can't grow into a plant without the right soil, light, and water, and that a feral dog won't behave like a pet, we resist recognizing the importance of environment in our own lives."[35]

Both psychological and neuroscience research have confirmed that learning is always rooted in the realities of the physical world, even if abstractly, though typically the relationship is extremely concrete. One of the classic examples of this relationship is Micronesian navigators, world renowned for their navigational abilities. They are regularly able to travel flawlessly from one small island to another across vast expanses of open ocean in situations where there is seemingly a total absence of landmarks or guideposts. Such navigation requires phenomenal skills in memory, inference, and calculation. However, in a research study in which these same individuals were administered standard tests of intellectual functioning, including tests of memory, inference, and calculation, they performed abysmally.[36]

More and more psychologists have discovered examples of individuals who perform poorly on a task in a laboratory situation but perform the same task quite well, often excellently, when in an appropriate, meaningful physical setting.[37] As suggested earlier in this chapter, neuroscientists have discovered a strong relationship between mental processing and environmental context. Learning appears to be context specific; in other words, it does not always easily or automatically transfer from one environmental context to another.[38] The failure to acknowledge that the physical context plays a central role in learning and that transfer is not automatic has profoundly affected educational practice.

It is fair to say that the overwhelming majority of educators do not fully understand or acknowledge the importance of physical context in learning. Most educators are willing to admit that physical context is important to a degree, but they basically believe that learning is somehow "immersed" within, rather than dependent upon, a physical context. If learning tasks are only "enveloped" by context, it should be possible to readily move the task, once learned, from one context to another, much as someone might remove a letter from one envelope and put it into another. This is clearly the operating assumption of most compulsory learning situations. Children are placed within the context of a school classroom and taught a variety of subjects, including history, science, art, foreign language, health, and even "life skills" such as babysitting and citizenship. The assumption is that these topics, once learned in the classroom, will be permanently stored in memory and available for use in other contexts, such as other courses, the home, or even the work environment. However, research would suggest that this is not the case, and when faced with evidence that children even have problems transferring information learned in one course to other seemingly similar courses, researchers have offered a variety of explanations.[39] The fact that children and adults are being taught concepts within decontextualized physical environments greatly impedes their ability to learn the material in the first place, let alone to transfer it to a new situation.

SITUATED COGNITION

Learning appears to be not just enveloped within a physical context but "situated" within the physical context. In fact, all learning appears to be inextricably bound to the environment in which it occurs.[40] The difficulty that people have transferring what is learned from one physical context to another is pervasive, including both the young and old, educated and uneducated, and those with high and low IQ. The inability to transfer learning from context to context is thus not an anomaly but the norm. A wide range of studies have found that students in schools and universities not only have difficulty transferring knowledge from one class to another but also find it difficult to transfer the general ability to solve problems in the real world.[41] On the basis of the available research, it appears that even students at good universities who take ample science, statistics, and math courses do not transfer the principles they learn in these courses to novel contexts.[42] Although it has been known for nearly a hundred years that training in such fields as Latin and math has no measurable influence on other cognitive functions,[43] belief in the value of teaching general problem solving persists. The fact is, "thinking depends upon specific, context-bound skills and units of knowledge that have little application to other domains."[44] The best evidence is that learning is generalizable to new situations only when the individual can recognize within the novel context elements of the context in which learning originally occurred.[45]

Perhaps it is not that this transfer is impossible, as the research cited would suggest, but that the transfer process needs to be facilitated. Research conducted at Bank Street College suggests that students learned most during school field trips when the work they did at the museum was interdisciplinary and closely related to what they had been doing in school.[46] In their efforts to involve students in creating interdisciplinary projects and activity-based experiences at school, teachers were actually helping students create relevant physical contexts for their own learning, resulting in greater transfer and subsequent learning. Arguably, when conceptual information or problem-solving ability is generalized to a new situation, it is as much the physical context that is being generalized as it is the information or some generalized problem-solving algorithm or strategy.

There exists a fundamental link between all learning and the physical environments and activities in which learning occurs. As stated by Tony Hiss in his book *The Experience of Place*:

> We all react, consciously and unconsciously, to the places where we live and work, in ways we scarcely notice or that are only now becoming known to us. Ever-accelerating changes in most people's day-to-day circumstances are helping us and prodding us, sometimes forcing us, to learn that our ordinary surroundings, built and natural alike, have an immediate and a continuing effect on the way we feel and act, and on our health and intelligence. These places have an impact on our sense of self, our sense of safety, the kind of work we get done, the ways we interact with other people, even our ability to function as citizens in a democracy. In short, the places where we spend our time affect the people we are and can become.[47]

Why should the physical context be so critical to life in general and learning in particular? To fully understand the key relationship between learning and the physical environment once again requires an evolutionary perspective.

EVOLUTIONARY ROOTS

As previously stated, learning is not a human invention; the roots of learning probably go all the way back to the beginnings of life itself.[48] Learning evolved as a mechanism to ensure the long-term safety of the organism. By recording events happening inside and outside itself, the organism could respond "intelligently" to future events.[49] For most organisms most of the time (including most humans for most of human history), the physical environment was not a particularly safe place. Nervous systems evolved to help organisms perceive threats, remember successful and unsuccessful strategies for dealing with threats, and generally keep one step ahead of death. The vertebrate brain in particular is a highly evolved perceiving and learning machine. Given that vertebrates as a group are large, long-lived organisms, evolution has provided them with a brain specifically designed to deal with a constantly changing, and frequently hostile, external environment. A fly that lives for only a day requires relatively little capacity for learning. A mammal that might live for twenty or thirty years and moves repeatedly from one environment to another requires a tremendous capacity for learning. The ability to remember smells, tastes, sensations, and sights is highly developed in all vertebrates but is particularly refined in mammals. This ability to learn from and about the environment, to make meaning out of the complex array of information that constantly bombards the animal, is as fundamental to all higher organisms as are breathing and eating. As it turns out, the need to make sense of the environment, to find pattern and make order out of chaos, is an innate quality of all mammalian brains.

For humans also, the search for meaning—the need to make sense of experience—and the consequential need to act on the environment are innate processes.[50] The brain needs and automatically registers the familiar while simultaneously searching for, and responding to, novel stimuli.[51] People make meaning through a constant process of relating past experiences to the present.[52] This process is at the root of all learning—learning is about meaning-making. People constantly attempt to place what they encounter in the world, whether it is a person, a place, a thing, or an idea, within the context of their past experience: "How is this like what I've seen before, how is it different?" The search for meaning cannot be stopped, only channeled and focused. "Meaning" is always relative to the individual, relative to self.

According to public historian Lois Silverman, "in every realm of activity, we seek and make opportunities to create, express, and affirm who we believe ourselves to be—our sense of self."[53] Learning, or meaning-making, is a process that evolved to help mammals understand and, to the extent possible, distinguish *self* from *nonself.* A child learns that it is safe to play in the backyard but it is not safe to play in the street. For the child, events in the backyard are controllable, while events in the street are not. Over time, the backyard becomes an extension of the child's self, while the street remains a part of nonself. Learning how to avoid or minimize noxious environmental conditions is a critical element in the development of a sense of personal self-efficacy.

For humans, learning is no longer primarily a vehicle for passively distinguishing self from nonself. Humans use learning to actively conquer nonself, in the process taking control over events in their lives. Much as a dog marks a territory and thus makes it its own, humans learn about their world and thus make it their own. For humans, whether it is a child in a backyard or an adult in a big city, feeling secure is knowledge dependent. Human learning has become a very sophisticated device for making the unknown known, for turning nonself into self. Present-day humans have such a voracious appetite for learning because today knowledge is power, knowledge is security, knowledge is the ultimate means to control fate. The more one knows, the greater control one has over events in one's life. The need for new knowledge is never-ending. As each day brings changes in telecommunications, health care, and interpersonal relationships, it is all too easy to become focused on this ever escalating demand for abstract and specialized knowledge. However, no matter how abstract human learning becomes, there remains a fundamental human need to know where one is within physical space.

Neuroscientists John O'Keefe and Lynn Nadel point out that everything that happens to humans happens in a physical space.[54] This is so fundamental that we tend to overlook it. Our human ancestors were acutely aware of their physical environment; not to be was to flirt with death. For early humans, day-to-day survival depended upon an intimate knowledge of the local and regional topography and geography. Every human needed to learn how to navigate through this world. Cities and farmland may have replaced forests and savannas, but humans today are just as dependent upon knowing about the topography and geography of their environment as ever. Fortunately, all humans are genetically endowed with the capacity to navigate through space. According to O'Keefe and Nadel, we do this by constantly mentally creating and testing spatial maps that give us information about our surroundings.[55]

This survival-oriented attention to the world occurs nonstop, even to a degree when we sleep.[56] Opportunities to explore the physical environment are an important element in the development of individual competency.[57] Environmental barriers or social regulations that restrict movement can adversely affect learning, particularly in young children. Research suggests that restrictions on exploratory behavior in infants are associated with delayed cognitive development,[58] while self-directed exploration is a critical component of spatial learning in young children. For example, restricting the exploratory behavior of young children results in reduced spatial abilities when they become adolescents.[59]

Neuroscience research has revealed that "spatial learning" is not just a specialized and isolated type of learning but is integrated with all types of learning; all learning is influenced by the awareness of place.[60] A key component appears to be the part of the brain known as the hippocampus. All memories of people, places, or events, if they are to become long-term memories, must pass through the hippocampus.[61] The hippocampus is located in a very evolutionarily ancient portion of the brain, the limbic area. As discussed in chapter 2, the limbic area of the brain is strongly associated with human emotional processing. Probably not coincidentally, then, it appears that in the process of becoming "permanent," a memory acquires both an emotional and a physical context stamp as it passes through the hippocampus.[62]

Investigators in a variety of fields have noted the strong relationship that exists between physical context and feelings.[63] Similarly, strong evidence supports the contention that learning occurs best under conditions of positive affect.[64] Given the connection between learning, the hippocampus, spatial mapping, and emotion, one would suspect that physical context, emotion, and learning are highly interrelated. Efforts to directly relate physical-setting characteristics known to be associated with negative affect, such as a lack of windows or "ugliness," have generally been unsuccessful when studied within the compulsory, school classroom environment.[65] However, there is limited evidence that when learning settings were made more comfortable and informal—in other words, when they no longer looked and felt like a typical school classroom—they were rated favorably by students and appeared to support increased levels of student-initiated discussion and learning.[66] In studies of out-of-school learning, Falk was able to show very strong correlations between positive affect, high levels of involvement with the physical context, and increased learning.[67] So tightly bound were these three dimensions that Falk suggested that any one could be used as a predictor of the other two.[68] Given that museums in particular, and other free-choice learning settings as well, have been consistently found to generate positive feelings and high levels of interaction with aspects of the physical setting, we have argued that they must also facilitate learning.[69] Consistent evidence for learning in museums is now being found, much of it showing these strong interrelationships between learning, affect, and setting.[70] This relationship is perhaps most strikingly recorded in a study of the long-term recollections of museum professionals:[71]

"I really don't remember how I decided to go to the DIA [Detroit Institute of Art]. I don't know how I figured out how to get there, but I walked. Maybe, I went with my class at school and wanted to return. I don't know. But I do know I used to walk from my home in 'the projects' to the museum several times a week (about 2 miles). I remember looking for hours at the Diego Rivera murals and pondering about what I saw.

"I remember sitting on a wrought iron circular staircase and marveling at the 'feeling' of the museum. What strikes me is that I was always alone. I do not remember seeing or talking to docents, interpreters or security staff. There was never anyone around. I found this to be pleasant, however, in retrospect, I wonder what type of influence 'the right person,' saying the 'right thing,' would have had upon me.

"I continued to visit the DIA after school once or twice a week for over a year, until we moved out of the area." (Forty-year-old female, recalling frequent visits to the Detroit Institute of Art)

"I don't remember going to many museums as a child. I grew up in southern Idaho and we didn't have any museums of any note in my town. Mr. Herrett, a jeweler, had a planetarium behind his store and I went there once in cub scouts to look at the stars through the telescope. It was in the early spring or late fall. The observatory was unheated, of course, and it was very cold.

"I remember being scared to look through the telescope—as if I would be sucked out into space through the telescope if I got close enough to look through it. . . . I don't remember much about it at all, except for there was one painting that showed Chinese laborers working in Rock Creek Canyon on the outskirts of the town I grew up in. I had no idea that there were Chinese in any quantities in this area during the late 19th Century." (Forty-year-old male, recalling a visit to a "funky" planetarium, as young Cub Scout)

"[I] saw [a] show about [the] death of the sun (a star)—[the] sky froze over and [the] room got cold and dark—very scary.

"For weeks after, my sister and I went around chanting 'Be quiet, the sun's about to die' in deep, Halloween voices.

"I don't remember what we did after the [planetarium] show. I do remember that I learned that the sun is a star and will die some time in the far distant future. I don't remember how far in the future, but I think it's billions of years from now." (Fifty-year-old female, recalling a visit with her family to the Hayden Planetarium at the American Museum of Natural History when she was nine or ten years old)

The links between places, emotions, and memories are strong. "The basic principle that links our places and states is simple: a good or bad environment promotes good or bad memories, which inspire a good or bad mood, which inclines us toward good or bad behavior."[72] We may not be conscious of the setting, but our brains are. Humans automatically form long-term, emotion-laden memories of events and places without deliberately attempting to memorize them.[73]

Take, for example, Sarah Minford's memories of the Glens of Antrim, transcribed at the beginning of this chapter. Sarah did not set out to memorize where she went and what she did, but in attempting to recall her experience—the memories of her teacher, the guide at the Glens, her schoolmates, the facts taught during the day, and the feelings she experienced that day—she also remembered the physical context. For example, her memories of what she learned about redwoods were tightly bound with her memories of place. And so it is with all our memories. The bond between the personal context (self) and the physical context (nonself) is a constant, stable basis of all thought. If people are arbitrarily cut off from the external world, deprived of physical context, as in sensory deprivation experiments, they literally go insane.[74] However, when the external world is thoughtfully constructed, the physical context can be manipulated to produce wonderful outcomes, including learning. This is what a well-designed museum is: a well-thought-out physical context designed to facilitate learning. The well-designed museum provides not just a supporting physical context but also a supporting personal and sociocultural context. In the next chapter we explore all three of these in detail.

KEY POINTS

- Learning appears to be not just "enveloped" within a physical context but rather "situated" within the physical context. All learning appears to be inextricably bound to the environment in which it occurs, generalizable to new situations only when elements of an old context are recognized in the new.

- The need to make sense of the environment, to find pattern and make order out of chaos, is an innate quality of all mammalian brains. For humans also, the search for meaning—the need to make sense of experience—and the consequential need to act on the environment are innate processes.

- Spatial learning is not just a specialized and isolated type of learning but is integrated with all types of learning; all learning is influenced by the awareness of place.

- Humans automatically form long-term, emotion-laden memories of events and places without deliberately attempting to memorize them.

NOTES

1. Post–field trip letter sent to the director of education, Glens of Antrim, Northern Ireland. Sarah Jane Minford is a pseudonym.

2 E.g., Fivush, Hudson, and Nelson 1984; Falk 1988; Falk and Dierking 1990, 1992, 1997; Stevenson 1991; Wolins, Jensen, and Ulzheimer 1992; McManus 1993.

3. Stevenson 1991.

4. McManus 1993; Falk and Holland 1994.

5. Falk, Luke, and Abrams 1996; Holland and Falk 1994.
6. Luke et al. 1999; Stevenson 1991; Medved 1998.
7. Bielick and Karns 1998; McKelvey et al. 1999.
8. Stanton 1994.
9. Medved 1998.
10. Abrams and Falk 1995, 1996; Luke et al. 1998; Medved 1998.
11. Barker and Wright 1955, 27.
12. Wicker 1979.
13. Barker 1968.
14. Gallagher 1993.
15. Falk and Dierking 1992.
16. Gallagher 1993.
17. Gallagher 1993, 12.
18. Lave 1991; Lave and Wenger 1991.
19. Lave 1991.
20. Gallagher 1993.
21. Ceci and Roazzi 1994.
22. E.g., Neisser 1976; Berry 1983; Charlesworth 1979; Cole and Scribner 1974; Irvine and Berry 1988; Sternberg 1985.
23. E.g., Piaget and Inhelder 1969.
24. Jackson and McClelland 1979.
25. E.g., Eysenck 1986.
26. E.g., Bayley 1970.
27. Ceci and Roazzi 1994.
28. Neisser 1976, 183.
29. Edelman 1987.
30. Ceci and Leichtman 1992; Ceci and Roazzi 1994.
31. Cf. Sternberg and Wagner 1986; Rogoff and Lave 1984; Brown, Collins, and Duguid 1989.
32. Falk and Dierking 1992, 1995.
33. Ceci and Leichtman 1992, 223.
34. Melton 1972.
35. Gallagher 1993, 47.
36. Gladwin 1970.
37. Labov 1970; Cole 1975; Scribner 1976; Gelman 1978; Gleason 1973; Shat and Gelman 1977; DeLoache and Brown 1979; Wellman and Somerville 1980; Ceci and Roazzi 1994.
38. Ceci and Roazzi 1994.
39. Ceci and Roazzi 1994.
40. Scribner 1986; Brown, Collins, and Duguid 1989.
41. Perkins and Salomon 1989.
42. Leshowitz 1989; Perkins and Salomon 1989.
43. E.g, Thorndike and Woodworth 1901; Thorndike 1923.
44. Perkins and Salomon 1989.
45. Perkins and Salomon 1989.
46. Wolins, Jensen, and Ulzheimer 1992.

47. Hiss 1990, xi.
48. Bonner 1980.
49. Bonner 1980.
50. Caine and Caine 1994.
51. O'Keefe and Nadel 1978.
52. Silverman 1995.
53. Silverman 1995, 161.
54. O'Keefe and Nadel 1978.
55. O'Keefe and Nadel 1978.
56. Caine and Caine 1964.
57. Evans 1995.
58. Wachs and Gruen 1982.
59. G. 1980, in Evans 1995.
60. O'Keefe and Nadel 1978
61. Hilts 1995; Rose 1993
62. Hilts 1995; Rose 1993; Calvin 1997; Aggleton 1992.
63. Cf. Evans 1995.
64. Isen, Daubman, and Gorgoglione 1987.
65. Ahrentzen et al. 1982; Sundstrom 1986.
66. Sommer and Olsen 1980.
67. Falk 1976.
68. Falk 1976.
69. Falk and Dierking 1992.
70. Falk 1999a.
71. Falk and Dierking n.d.
72. Gallagher 1993.
73. Caine and Caine 1994.
74. Bexton, Heron, and Scott 1954; Suedfeld 1980.

5

Museums and the Individual

> While each [museum] has something to offer to some people, what
> they offer is neither the same, nor of interest or value to all.
> —Bruno Bettelheim, "Curiosity—Its
> Applications in a Museum Setting"

If all learning is contextual, then it goes without saying that where and
with whom someone learns profoundly affects learning; even attributes
normally considered fundamental to the individual, such as attributes of
self and learning styles, vary as a function of situations.[1] Thus, understanding learning in museums cannot merely rely on generalized notions
of how humans learn. While the preceding three chapters lay out a general understanding of how people learn from museums, they only provide a broad framework within which to think about the topic. To make
our understanding of learning from museums useful, we must be more
specific. A realistic understanding of learning from museums is not deriv-
able from factors common to all learning but rather must come from personal, sociocultural, and physical contextual factors unique to museums.
In this and the next two chapters we will attempt to describe what we currently understand to be the relevant factors and research applicable to the
specifics of learning within a museum context.

Three major suites of factors contribute directly to issues of learning
from museums, all of which can be generally placed into what we would
call the personal context: (1) a person's motivation for, and expectations
of, a visit; (2) the knowledge, interests, and beliefs a person brings to a
visit; and (3) the personalized way learning occurs in museums, especially the opportunities for choice and control over learning that are central

to most people's museum experiences. These three factors are not equally understood or researched.

MOTIVATION AND EXPECTATIONS

In an interview conducted at her home, Florence Mathews,[2] a twenty-five-year-old housewife and frequent visitor to the National Gallery of Art, reflected on her love of art and how free-choice learning experiences such as reading the newspaper and visiting museums have played an important role in developing and supporting her art interests:

> We had these nice dreams [professional degrees and careers] you know, when we were young. [Dreams] of doing these nice things. But the love of art remained on. I mean from Dad taking me to museums and then I started reading the newspaper a lot more. And I read it a lot more, even more than before, and that gives me information. And now the newspaper reading is something that both of my parents did, because Dad subscribed to three newspapers, the *Washington Post, Daily News,* and *Evening Star.* And he read all three! Yeah, because that way he figured he could get the straight story, because everyone is slightly biased and he wanted to get that information. And my mother who, of course, would [also] read the papers. So between the two of them and then being young at the time and of course [I] didn't want to do it, you know, when I was my children's age. But as I became an adult and then I started saying, oh, you know, "Read this and read that" and I'd get these bits of information, and um, yeah, so that's what started me. I found the listing in the paper about museums, and then that's where I would find out about special exhibits going on. And I'd say I want to see that. . . . So, uh, now it's my habit just to read, I guess you might call it the entertainment section, to find out, 'cause I want to find out what's going on. Like right now, I know about the first Mrs. [Woodrow] Wilson; finding out that she was an artist who suppressed her art work career to raise a family and support a husband. And I'm thinking, "Gee, I'm not the only person who did that." Of course, she later picked up on her art work and now it's on exhibit at the Woodrow Wilson House downtown. So, um, I never even knew that until I read it in the *Post.* So you know, I read about, and, of course, that's where I found [out] about *The Greek Miracle* and *1492* [exhibitions at the National Gallery of Art] and other special exhibits that have been there at the museum. And that's when I take my children.

This excerpt is informative on many levels, particularly as we explore how what has happened in people's lives before going to a museum strongly shapes their in-museum experiences. Florence's conversation provides insights into the important roles of motivation and expectations surrounding and preceding a visit to a museum.

As discussed in chapter 2, it is not possible to understand learning in the absence of understanding an individual's motivation for learning. Museums are free-choice learning environments—not only places where individuals can freely select what to learn but also places where individuals freely choose whether to come in the first place. To understand museum learning requires an understanding of why someone would choose to go to the museum and what effects those factors have on learning once the person gets there.

Why would anyone want to go to a museum? Clearly many people seem to have a reason for doing so. According to the American Association of Museums, in 1998, 865 million visits were made to some type of American museum.[3] Profiles of museum visitors reveal that they have a number of characteristics in common. Many of these relate to demographic factors such as income, education, and occupation. Dozens of studies have established that, on average, museum-goers are better educated and more affluent and tend to be employed in more professional-level jobs than people who do not visit museums.[4] However, demographics do not ultimately have much to do with why people go to museums; they tell only superficial facts about visitors such as what they look like or how much money they earn. A case in point is Florence, the woman quoted at the beginning of this chapter. Judging from demographic factors alone, she should not be a frequent museum-goer. Her roots are working class, her income and education would place her in the lower middle class, and yet she and her husband are both avid museum-goers. Ultimately, if we want to know why people go to museums, we need to know something about visitors as individuals—their personal motivations, values, and interests; their personal history relative to museum-going; and their general awareness of museums and receptivity to the museum-going experience. Then, and only then, can we determine what effects these factors will have on museum-going and the learning that ensues.

MOTIVATION AND LEISURE VALUES

The most direct way to determine why people go to museums is to ask them. Many investigators have done this, and the results include a wide range of answers, including social and recreational reasons, educational/learning reasons, and reasons related to culture, awe, and reverence.[5] On the basis of a thorough review of the literature, coupled with open-ended interviews with hundreds of visitors at a range of museums in England,

Theano Moussouri, as part of her doctoral work at the University of Leicester, concluded that all the reasons given for visiting museums could be placed into one of six general categories.[6] These categories reflect the functions a museum is perceived to serve in the social/cultural life of visitors: *education, entertainment, social event, life cycle, place,* and *practical issues.*

Education represents a category of reasons related to the aesthetic, informational, or cultural content of the museum. This was the most frequently cited motivation for visiting a museum. Most visitors mentioned that they go to museums to learn more about something—occasionally something in particular, more often just "stuff" in general. Occasionally, or alternatively, visitors expressed a desire for an emotional/aesthetic experience. Reasons of this sort were also grouped under education. *Entertainment,* the second most frequently cited motivation, refers to leisure-related reasons for visiting a museum. Most visitors mentioned that they go to museums in their free time to have fun and/or to see new and interesting things in a relaxing and aesthetically pleasing setting.

Museum-going was also commonly viewed as a *social event.* Visiting a museum was widely perceived as a "day out" for the whole family, a special social experience, a chance for family members or friends to enjoy themselves separately and together. A related but separate category was what Moussouri called *life cycle.* Distinct from normal social experience, some people seemed to view museum-going as an important marker event, taking place at certain phases of one's life, usually related to childhood (e.g., "I was brought to the museum as a child, and now I'm bringing my child to the museum").

Moussouri categorized under *place* the cluster of reasons given by individuals when they categorized museums as leisure/cultural/recreational destinations emblematic of a locale or region. Many people visit museums for this reason, including those on holiday or day trips or those who have out-of-town guests. Finally, the *practical* side of a museum visit also factored into some people's motivations for visiting. Practical external factors such as weather, proximity to the museum, time availability, crowd conditions, and the entrance fee contributed to many visitors' decision-making process.

In a follow-up study conducted at the Smithsonian Institution's National Museum of Natural History, Moussouri and Falk discovered that virtually all visitors cited the first two motivations—education and entertainment—as reasons for visiting the museum.[7] In fact, contrary to popular belief, there was no evidence that visitors came *either* to learn or to have fun, but almost without exception visitors came *both* to learn and to have fun. The individuals who chose to go to the museum were seeking a *learning-oriented entertainment experience*. The museum-going public's idea of entertainment, at least for that time when they are at the museum, is not the same as the theme-park-going or shopping-mall-going public's idea of entertainment. As one visitor in the study aptly stated, "We really enjoy it when we're here . . . and also learning. So it's educational, not just a theme park type-like place."[8] Most museum visitors saw no apparent conflict between fun and learning, as was succinctly summarized by one visitor: "We expect to enjoy ourselves and learn new things."[9] People who enjoy learning in their free time consider learning in a museum entertaining. Hence, for the overwhelming majority of museum visitors, education and entertainment are not mutually exclusive motivations for coming to the museum but are complementary aspects of a single, complex leisure experience.

However, the reasons people go to museums are much more complex than merely to satisfy educational and entertainment needs. In the 1970s a number of researchers began to try to investigate more analytically the nature of leisure experiences. In *The Museum Experience*, we reviewed in detail several of these early works. Although some researchers have asserted that leisure values such as a concern for learning and an interest in doing something challenging and worthwhile in their leisure time are held by only a small minority of Americans, especially those who frequent museums,[10] Falk and others have found evidence that these values are currently shared by half or more of the public—infrequent and frequent museum-goers alike.[11]

In addition to valuing learning in general, today's museum-goers share a fourth value, a perception that learning is a lifelong activity and not vested exclusively in the schools.[12] Individuals who go to museums are significantly more likely than people who do not to read books, watch educational television, use the Internet, listen to educational radio, read the newspaper, and generally engage in free-choice learning.[13] Regardless of the activity, people inclined to go to museums do so because they perceive learning experiences to be an important thing that museums, along with a wide range of other institutions, offer. This was confirmed in a recent preliminary study conducted by Australian museum researcher Janette Griffin and Lynn Dierking.[14] Such characteristics are shared by a variety of people, including people of both genders and all races/ethnicities, incomes, levels of educational attainment, and ages.

People who are inclined to go to museums think that they and their children need to be continually learning, continually searching for new information and connections, continually intellectually and aesthetically stretching, and they perceive museums as places to engage in this meaning-making. As previously mentioned, dozens of studies document that the primary reason most people attend museums, whether for themselves or for their children, is in order to learn. The high value that museum-goers place on learning accounts in large part for the high correlation between museum-going and level of education. It is not that one needs a college degree to think learning is important; rather, people who find learning important are more inclined to pursue higher education than are those who perceive advanced education as unimportant. Individuals who value learning seek it in many forms—through pursuing higher education; by watching educational television; by reading books, magazines, and newspapers; and by visiting museums. In other words, visitors to museums are a self-selected population, a population already predisposed to learning. Those individuals not so predisposed—and there are many who fall into this category—by and large do not attend museums in their leisure time.

PREVIOUS EXPERIENCE AND PERSONAL HISTORY

Of course, the caveat to all of this is that in order to utilize museums for personal learning, an individual needs to appreciate that museums exist, that they are readily accessible, and that they have the capacity to satisfy the individual's personal needs and interests. This awareness does not just happen; for most people it comes about through a recent or past (i.e., family) history of museum-going. In other words, people who have gone to museums in the past are the most likely to go in the future. Leisure behavior is especially influenced by early childhood experiences and parental modeling. As illustrated by Florence and confirmed in other research studies, we now know that a range of early childhood leisure behaviors seems to be correlated with adult museum-going.[15] These behaviors include reading, taking family trips, and participating in clubs, associations, or scouts.[16] However, one of the best predictors of whether adults will go to a museum is whether they were taken to museums *by their parents* when they were children.[17] Unfortunately, this is an area where not all Americans have had equal opportunity. Historically, many minorities, recent immigrants, and the economic underclass have had fewer opportunities than the more affluent majority population to visit museums with their families as children. A range of factors conspired to prevent earlier generations of whole groups of Americans from visiting museums. These factors included racism, growing up in rural areas or foreign countries where few museums exist, and poverty. Overall, it is fair to surmise that proportionately fewer minority, immigrant, and poor children went to museums with their parents a generation ago than did affluent majority children. This history directly influences current adult museum-going behaviors.

In addition to family leisure history, recent leisure behaviors also are a factor. Although family modeling influences future leisure behaviors, that influence is not absolute. All of us can think of things we do in our leisure time that our parents did not do, perhaps even museum-going. Sometimes this is because of changes in availability; for example, our parents did not surf the Internet because there was no Internet twenty years ago. At other times, leisure behaviors change because of changes in personal interests and lifestyle. A notable example has been the increase in physical exercise during leisure time, something that earlier generations could have done but by and large did not. Museum-going as a leisure behavior appears to be on the upswing. Another complementary explanation for this can be found in the theory proposed by businessmen Joseph Pine II and James Gilmore in their book *The Experience Economy*.[18]

MUSEUM-GOING AS LEISURE EXPERIENCE

Pine and Gilmore's basic premise is that Americans are more and more seeking experiences, rather than merely services or products; experiences are a more highly valued, more desirable economic product. According to Pine and Gilmore, there is a hierarchy of economic offerings, beginning with commodities (e.g., iron ore and tomatoes), then goods (e.g., automobiles and cans of tomato soup), then services (e.g., rental cars and restaurants), and finally experiences (e.g., limousine services and dinner theaters). At each level, the price goes up an order of magnitude and so does perceived value. "While commodities are fungible, goods tangible, and services intangible, experiences are *memorable* . . . revealed over a duration of time. Experiences are events that engage individuals in a personal way."[19]

This simple distinction clarifies both the current reality and future promise of museum-going as leisure experience. The public's increasing appetite for experience has propelled them to discover or, in many cases, rediscover the museum. This has dovetailed well with many museums' efforts to become more experience based. For those institutions that have not yet made such an effort, the experience construct is probably an excellent way to get out of the learning-versus-entertainment bind so many seem to find themselves in. As we suggested earlier, there is compelling evidence that in visitors' minds, learning and entertainment are not an *either-or* but a *both-and* phenomenon.[20] The experience construct developed by Pine and Gilmore emphasizes that experiences are not about *entertaining* or *teaching* people, they are about *engaging* people. Taking this thesis one step further, museums should strive neither to entertain nor to teach but to engage people in educationally enjoyable experiences *from which they can take their own personal meaning*. In fact, Pine and Gilmore argue that when museums are successful, they go one step beyond experience and provide the ultimate offering, *transformation*. Transformations are enduring memories and benefits, lasting changes in individuals, which result from highly engaging and personalized experiences. It is the expectation of an experience, or transformation, revolving around a personal interest that primarily motivates people to visit museums. These motivations and expectations turn out to directly affect learning.

EXPECTATIONS AND LEARNING: THE VISIT AGENDA

An individual's motivations, interests, and prior museum experiences all combine to create expectations for the visit; collectively these have been referred to as the visitor's agenda.[21] It has been argued for a number of years that not only do visitors have an agenda for their visits but also that these agendas directly influence visitor behavior and learning.[22] This idea was initially described by Falk and his colleagues on the basis of a major study conducted in the late 1970s with schoolchildren visiting the National Zoo in Washington, D.C.[23] As a result of Falk's and others' studies, Falk and John Balling had come to believe that previous experiences, not only intellectual but also physical and social ones, significantly affected the visitor's museum experience. The 1970s zoo study explored the impact of these different kinds of "advance organizers" on children's behavior during the visit and on their learning and attitudes toward a zoo field trip.

Discussions with children prior to the study indicated that they began a field trip with two agendas. One was very child centered and included seeing favorite exhibits (or, in the case of the zoo, favorite animals), buying something at the gift shop, having fun on the bus, and getting a day off from the usual school routine. The other agenda was similar to that of the school and the zoo: meeting zoo experts and learning more about the "stuff" there. Falk and Balling believed that the interaction between the children's "ideal" experience, as expressed by their hopes and expectations, and their "real" experience, as expressed in the events that actually occurred, should significantly affect the outcome of the trip. This study was designed specifically to investigate how manipulating these agendas through pretrip orientations would affect children's learning and behavior.

The results were informative and complex. First, all groups that visited the zoo, including a comparison group that received no orientation, showed significant learning in the three areas investigated: content, observational skills, and knowledge of setting; the groups with an orientation learned significantly more than the comparison group with no orientation. In addition, as demonstrated by a second assessment three months later, learning persisted. Also, on the basis of attitudinal questions, all groups showed significant positive changes in their attitudes toward animals in general and zoos in particular. The only group that did not show any significant learning was a second comparison group that did not visit the zoo at all.

Most notably, the group that was provided with the child-centered orientation—intended to set the children at ease about the trip by informing them about the practical aspects of their zoo visit, such as how they would get there, where they would enter, what they would see, what they could buy, and what they would have for lunch—demonstrated significantly more learning than any other group. They performed better on the cognitive test of zoo animals than the group that was provided cognitive facts and concepts as an orientation and significantly better on the observational skills than children provided an observation orientation session. Balling, Falk, and Aronson's explanation for this counterintuitive finding was that every child on that field trip began with a personal agenda of what he or she hoped to do or see. The child-centered orientation set the children's mind at ease so that they could concentrate on the experience once they were at the zoo. The other children kept wondering the whole time whether they would see a panda or get to buy something at the gift shop. Observations of the children over the course of the field trip seemed to support this interpretation. The child-centered orientation group seemed more relaxed and attentive to the docent than did the other groups. It is important to know that most of these children had visited the National Zoo before. Those who had not received the child-centered orientation seemed to grow restless during the lesson at the zoo; they knew from previous experience what they wanted to see and do but were not sure whether they would be able to do so on this visit.

As provocative as these results were, the conclusions were reached by inference rather than direct measurement. Thus, in an effort to further understand the role of visitor motivations on learning, Falk and Moussouri attempted to directly investigate the effects of different museum visit agendas on visitor learning.[24] This research study was conducted with visitors to the newly reopened *Janet Annenberg Hooker Geology, Gems, and Minerals Hall* (GGM) exhibition at the National Museum of Natural History. As previously noted, Moussouri had segmented all of the motivations people give for visiting a museum into six categories: education, entertainment, social event, life cycle, place, and practical issues. The researchers developed a "visitor motivation" instrument to delineate visitor agendas. The instrument allowed visitors to assess the relative importance of each of the six reasons for visiting the museum. These motivations were then compared with visitor learning, as "measured" by Personal Meaning Mapping, a methodology created by John Falk and designed to document the personal construction of understanding by an individual.

Overall, there was evidence that significant learning about gems and minerals occurred as a consequence of a visit to the GGM exhibition. When visitor learning was compared with each of the six motivational categories, only education and entertainment emerged as significantly correlated with learning. Although the social event, life cycle, place, and practical motivations were prevalent among visitors, there was no evidence that the presence or absence of these motivations influenced whether or not a visitor learned. However, this was not the case with the motivations of education and entertainment. It was possible to divide the adults in the sample into four nearly equal "agenda" groups by using each visitor's self-rated sense of how important "education" and "entertainment" were in the decision to visit the museum that day: individuals with low entertainment and low education agendas (20 percent of the visitors); those with a low entertainment and a high education agenda (25 percent of the visitors); individuals with high entertainment and low education agendas (25 percent); and those with both a high entertainment and a high education motivation agenda (30 percent). The researchers were able to document significant learning in virtually all the visitors to the exhibition, but not all. The individuals who self-identified as having a high education motivation demonstrated significant learning via their personal meaning maps, as did the individuals who self-identified as having a high entertainment motivation. Even some individuals who defined themselves as having either a low educational or a low entertainment motivation (with a corresponding high entertainment or high education motivation) showed significant learning, but the 20 percent of individuals who said they had both a low education and a low entertainment motivational agenda did not demonstrate significant learning.

This study confirmed the hypothesis that an individual's motivation for visiting a museum significantly influenced how, what, and how much he or she learned at that museum. As would be expected, individuals voicing a strong educational motivation demonstrated significantly greater learning than did those expressing a low educational motivation. However, less expected, a similar relationship was found among those individuals voicing strong entertainment motivations. These significant differences were independent of the individual's expressed educational motivations.

Visitors intent on learning about gems and minerals focused on the conceptual information provided in the exhibition. These individuals added whole new conceptual categories to their repertoire. Visitors' educational motivation, high or low, did not appear to significantly influence how much time they spent in the exhibition. By contrast, those individuals intent on an enjoyable and entertaining experience seemed to focus more concretely on the objects. As a result, there were significant gains in these visitors' ability to describe and list different kinds of gems and minerals after the visit, as well as a significantly improved ability to talk about gems and minerals. Perhaps what could be characterized as a greater enthusiasm for the experience also manifested itself in the way this group of visitors utilized the exhibition. Individuals with a high entertainment motivation spent significantly more time in the exhibition than did individuals with a low entertainment motivation (even longer than those with educational motivations). Thus, individuals who placed a high value on the entertainment and enjoyment aspects of the exhibition spent more time in the exhibition and demonstrated greater learning than did those who were less concerned with entertainment. As illustrated by this study, the suite of characteristics referred to as the visitor agenda—personal interests, values, prior experiences, visit motivations, and expectations— influence not only why people go to museums but also what they do and learn once they get to the museum. Once the visitor is in the museum, though, other personal context factors also influence learning.

PRIOR KNOWLEDGE, INTEREST, AND BELIEFS

Visitors to museums do not come as blank slates. They arrive not only with expectations and motivations for a visit but also with a wealth of previously acquired knowledge, interests, skills, beliefs, attitudes, and experiences.[25] All of these combine to affect not only what and how visitors interact with educational experiences but also with what meaning, if any, they make of such experiences.

For example, a recent research study at the National Aquarium in Baltimore revealed that visitors to the aquarium were generally more knowledgeable about, more concerned about, and more inclined to be involved in conservation-related issues than the general public.[26] Visitors easily identified conservation as a term and a concept and shared multiple thoughts when asked what conservation meant to them. Their conceptual understanding was consistent with the meaning of conservation for zoological institutions: the preservation of biodiversity. Visitors also had a strong positive attitude toward conservation issues and the roles and responsibilities of people influencing the world around them, both locally and globally. Nearly all the visitors readily perceived connections between conservation issues and their everyday lives, and most could readily articulate their thoughts with specific details and examples. All of these findings placed aquarium visitors above national norms relative to knowledge, interest, and attitudes.[27] Related to their general knowledge, personal experience, attitudes, and concerns, National Aquarium visitors also perceived themselves as generally active in conservation issues. Aquarium visitors were more frequently engaged in conservation actions than the general public, according to criteria from national studies of conservation actions.[28]

Thus, aquarium visitors were neither uninformed nor "typical" with respect to the issues forming the core of the National Aquarium's mission and major messages. Neither, however, were they expert ecologists or conservationists. For instance, although the vast majority of visitors were concerned about multiple issues, most were generally unable to express their concerns in much detail or relate them to root causes, such as overpopulation. The visiting public generally lacked sophisticated understanding of ecological and conservation principles and issues, as well as an understanding of the terminology used by professionals in these areas. Finally, in the area of conservation action, although most visitors perceived themselves as fairly active, relatively few discussed behaviors or changes in lifestyle beyond cursory awareness, such as recycling or not polluting. As mentioned earlier, museum visitors can be characterized as having high to moderate interest and low to moderate knowledge; the National Aquarium study merely puts a little more specificity on this generalization.

Although it can be predicted with certainty that visitors' entering knowledge, interests, and beliefs can and do affect learning from museums, in exactly what ways is harder to predict. To date, the vast majority of studies on the role of prior knowledge have been conducted in the domain of science and mathematics, most of these in either school or laboratory settings, most with a focus on student misconceptions.[29] These studies began in the 1970s with initial work in the area of Newtonian physics;[30] however, today studies of prior knowledge can be found across a wide array of science and mathematics topics including biology,[31] heat and temperature,[32] electricity,[33] mathematics,[34] probability,[35] statistics,[36] and computer programming.[37] More recently, studies on the public's knowledge of history have also been conducted; these studies suggest that people, particularly children, hold misconceptions that sometimes make it difficult for them to learn history at particular developmental points in their life.[38] Although it was hoped that these more traditional prior knowledge investigations would provide a wealth of information on visitors' entering understandings, because of the contextual nature of learning, most of these findings are difficult, or impossible, to apply to learners within the museum context.[39]

However, one study focused specifically on the problem of visitor "misconceptions." Museum researchers Minda Borun, Chris Massey, and Tiuu Lutter conducted a multiyear investigation aimed at identifying what they claimed were widespread misconceptions about gravity, with the goal of "correcting" and overcoming these misconceptions through exhibitions.[40] According to the researchers, visitors consistently shared the same basic misconceptions, which often were based on a "shared error in reasoning and sometimes on misinformation."[41] A sample of visitors was asked to explain gravity. Analysis of the in-depth study revealed that (1) only a third of the visitors understood that gravity was related to mass, and only one in seven visitors could be said to have had no misconceptions; (2) misconceptions were equally prevalent in adults and children, males and females; and (3) misconceptions sometimes appeared to be part of a well-developed view of the world and other times consisted merely of vague ideas. The ultimate goal of the project was to correct visitors' misconceptions so that they would be more receptive to expert explanations of gravity. Results appeared to support this goal.

As suggested in chapter 2, a number of investigators have criticized this approach to addressing prior knowledge, both in classrooms and in museums.[42] To begin with, research on prior knowledge suggests that most knowledge structures are firmly held, making them very resistant to change, even after long and concentrated instruction designed to effect change.[43] Thus, although visitors could be "led" to new conclusions about gravity during the experiment, there was no evidence that their long-term understanding of gravity would actually change. Another dimension of the problem is that this research has tended to be very reductionist, focusing on a very small number of knowledge elements and attributing great power to each. Finally, this approach to knowledge construction has been fundamentally negative and heavily value laden. Terms like "preconceptions," "alternative conceptions," "naive conceptions," "misconceptions," "alternative theories," and "naive theories" misleadingly focus on the failings of knowledge construction rather than the successes. If, instead, successes were investigated, these would be the consequence of prior knowledge also. Investigating prior knowledge is a valuable tool for understanding how learning occurs from museums, but approaches need to be holistic and respectful of the personal construction of knowledge.

A recent doctoral dissertation by David Anderson attempted to take such an approach by documenting both the successes and the failures of constructing knowledge from museum experiences.[44] Although we describe Anderson's research in greater detail in chapter 9, we will briefly outline some of his findings here. Anderson investigated the relationship between previsit and postvisit experiences for twelve students attending field trips to the Queensland Sciencentre, developing in-depth case studies for five of these students, with the goal of documenting changes in students' understandings of electricity and magnetism. This study not only demonstrated that a science center experience can play a significant role in facilitating understanding of particular science topics, it also demonstrated very specifically how prior knowledge and understanding combined with the in-museum experiences to effect personal meaning making. All five students constructed knowledge about magnetism and electricity as a result of their Sciencentre experience, but this knowledge construction was revealed to be exceedingly personal and inextricably connected to the prior knowledge and understandings they brought to these experiences. In some cases, the museum exhibitions refined and extended the children's prior understanding of scientific concepts, and in a few cases the exhibits reinforced preexisting ideas and knowledge structures that differed from traditional scientific explanations.

The experience of one student, Andrew, illustrates the refinement and extension of a concept:

> Andrew's understandings of how dynamos and generators produce electricity expanded and increased during his visit. Analysis of the pre-visit data sets indicated that Andrew [believed] that a dynamo turns turbines to generate electricity. It was also clear that he held detailed understandings of the operation of motors and the role of magnets in the mechanical processes, as exemplified by his discussion of disassembling slot cars with his brother Jacob. . . . The understanding that dynamos were devices that produce electricity appeared to be further developed by Andrew's related

learning experience at the live, facilitator-led, science demonstration which followed student's free-choice interaction at the exhibits, as well as with his interaction at the Electric Generator exhibit. Analysis of the post-visit data sets indicated that Andrew had developed the concept that generators generate electricity from these experiences. Andrew's post-visit interview showed that he described his understandings of generators and dynamos in a much more explicit way than presented in his initial interview.[45]

Roger's experience shows the reinforcement of a previously held idea:

When recalling his visit to the Sciencentre, Roger described his interaction with an exhibit which was intended to demonstrate the effect that heating of metals has on their ability to be attracted by magnets. The exhibit, entitled Curie Point, consisted of a coil of wire suspended in an elevated position, to which a small bar magnet was magnetically attracted and in contact. The visitor presses a button which causes the wire to heat up to a point where it glows red hot and loses its magnetic properties, resulting in the magnet falling away. Many students who interacted with this exhibit, including Roger, constructed their experiences at the exhibit in terms of heat being a 'repelling force to magnets.' When questioned about the exhibit, Roger expressed the view that heat was in some way involved with the process of magnetic attraction and repulsion. . . . [T]his [experience as well as a post-visit activity] appears to have entrenched Roger's association of heat with magnetic attraction and repulsion.[46]

Unfortunately, museum-focused studies of the depth of Anderson's are few and far between. Although a growing number of museum-based studies have been conducted on topics ranging from health[47] to astronomy[48] to optics,[49] many of these studies are not very comprehensive or rigorous, and most have focused on the construction of content knowledge, rather than investigating other dimensions as well.[50] Clearly there is a need for additional studies that demonstrate the role of prior knowledge, studies that do not merely investigate prior content understanding but also include investigations of visitor attitudes, interests, and beliefs.

Another startlingly simple, but profound, influence on learning from museums relates to people's personal interest in the topics presented there. This personal interest plays an important role in shaping what people do and what they take away from such experiences. The interview with Florence presented earlier in this chapter eloquently illustrates the close interrelationship between interest and action, in this case between a love of art and a desire to visit art museums. Falk found that when visitors to museums were asked to rate their interest in the subject matter presented there, roughly 98 percent indicated a very high or a moderately high interest in the topic (the other 2 percent said they were accompanying someone who had a high interest).[51] Individuals interested in the topics presented by museums are the individuals who go to museums—people who visit history museums enjoy history, people who visit art museums enjoy art, and people who visit science museums enjoy science.

Personal interest also influences what people choose to look at and do in the museum. During a front-end study at the National Museum of Natural History, Dierking and Holland found that visitors were self-selecting what galleries to visit once they were inside the building; 40 percent of the visitors to the *Geology, Gems and Minerals Hall* in the morning were choosing to visit that second-floor exhibition *first*, and another large percentage were visiting it *second*, after visiting the *Dinosaur Hall*. These visitors were interested in geology, fossils, and earth history and were voting with their feet.

However, it is important to note that interest is not the same as knowledge, although there is a correlation. Museum-goers who self-reported high to moderate interest in science, art, or history at the museum were likely also to self-report that they possessed only a low to moderate knowledge of these topics.[52] These individuals were at the museum to further their interest in, and general knowledge of, the topic; they were not experts, and they did not visit the museum with the expectation of becoming experts.[53]

Despite a plethora of studies, it is probably fair to state that the influence of visitors' prior knowledge, interest, and beliefs on learning from museums currently exceeds our understanding of the topic. However, one insight we do have is that visitors are much more likely to focus their in-museum attention on familiar topics and objects than on those with which they are unfamiliar.[54] Ironically, visitors are much more likely to utilize museums to confirm preexisting understanding than to build new knowledge structures. In short, learners within the museum context actively select what to attend to and what to ignore, what to learn and what not to learn.

CHOICE AND CONTROL

Museums are learning settings in which visitors have the opportunity to exercise considerable choice over what they will learn, or, framed in another way, visitors have the opportunity to control their own learning.

Both of these ideas are at the heart of what we call free-choice learning. Choice and control are fundamental, but understudied, variables in learning from museums. As we discussed in chapter 2, a whole range of important variables play a role in visitor choice and control, including interest, motivation, self-concept, attribution, and locus of control. Most of the research on these variables has been conducted in laboratory or school settings, situations in which learning is often constrained and imposed, so it is perhaps not surprising that it was found that not all learners seemed to be intrinsically motivated to learn and that not all possessed positive motivations, self-esteem, attributions, or locus of control. One could hypothesize that when learning occurs in a free-choice setting like a museum, learners should exhibit more intrinsic motivation and greater self-esteem, attribution, and locus of control. This greater sense of control over learning should lead in turn to more successful learning. In the few cases where this has been investigated, this is exactly what has been found. Unfortunately, control and choice have been investigated only rarely within the museum context.

One important example is research conducted by Deborah Perry as part of her doctoral work at Indiana University. Perry found that the confidence that came along with free-choice learning, coupled with the motivation to control one's environment, was among the most important variables determining successful learning from a children's museum exhibit.[55] Perry discovered that six motivational variables played major roles in museum learning. Although it was not surprising that motivations such as curiosity, challenge, and play had a role in learning within a children's museum context, the need for children to feel in control and confident about their environment was surprising. A final variable that emerged as important was the interpersonal need to communicate with others. Together, these six factors were important determiners not only of the perceived quality of the exhibit by learners but also of children's learning.[56]

Perhaps one of the reasons so little attention has been focused on choice and control in museum learning is because they are almost too obvious. Since these variables tend to be intrinsic to the museum experience, it is perhaps all too easy to overlook how important a contribution they make to most museum-based learning. Investigations by Finnish museum researcher Hannu Salmi confirmed that museums can use the motivating effects of freedom and control over the environment to enhance student learning.[57] In fact, these motivational attributes of museums have been observed by a wide range of investigators and used as a justification for school field trips.[58] But it is when free choice is denied—for example, during overly structured school field trips—that the true importance of choice and control in museums emerges. Some of the most interesting research in this area has involved investigations of school groups, comparing learners when learning was prescribed with learners when the visit was self-directed.

Australian museum researcher Janette Griffin investigated matched groups of schoolchildren in museums under two conditions. The first condition was an organized, traditional, teacher-directed school field trip. In the second condition students were freed from the typical constraints and structures imposed by teachers and allowed to define their own learning agenda in the museum. The second condition was not only perceived by the students as more enjoyable, but it also actually facilitated learning.[59] Students in this second situation were observed to behave and learn in ways similar to children in family groups.[60] Griffin identified three variables important to students in these learning situations: choice, purpose, and ownership. Given ownership of learning, learning and enjoyment became intertwined and, according to Griffin, ultimately inseparable in the minds of the children.

A study of schoolchildren in New York City found that children preferred going to museums with their family over school field trips. Choice and control were key factors for all the children; they preferred family trips because they could choose what to look at and do, set their own pace, and eat when they were hungry. Once again, implied social variables were important—things like being with family and friends (people you like and have chosen to be with), sharing with family members, and being part of a small group rather than a large one, which suggests less waiting time and less crowding. Children also hated the work sheets that they felt were the teacher's agenda rather than their own. These autonomy issues mirrored the findings of the Griffin study.[61]

An interesting twist on this study was an action research project conducted at the Liberty Science Center in New Jersey, where pilot studies sought to affect children's learning from a school field trip by influencing school groups' planning, self-monitoring, and reflection process.[62] In the words of the authors, "the more students and teachers attend to the nature, direction, and outcomes of their free choices, the greater the chance those experiences will coalesce as part of sustained and integrated . . . learning."[63] Preliminary results suggest their hypothesis is correct. Enhanced learning resulted when more free-choice museum-based school experiences were provided and students and teachers were given tools that enabled them to utilize that choice productively.

Clearly, choice and control influence learning from museums, but, as with prior knowledge, interest, and beliefs, much remains to be investigated to fully understand the role that they play in such learning. There is a huge void in the literature in this area and a critical need for further study. Throughout this chapter we have discussed a range of personal context factors that affect learning from museums. We have treated these factors as though they were independent, exclusive attributes of the individual. However, all these factors are actually intertwined and inextricably linked to the individual's sociocultural world. For example, leisure behavior, in general, and museum-going, in particular, are largely social experiences played out within a larger sociocultural context. Our knowledge, interests, and beliefs are molded by those around us. Our self-concept and self-esteem are greatly influenced by the feedback we receive from others. Even the choices we make within a museum, and our sense of control over them, are formed, constrained, and experienced through the influences of friends, family, and the staff of the museum. We explore these effects in the next chapter.

KEY POINTS

- To understand museum learning requires an understanding of why someone would choose to go to the museum and what effects those factors have on learning once the person gets there. Important factors include an individual's personal motivations, values, and interests; personal history relative to museum-going; and general awareness of museums and receptivity to the museum-going experience.

- Contrary to popular belief, there is no evidence that visitors come to museums either to learn or to have fun; almost without exception, visitors came both to learn and to have fun. The individuals who choose to go to the museum seek a learning-oriented entertainment experience.

- Visitors to museums do not come as blank slates. They come with a wealth of previously acquired knowledge, interests, skills, beliefs, attitudes, and experiences, all of which combine to affect not only what and how they interact with educational experiences but also what meaning, if any, they make of such experiences.

- Visitor choice in what and when to learn and perception of control over learning tend to be intrinsic to the museum experience. Perhaps because they are almost too obvious, the critical importance these variables play in museum-based learning has often been overlooked.

NOTES

1. Dweck and Elliott 1983; Harter 1983; Rosenberg 1979.
2. "Florence" is a fictitious name. She was part of a pilot study conducted by Falk and Holland 1997.
3. Lusaka and Strand 1998.
4. Falk 1998.
5. Falk 1998; Falk and Dierking 1992; Gore et al. 1980; Graburn 1977; Hood 1983; Macdonald 1993; McManus, 1992; Merriman 1991; Miles 1986; Moussouri 1997; Prentice, Davies, and Beeho 1997; Rosenfeld 1980.
6. Moussouri 1997.
7. Falk, Moussouri, and Coulson 1998.
8. Falk, Moussouri, and Coulson 1998.
9. Falk, Moussouri, and Coulson 1998.
10. Hood 1983; Marilyn Hood, personal communication, June 16, 1999.
11. Falk 1993; Falk unpublished data 1998; BBC Research and Consulting 1997.
12. Falk 1993.
13. Falk, Brooks, and Amin in press.
14. Griffin and Dierking 1999.
15. Cf. Falk 1993; Smith, Wolf, and Starodubtsev 1995.
16. Falk 1993.
17. Falk 1993; Smith, Wolf, and Starodubtsev 1995.
18. Pine and Gilmore 1999.
19. Pine and Gilmore 1999, 11–12.
20. Falk, Moussouri, and Coulson 1998.
21. Cf. Falk and Dierking 1992.
22. Balling, Falk, and Aronson 1980; Falk and Dierking 1992; Anderson and Lucas 1997; Macdonald 1993; Moussouri 1997.
23. Balling, Falk, and Aronson 1980.
24. Falk, Moussouri, and Coulson 1998.
25. Doering and Pekarik 1996.
26. McKelvey et al. 1999.
27. McKelvey et al. 1999.
28. McKelvey et al. 1999.
29. Cf. reviews by Confrey 1990; McDermott 1984; Eylon and Linn 1988.
30. Cf. Larkin et al. 1980; Larkin 1983.
31. Carey 1985; Keil 1979.
32. Lewis 1991; Wiser and Carey 1983.
33. Cohen, Eylon, and Ganeil 1983; Gentner and Gentner 1983.
34. Resnick and Ford 1981; VanLehn 1989.
35. Shaughnessy 1985.
36. Teversky and Kahneman 1982.
37. Spohrer, Soloway, and Pope 1989.
38. Ravitch and Finn 1987; Rosenzweig and Thelen 1998; Egan 1998.
39. Dierking and Pollock 1998.
40. Borun, Massey, and Lutter 1993.

41. Borun, Massey, and Lutter 1993, 210.
42. E.g., Feher 1993; Roschelle 1995.
43. Roschelle 1995.
44. Anderson 1999; Anderson et al. in press.
45. Anderson 1999, 241.
46. Anderson 1999, 286.
47. Giusti 1996; Falk, Luke, and Abrams 1996.
48. Tisdal and Gang 1994; Korn 1992.
49. Feher and Rice 1988; Feher and Rice Meyer, 1992.
50. A review of these and other studies can be found in Dierking and Pollock 1998.
51. Falk 1993.
52. Falk 1993; Dierking and Holland 1994.
53. Falk 1993; Dierking and Holland 1994.
54. Dierking and Holland 1994.
55. Perry 1989.
56. Perry 1989.
57. Salmi 1998.
58. Rennie and McClafferty 1995.
59. Griffin 1998.
60. Griffin 1998.
61. Jensen 1994.
62. Lebeau et al. in press.
63. Lebeau et al. in press.

6

Communities of Learners

What would happen if a different eye . . . were turned on specific contemporary cultural and historical features of learning processes...in the
United States? Rather than turning to school-like activities for confirmation and guidance about the nature of learning, . . . it would draw
on what is known about learning in forms of apprenticeships . . . to
consider learning in our own sociocultural, historically grounded
world. Such a view sees mind, culture, history and the social world as
interrelated processes that constitute each other.

—Jean Lave, "Situating Learning
in Communities of Practice"

Although the institutions may vary from science, history, art, or children's
museum to zoo, historic home, or nature center, fundamentally museums
are sociocultural environments.[1] Although more than half of all museum
visitors arrive as part of family groups,[2] all-adult groups, school groups,
scouts, day-camp groups, and, increasingly, organized groups of senior
citizens also make up large percentages of museum visitors. And since the
museum environment itself is a sociocultural one, all visitors, even those
who choose to visit alone, find themselves quickly immersed in the sociocultural milieu of other visitors and museum staff and volunteers.

Spend any time watching visitors in museums and you recognize the
social nature of these experiences. A closer look reveals that much of the
social interaction is a way for visitors to connect and find meaning; it is a
form of the distributed meaning-making discussed in chapter 3. Although
one also observes the usual social maintenance behaviors expected of
people—for example, within families, behavior management such as
checking to see if children are hungry or need to use the rest room—much
of the social behavior observed within and among groups is learning oriented. For example, a couple talks together about what they are viewing,

adults and children interact with one another at a hands-on exhibition, or a group of friends relate objects or ideas to their own concrete experiences: "Gee, remember when we were camping last year, we saw a bird that looked like that!"[3] If one takes the notions of sociocultural constructivism to the extreme, even when a visitor is alone and there is no direct social interaction, there is indirect interaction. The museum itself is a socioculturally constructed product. As solitary visitors read, interact with the exhibition, and attempt to find personal meaning, they bring their own experience, emotions, and values to the fore, all mediated by their own sociocultural background.[4]

This sociocultural mediation, either direct or indirect, plays a critical role in personalizing the museum experience for visitors, facilitating their efforts to learn and find meaning from museums. The sociocultural dimension of the experience is an important component of the "contextual stamp" that enhances people's ability to remember the experience and shapes subsequent experiences with the same objects, ideas, or events. Learning is a special type of social behavior, and museums represent a special kind of institution that facilitates such learning.[5] As sociocultural researcher Gaea Leinhardt suggests: "Museums are our preeminent institutions for learning. Museums are where our society gathers and preserves visible records of social, scientific and artistic accomplishments; where the society supports scholarship that extends knowledge; and to which people of all ages turn to build understandings of culture, history, society and science."[6]

At a fundamental level, museums support the participation of visitors in diverse learning communities.[7] This participation can take many forms, including pursuing inquiries, making connections among various contexts, sharing interests with others, and learning how to learn and how to assist and collaborate with others. Let us see how participation among these communities of learners occurs within the social configurations commonly found in museums—families, all-adult groups, and school groups—as well as how participation within the museum's community of practice is affected by interactions between these groups and museum staff and volunteers.

WITHIN-GROUP SOCIOCULTURAL MEDIATION

Families

Proportionately, families are the largest museum audience, and as we have suggested, most come to learn. However, this is an implicit, not an explicit, goal. As our colleague Samuel Taylor likes to quip, few families wake up on Saturday morning and say, "Hey, let's go to the aquarium today and learn about teleost fish!" Similarly, families do not say, "Hey, let's go to the museum and participate as part of a community of learners today!" However, interviews with parents in museums consistently demonstrate that their decision to visit is strongly influenced by their perception that these settings are "good places to take children to learn," and several studies support the idea that families use museums as socially mediated meaning-making environments.[8] In other words, many families perceive museums as good settings in which to learn together.

One need only briefly watch a family in this setting before observing a variety of behaviors that suggest that they are participating as members of a community of learners. Families spend a majority of their time in conversation, sharing what they know and trying to find out more together. They ask questions among themselves, either about the exhibitions in general or about specific content. Questions tend to deal with concrete information about specific objects or, in the case of zoo and aquarium visits, specific questions about the species of animal or the animal's care.[9] For example, when conducting his doctoral research on families visiting the Steinhardt Aquarium in San Francisco, Taylor observed that the most frequently asked questions concerned concrete, visually verifiable aspects of the fish exhibits.[10]

Because much of the social interaction observed within the museum is conversation, analyzing family conversations has been the focus for many researchers interested in family learning in these settings. This is in keeping with sociocultural approaches that emphasize the role of Conversational Elaboration, that is, talk occurring during and after a museum visit that demonstrates how meaning, experiences, and interpretation develop and are intertwined. Conversation is a primary activity of knowledge construction.[11] The research suggests that families with children interact, converse, and provide information to one another in recognizable, patterned ways that are repeated throughout the visit. In fact, the entire visit can be characterized as one single, large-group conversation, even though, as families move through exhibitions, they engage in numerous small conversations that are constantly beginning and ending.[12]

The role that prior knowledge and experience play is also clearly evident. Family members talk about what they know from previous experiences, discussing the exhibitions and programs in terms of these experiences and memories. As researchers have observed, these discussions provide opportunities for parents to reinforce past experiences and family history and develop a shared understanding among family members,[13] the "funds of knowledge" described by Luis Moll and James Green-berg.[14]

Research also suggests that families' conversations tend to be close and personal. Although they talk about topics described in labels on exhibits, they do not read/pay attention to the entire text if doing so interferes with the group's ability to enjoy and maintain social relationships. There is also some evidence that many of these conversations continue once families are back at home.[15]

Museum researcher Minda Borun and a group of researchers in the Philadelphia/Camden Informal Science Education Collaborative have focused on documenting family learning. Their studies demonstrate that when experiences were designed to facilitate social interaction, learning and meaning-making actually did result. The learning observed was related to specific behaviors, including asking and answering questions, commenting on the exhibition, and reading the labels aloud—all social behaviors (even the solitary behavior, reading labels silently, occurred in the context of a social group).[16]

Not all of the behaviors observed in these communities of learners are verbal; family members also watch one another, other groups, and muse-um staff. This "people watching" often results in modeling, also called observational or social learning. Family members observe one another, other groups, and staff to figure out how to manipulate interactive exhi-bitions and behave appropriately in the setting, and thus participate in the community of practice that the museum embodies.[17]

Families also engage in behaviors that are unique and special to them, and museums afford rich environments in which to share, interact, and reinforce these behaviors. For example, Dierking observed that modeling played an important role in the types of learning observed among fami-lies visiting museums. Some families were highly collaborative through-out the visit, staying together and interacting at all exhibitions as a group. Other families split up and interacted with exhibitions more inde-pendently, meeting on occasion to talk about what they were experienc-ing, sharing, and even showing other family members what they had done. From these data, Dierking developed a continuum of family learn-ing styles that ranged from "collaborative learning" to "independent learning."[18] Findings suggested that teaching and learning were taking place across the whole continuum and that modeling played a critical role in the process.[19] For example, in collaborative-learning families, fam-ily members, through conversation and modeling, learned not only about what was in the museum but also that museums are good places for families to learn together. They learned about one another, including each other's interests, preferred ways of learning, and favorite exhibitions. In independent-learning families, through modeling and to some degree through conversation, children and adults independently learned about what was in the museum and about one another; they learned that museums are interesting places, that people learn in different ways, and that adults like to learn as well. Similar styles of family learning have been independently observed by museum professionals working with families during parent-child workshops.[20]

Research on how families participate in communities of learners in museums is also benefiting from the focused application of sociocultural approaches. Researchers are exploring a variety of topics, primarily investigating Vygotskian constructs such as scaffolding, families' notions of museums as places of learning, or the role that different museums play in family activity and conversation. Some of the emerging research findings suggest that:

- Parents can be effective facilitators for their children's learning when exhibitions are designed with collaborative learning in mind and when adults feel comfortable with the content and experiences provided in the museum.[21]

- Adults' perceptions of a body of knowledge—for example, understanding the tentative nature of scientific knowledge versus considering it static—influence the ways that parents interact with their children and facilitate their learning, as well as influencing how adults convey process and the epistemology of knowledge to their children.[22]

- Parents are far more willing to take advantage of in-house library materials, family activity kits, and other opportunities to participate in this community of practice if they know that these materials are available and understand their role in providing assistance to their children. (Such participation seems to facilitate deeper levels of learning.)[23]

- Family members focus on and notice different aspects of an exhibition's theme and as a group consolidate their experience to construct a shared meaning for the exhibition.[24]

- Museums are clearly a part of a larger context constituting the family's free-choice learning activities. (Interestingly, not all families perceived museums as free-choice learning settings; some saw them as more formal learning environments.)[25]

Although sociocultural mediation is clearly an important aspect of family learning and meaning-making and directly affects the ways family's participate peripherally in this community of practice, many museum exhibitions and programs are clearly not designed to facilitate distributed meaning-making and collaborative learning. In fact, it is not uncommon to observe exhibition designs that actually impede the collaborative learning process by preventing meaningful interaction among family members or that encourage parents and children to adopt opposing learning goals rather than complementary ones. Fortunately, a few research efforts are focusing on how to influence the quantity and quality of social interactions within family groups so that collaborative learning is facilitated. For example, a study conducted by researchers John Falk, Kenneth Phillips, and Jennifer Boxer Johnson in the *Electricity and Magnetism* exhibition at the California Science Center (at that time the California Museum of Science and Industry) found that exhibitions could be designed specifically to facilitate social interaction, increasing the probability that learning and meaning-making would occur.[26]

At the time of this study, roughly 40 percent of the visitors to the museum were Hispanic families for whom English was not a first language; in fact, many of the adult visitors were believed to be nonreaders. Initial observations of the exhibition determined that children were the primary facilitators of the experience for adults. Children conversed in Spanish, apparently explaining the phenomena represented by the exhibits to family members; this assumption was confirmed by Spanish-speaking museum staff assisting with data collection. The abstract nature of the exhibition content, coupled with a general absence of appropriate explanatory text even in English, resulted both in confusion as to how to appropriately use the mechanical interactives in the exhibition and in poor understanding of the concepts presented. Baseline data revealed that most visitors spent less than four minutes in the exhibition and fewer than one in five visitors were using the exhibits as intended; conversations with families after the experience indicated that only a quarter were able to understand the concepts presented in the exhibition.

Researchers proposed changes to the exhibits, particularly modest labeling in both English and Spanish, to focus the children and adults on what they should do with each interactive and what the resulting phenomenon meant. Families were again observed and interviewed by bilingual data collectors after these changes were made. The modifications resulted in a 50 percent increase in the amount of time visitors used the exhibition, a 200 percent increase in the intended use of exhibit elements, and a 136 percent increase in conceptual understanding of the exhibition as a whole; increases for Hispanic families were even greater. The addition of more effective labels, provided in English and Spanish, improved the quality of meaningful social interaction between children and adults, which resulted in improved learning and meaning-making.

Kevin Crowley and Maureen Callanan conducted research at the *Map Your Head* exhibition at the Children's Discovery Museum in San Jose, California, where, as is the case in many children's museums, the focus of exhibition design was often on child-directed rather than collaborative learning.[27] In this formative evaluation study, the prototype design seemed actually to encourage children and adults to adopt conflicting learning goals for the exhibition. As researchers observed videotapes they had made, they realized that this could be traced to "misguided" parental guidance. The exhibition was designed in such a way that only the child "climbed" inside the exhibit enclosure where the major goal of the exhibition was most apparent. The exhibition was complex, and most children needed some facilitation in order to interact as intended, but because the design prevented parents from really seeing inside, they often entirely misinterpreted the goal of the exhibition.

However, using the information gathered from the study, researchers were able to recommend some simple revisions that encouraged parents and children to adopt complementary learning goals. The revision opened the exhibition up so that the child was not isolated from the parent and they both could enter if they chose. The enclosure was also constructed out of Plexiglas so that visitors, including parents, could see what was going on inside. Observations of the revised exhibit indicated dramatic changes in the use of the exhibit and visitors' understanding of its major goals. Only one in eight children who used the first prototype had participated in the intended activity; nearly seven in eight children did so using the revised version. Parents' conversations changed also, becoming more supportive of the intended goal, rather than hindering it as they often had with the prototype. By revising the exhibition, the project team created a new design that better supported collaborative learning goals, goals that the museum had not previously considered. Sally Osberg, director of the museum, felt that one of the benefits of participating in this research was that guided, careful looking helped the staff think of ways to include parents in exhibition experiences, rather than excluding them as they typically had.[28]

Clearly, museum exhibitions and programs, when done well, support opportunities for families to participate in and become more effective communities of learners, allowing group members to share, watch one another, have a new and novel experience, reinforce something they already know, or see something in a new way. By looking at objects together, reading labels, manipulating interactives, participating in a program, watching others, and/or talking with each other, family members have increased opportunities to incorporate new ideas and information into existing frameworks, negotiate personal and cultural meaning as it relates to the family's own experience and worldview, and transform their participation as they assume more responsibility for their own learning. All of this contributes to a highly personal experience, which is all-important if meaningful learning is to occur.

Adults

Groups of adults are another important audience that participates in the community of practice we call the museum. Although most of the social interaction research in museums has focused on families, the few studies that have examined social interaction in all-adult groups suggest that, as for families, it is an important way that adults relate to exhibitions and share their experiences with companions. Two studies contrasted all-adult groups with family groups, observing interesting differences in their patterns of interactions. Findings in the first study suggested that all-adult groups did not necessarily interact with all the exhibitions they viewed; instead they scanned an exhibit, perhaps looking briefly, but if nothing piqued the interest of someone in the group, they quickly moved on. In contrast, once a family group was attracted to a particular exhibition, they remained, interacting with the exhibit in a fairly stereotypical manner. In the second study, the roles of group members, particularly women, varied depending upon whether they were in all-adult or family groups. In family groups women concentrated their interactions on their children, focusing learning behaviors at the child's level, while women in all-adult groups focused on their own learning, often engaging in conversations with companions as they made sense of the exhibitions they encountered.[29]

Another study specifically focused on analyzing social interaction in all-adult groups. In an effort to better understand how adult visitors learn and make meaning in the museum, public history researcher Lois Silverman utilized a mass communications framework, suggesting that museums share many of the purposes of the mass media, including providing opportunities for people to gain information, enjoy recreation, and arrive at shared cultural meaning.[30] The study supported the view that museums facilitate meaning-making processes by housing many of the symbolic objects important to a culture and thus to such communication. Silverman, like others before her, found that the presence of companions, particularly family members or close friends, contributed greatly to learn-ing. Learning from the museum appeared to be primarily an interactive, creative process that took place through social interaction with compan-ions. This social interaction actually increased both the likelihood of learning in general and the likelihood that learning would include a num-ber of possible meanings for a particular message rather than just a single meaning.[31] Finally, using this mass media perspective, Silverman con-cluded that social interactions not only resulted in the sharing of new information but also served to maintain social relationships, forging new sociocultural bonds and reinforcing old ones. This sociocultural bonding occurred through the communication and shared reinforcement of known information, such as memories and experiences, shaped by the socio-cultural milieu of the visitor and the institution itself.[32]

Some of the most interesting family and all-adult group studies focused on the sociocultural context are just beginning. For example, sev-eral studies in their pilot phase are focusing on how individual and group identity shapes the conversations and meanings visitors make of museum experiences. Not surprisingly, identity, including gender, race, self, fami-ly, age, and historical components, emerges as a variable that significant-ly influences the meaning that is made from the museum experience.[33] As with the family research, most of the studies on adults have focused on analyzing conversations, but researchers Gaea Leinhardt and Carol Tittle are exploring the use of diaries as a methodology for understanding the effects of identity and personal history on adult museum-goers, ranging in age from twenty to seventy.[34]

One way to make these ideas of sociocultural context more concrete is to examine some real data from an all-adult group. To this end, we share findings from an all-adult group who participated in the 1994 study at the National Museum of Natural History that we described in chapter 1. This group provides useful insights into the social dimensions of such groups. Group members were tracked throughout their visit, and one, Jean Guil-iani, was interviewed during her visit and again by phone several months later.[35] The following transcript briefly summarizes the findings:

> Jean, along with her husband and sister, visited the National Museum of Natural History in the fall of 1994. Jean lives in New Orleans with her hus-band, Will; her sister, children, and grandchildren all live nearby. She enjoys traveling and she and her husband, Will, travel quite a bit whenev-er they can.
>
> The Natural History Museum is one of Jean's favorite museums. She and her husband had been to the museum two times before and are "almost always impressed with all museums." She claims to not have any particular

interest in science but loves to see the many impressive things the Smithsonian has. Since they were passing through Washington (on a trip to drive Jean's sister from Buffalo to New Orleans), they just had to stop, for "a quick refresher course." Besides, Jean's sister had never seen Washington, and they took this trip primarily to show her around. They were only in town for a day. But, "a few years ago" (actually 1976), Jean and her husband spent 10 days in Washington and "saw everything." Jean's husband especially liked the "South Seas" exhibition [*Pacific Island Cultures Hall*], because that is where he was stationed when he was in the Navy during the Second World War. He and Jean traveled to Hawaii a few years ago, but it did not look anything like how he remembered the South Pacific. However, he enjoyed the exhibition because it had more of the flavor he remembered, even if he was not familiar with the specific objects. On this particular day, Jean and her sister spent a considerable amount of time in this exhibition so that Jean's husband could reminisce and explain some of the objects to them.

Several months later when we talked to Jean by phone in New Orleans, she said that it was nice that the museum had an exhibition on the South Pacific. She said she enjoyed hearing her husband reminisce about the war and share his experiences with her sister and her. It was one of the first times her sister got to hear some of her husband's war stories, although Jean felt that she had heard them all before.

According to Jean, her sister loved the gems, especially the Hope Diamond. That was what she wanted to see even before she got to the museum. In her interview, Jean stated, "We barely got to see it [Hope Diamond]. I heard it was moved shortly after we visited. And we saw fossils, stones and scenes with native peoples. My sister was most impressed with the jewelry. Any woman would be. I was impressed with the crystallized stones and that beautiful stuff. But the visit wasn't really for me to see things." Talking later about the Hope Diamond, Jean stated that she and her husband were not thrilled with how it was displayed this time—they remembered it being less recessed during previous visits. Jean felt that the way it was currently displayed "makes it so the full beauty of the gem's color isn't as apparent, and the chain didn't seem as striking either." But maybe it was her imagination, she said: "The diamond is spectacular and wonderful regardless of display." Jean reiterated that she felt that the gem and mineral exhibition was one of the most important things for them to see in the museum. She said she enjoyed the "beautiful quartz stones that you have and all the jewelry." Still later in the conversation, Jean said that a few months after her visit, she had noticed in the newspaper that the gem [Hope Diamond] had been moved. She said that she had commented at the time to her husband, "Maybe it was displayed better now."

Not only do Jean and her sister like gems and minerals, but according to Jean, her 10-year-old granddaughter "loves collecting pretty rocks and especially likes breaking them open to observe their contents." When she got home, Jean told her granddaughter all about the Natural History Museum, particularly the rocks and minerals exhibition, and told her that she would really enjoy visiting the museum someday. Knowing her granddaughter's interest, she had also specifically gone to the museum shop and purchased a rock as a gift for this particular granddaughter. Jean said that the highlight of the museum visit was seeing the look in her granddaughter's eyes when she opened up the box and saw that beautiful rock.

Jean also remembered how impressive the bones were, in particular the dinosaur and whale bones. She could not really say she learned anything specific; she just wanted to see all the impressive things displayed there. She said they have dinosaurs in the Buffalo Museum too, but "nothing compares to the Smithsonian. It's outstanding." Following up on her comment about the Native American exhibits, we asked Jean if she recalled anything in particular from this part of the museum. She said, "I just think of the way they [Native Americans] dress, the food they cultivated, their family-type life." But she could not provide any additional details.

For many adults , the social reasons for their visit are so dominant that it is these aspects that are the take-away messages from a museum experience. Certainly in Jean's case most of what she did at the museum, what she saw, and even what she remembered was framed in terms of her social reasons for being there in the first place. She went to the museum for her sister's benefit; she spent a good deal of time in the South Pacific exhibition area for her husband's and sister's benefit. Seemingly, the visit to the Hope diamond exhibit was both for her sister's and her own benefit. Clearly, the sociocultural context of this visit not only facilitated the choices of what to look at, and presumably what was learned and remembered, but also served to maintain the social relationships among this group, forging new bonds, for example, between Jean's husband and her sister and reinforcing old ones between Jean and her husband. Social bonds were even reinforced through modeling with family members not present. The highlight of Jean's experience was being able to purchase some gems for her granddaughter who was interested in geology at the time, share them with her back at home, and tell her all about the museum. It probably is not too large a stretch to imagine this young girl growing up with the desire, somewhere in the back of her mind, one day to visit the museum that her grandmother had told her so much about when she was a child. This form of modeling is one important way that museum-going/ free-choice learning cycles continue in families. Overall, Jean's experience illustrates how museums help to build identity—identity between individuals within and across generations, and between and within members of the society. However, this example probably raises as many questions as it answers. The general paucity of research on all-adult groups, particularly groups of older adults, is a significant deficit in our understanding of museum visitor learning.

This lack of understanding becomes of even greater concern given the aging of the American population. All-adult groups are becoming a more numerous and more important museum audience, with older adults representing a huge, virtually untapped source of new museum visitors. But not all adult users are to be found in the exhibition halls. A team of researchers at the Museum of the Rockies recently investigated the motivations of adults who participated in a diversity of museum programs across a range of museum types.[36] The adult learners in this study were categorized into four types: (1) learning lovers who saw the museum as a place to satisfy their learning needs; (2) museum groupies who enjoyed spending time at museums; (3) skill builders who participated in certain programs to learn specific skills; and (4) socializers who were using the experience as a way of meeting people. Consistent with the findings presented in the previous chapter, these motivations affected what and how these adults learned. Although a preliminary investigation, this research is one small step toward filling the gap in our understanding of adult museum learners.

School Groups

After families, the most frequently studied museum visitor groups are school groups. Despite this, very little research has focused on, or even considered, the sociocultural context of school field trips and the role it plays in children's learning. We suspect that this is because of educational researchers' historical lack of appreciation of the important role social mediation plays in learning. Early studies had experimental designs that focused on variables such as the advance preparation of students or docent teaching styles, assessing their effects on fairly narrowly prescribed learning outcomes. The social nature of the field trip experience was at best disregarded and at worst considered a confounding variable.

However, recent research suggests that social interaction, that sense of participating in a community of learners, is an important aspect of field trips for children also and, if respected and capitalized upon, can result in increased learning. For example, several studies suggest that recognizing and accommodating children's social agendas can result in significant learning and that when children have opportunities to explain their learning to other children or to adults, they remember their discoveries better and are also more likely to transfer the new insights to new situations.[37] It is also clear that children are able to talk about their learning in such settings, indicating that social mediation plays an important role in the process.[38] Specifically, children suggested that they (1) enjoyed seeing and learning about new things and perceived museums as places to do so; (2) preferred to share what they were learning with others, particularly peers, rather than listen to adult docents; (3) were able to define specific places and conditions in which they could best share what they were learning; and (4) appreciated that there were optimum conditions under which to visit the museum by expressing dislike for certain negative aspects of museums, such as crowding, that hindered their ability to look.[39]

In a longitudinal study at Bank Street College in New York City, researchers found that children remembered most about visits to museums when there were multiple visits, when the teacher linked the visit to the school curriculum by embellishing the unit with many varied classroom activities and group projects, and when there were opportunities for children to exercise choice and personalize the experience.[40] The museum activities that allowed children to interact socially with one another, talk to one another about what they were seeing, and engage in related learning experiences back at school were, for the most part, the most remembered.

Consistently, opportunities to interact with peers, in activities of their own choice, emerge as important to children's learning in school groups. These findings are consistent with research indicating that when children collaborate with each other or with their parents, their learning is more advanced than when they think and learn alone.[41] In one study, children were observed during free exploration and then interviewed one week after their visit.[42] Although the children's behavior during free exploration time seemed chaotic and random, after at least ten minutes of observation the researcher found that the children returned to interactive exhibits that they had "sampled" earlier and spent more focused time at their favorites, often with peers. The researcher surmised that children most likely wanted to see what the options were before settling down to interact with a particular exhibit. Findings suggested that interactions between students enhanced their interactions with individual exhibits. A great deal of peer teaching was observed; in some cases the interactions seemed to stimulate label reading, and attitudes were more positive. Pupils' recall showed that they remembered and could talk about the exhibits where they had spent the most focused time with peers and that required the most active participation.

Conversation-analysis techniques utilized to understand family learning have also been used to investigate how social interaction between child peers, between children and teachers, and between children and adult chaperones influences the outcomes of visits to zoos. One group of studies demonstrated that the conversations between children were often more focused than were conversations with adults. In a study at a zoo, teacher-led groups generated more "dislike-comments" than did groups of students alone.[43]

Two additional studies, discussed to some degree in the previous chapter, support the notion that learning is enhanced on school field trips if children have opportunities to interact socially in meaningful ways that relate to the exhibitions. Science education researcher Janette Griffin conducted a dissertation study in which she created field trip experiences that were more like family visits, with opportunities for choice and social interaction.[44] Children not only preferred these kinds of school trips but also learned far more on them, when compared to a matched group of students participating in more traditional trips. Science education researcher David Anderson focused his doctoral dissertation study on developing in-depth case studies of a small group of students visiting an interactive science center.[45] This focused, qualitative approach demonstrated clear relationships between learning and the social dimensions of the visit, as well as showing the role that social interaction had played in constructing prior experience and knowledge. Because this study investigated the effect of postvisit activities designed to reinforce the science center experience, it also documented the impact of social context on subsequent learning.

As these studies are beginning to demonstrate, social context plays an important role in facilitating learning during children's field trip experiences. However, there is still much more that can be investigated; important social processes such as modeling, for example, are barely documented. This is also an area of research that could benefit from a focused sociocultural lens. However, most of the Vygotskian theory has focused on adult-child interactions—for example, how parents structure tasks for their children or how teachers create contexts that facilitate students' understanding. Methods are only now being developed to investigate how children interact with one another and construct knowledge jointly.[46] As suggested here though, it is highly likely that, just as in the case of family and adult visitors, a host of sociocultural factors influences the learning of children visiting as a part of school groups.

School groups are not the only child–child groups visiting museums. Increasing numbers of camp, scout, boys and girls clubs, and after-school groups now regularly utilize museums. Museums are also developing intensive programs for children and youth that allow them to become involved in the activities of museums in meaningful and productive ways. One very successful apprenticeship program for low-income youth, the American Association of Science-Technology Centers' YouthALIVE! program, which is supported by the Dewitt Wallace Reader's Digest Fund, with additional funding from the Hitachi Foundation, has made a difference in a number of young people's lives throughout the country. Preliminary research suggests that after young people had participated in the program for one to two years, their interest in, and attitudes toward, science improved; they developed communication, career preparation, and other life skills; their self-confidence was strengthened; and many learned science as well, although that was not a major goal of the project. There is even the sense that some participants performed better in school or were transformed in other ways as a result of the program.[47] Project staff attribute many of these effects to the opportunities provided youth to participate in a supportive social environment among the various communities of learners found in museums. Clearly the sociocultural dynamics of these groups are quite different from those of school groups; nor is it an exaggeration to say that little is known about the ways learning in these groups differs from that in school-organized child–child groups. This area, also, is ripe for additional research.

SOCIOCULTURAL MEDIATION BY OTHERS

Other Visitor Groups

If indeed the museum represents a community of practice in which myriad communities of learners mingle and learn, then it is important to understand the influence of the social interaction between these visitor groups and between visitors and museum staff and volunteers. This is also an area that has only begun to be investigated. There is essentially no research on distributed meaning-making between different families and/or all-adult groups. Exceptions are two studies, summarized in *The Museum Experience,* conducted at the Florida Museum of Natural History. These studies explored the effects of modeling on the visitor experiences of both families and all-adult groups. As with family members in family groups, modeling seems to be an important between-group behavior in museums. Visitors watch other people and often indicated in interviews that this was something they did frequently and was an important ingredient in their sense of satisfaction with the visit.[48] How this modeling influences learning outside one's immediate family or social group has not been well documented; however, preliminary data from these studies suggests that museum visitors attend to other visitors and often seem to be observing one another to gain information or knowledge.[49]

Despite the sense that social interactions between groups might positively influence the experience and result in subsequent learning, there is also evidence that groups in museums actively avoid such interactions. Some groups choose not to interact with other groups and have been observed going to some lengths to avoid interacting at all.[50] Findings also suggest that some social interaction factors can inhibit the positive sense of being part of a community of learners that many visitors seek in museums. Crowding is often a major problem, and families tend to walk past exhibits when other visitors are blocking their view, stopping only when they find an empty space. Taylor found that in a museum layout with a one-way traffic pattern, a new family group arriving at an exhibit would "bump" the current family on to a new exhibit, limiting their time at a display. There is no question that visitors pay attention to what other visitors are doing and that this social interaction influences visitor behavior and, by inference, subsequent learning. Currently, the details and relative importance of this sociocultural behavior are virtually unknown.

Social Interaction and the Single Visitor

Clearly, social interaction plays a critical role in mediating and influencing learning within and between groups, but what role does it play for the lone visitor immersed in the sociocultural milieu of other visitors, staff, and volunteers? There is essentially no research on interactions between lone visitors and other visitors, although there is evidence to suggest that some visitors go to interpretive settings specifically to meet others,[51] and many interpretive settings have built popular and profitable programming around the single adult's desire to meet someone interesting.

However, some visitors prefer to visit a museum alone, seeking its solitude and restorative power. According to educational researcher Howard Gardner, there are people who prefer to learn by themselves (what he refers to as intra-intelligence).[52] Think back to the young woman from the projects describing her experiences visiting the Detroit Institute of Art alone, enjoying the quiet privacy (see chapter 4); or consider the visitor who purposely visits a museum when he knows only a few people will be there. Although radical sociocultural psychologists would still argue that sociocultural factors influence such a visit, clearly not all learning is directly influenced by social interaction, nor do all learners actively seek such learning situations.

Museum Staff and Volunteers

Given that more than a hundred years of educational research documents the important role of "teachers" in facilitating learning, it is amazing how little research exists on the role that museum staff—volunteers, guides, explainers, demonstrators, and performers—play in facilitating learning from museums. The few studies conducted with casual visitors suggest that staff and volunteers positively influence the experience, particularly when they are skilled interpreters, helping to facilitate and make the experience meaningful for visitors. For example, studies in a wide range of museums showed that when a staff member or docent was available to answer questions informally for families, the time spent at individual exhibits increased to as much as twenty-two minutes.[53] Researchers have consistently observed that families spend more time at exhibitions involving interaction with other visitors or docents or staff. Museum researchers Robert Wolf and Barbara Tymitz observed that visitors to zoos initiated informal conversations with zoo personnel to inquire about the animals. These conversations were often repeated to family members who had not heard the discussion, and following the conversation, children often continued to question their parents.[54]

This research suggests that investing effort in having knowledgeable and skilled interpreters available to assist visitors is one way to communicate that the museum is a place for learning, a community of practice. Also, in the truest sociocultural sense, staff and volunteers are members of the community of learners themselves, a part of the community of practice we call the museum. They are also transformed by the interactions they have with visitors, in the same way that visitors are transformed and affected by interactions with them. Findings also suggest that staff and volunteers have a nonverbal role to play in supporting the many communities of learners present at any one time at the museum by modeling effective inquiry strategies.[55]

One increasingly common form of social mediation between staff and visitors in museum settings is the use of theater, performance, film, or first-person interpretation as an interpretive strategy. A body of research is beginning to be developed demonstrating that this approach is effective in communicating and connecting to visitors.[56] Specific findings indicate that participants' general perception is that these experiences are informative, educational, and valuable. There is evidence that these experiences enhance visitors' learning of content, as well as their ability to articulate complex issues and ideas.[57] As chapter 3 suggested, there are reasons theater and performance might be powerful mediators for learning, since cognitive research universally demonstrates that people can effectively organize information mentally if it is recounted to them in a story.[58] Social narrative forms, such as plays or performances, have ancient roots and have evolved over time as mechanisms for sharing culture. Consequently, they are extremely powerful tools for meaning-making.

Researchers recognize the importance of such narratives; museum researchers Zahava Doering and Andrew Pekakirk call the unique story lines that visitors bring to the museum "entrance narratives."[59] Museum researcher Lisa Roberts has suggested that each museum visitor comes away "with an individually unique experience and interpretation because every visitor is engaged in constructing a narrative about what he or she sees."[60] A recent dissertation study investigated how children involved in a unit of study on Pueblo history conceptualized, constructed, and found meaning in the past. Two primary methods were observed: a linear form consistent with the way history is taught in schools and a nonlinear, or "diachronic," form. Given a choice, students preferred to create nonlinear collages of the Pueblo past. Their narratives included information from diverse time periods and cultures and reflected issues of personal identity and culture, not because of misconceptions, but because of personal choice.[61]

A planning grant from the National Science Foundation allowed researchers at the Arizona Science Center to examine the feasibility of introducing interdisciplinary narratives into a science center visitor's experiences.[62] The narratives were generated by experts with diverse life experiences and perspectives—Native American, African American, Hispanic, and feminist—and were presented to, and validated by, the public. What emerged were guidelines for successful narratives that suggest that it is important to (1) include a variety of voices, images, and experiences to help everyone find personal meaning in science topics; (2) blend narrative art and science content and maintain high quality in each; and (3) help the public connect their museum experiences with responsible thinking about the world around them that deepens with each visit. Future research will explore the role of narrative in engaging the interests of diverse audiences.

There is evidence that social interaction between museum staff and visiting groups has positive effects on learning, but there is still much more to learn about how to facilitate such interaction. In a study of families at zoos, Sherman Rosenfeld observed that families did not listen to the commentary by the trained guides on the zoo train, nor did they ask questions.[63] Taylor found that volunteer interpreters frequently did not have enough content background or training to respond effectively to visitor questions and perceived their role as policemen rather than facilitators of collaborative learning.[64] A better understanding of how social interaction between staff and visitors affects learning and under what circumstances could lead to significantly better practice.

In conclusion, whether between groups or within groups, it is clear that sociocultural mediation plays a major role in affecting learning from museums. However, there are currently two serious impediments to a better understanding of the sociocultural nature of museum learning: the need to better define and operationalize what learning is from a sociocultural perspective and the need to develop better tools to investigate such learning. Most sociocultural researchers' notions of learning diverge significantly from the perspective of most cognitive psychologists. Sociocultural researchers take the position that learning is much more about process than product; it is about transformation and distributed meaning-making. For example, Rogoff identifies a number of transformations in participation that might be observed and thus, from a sociocultural perspective, be considered as evidence of learning: (1) an individual's contributions to the effort, (2) individual initiative or commitment to the effort, (3) leadership and support of others' roles in the effort, and (4) the understanding of complementary roles in the effort.[65] Although most researchers could accept that these transformations are part of the learning process, few outside the sociocultural community would view these transformations alone as sufficient evidence of learning.

Also, although sociocultural mediation seems to play a critical role in personalizing experiences, facilitating the process and products of learning, our ability to document this and determine in what ways it is an influence is still limited. As much of the research shared in this chapter suggests, researchers are trying to create new approaches, utilizing tools such as in-depth interviews, videotaped observations, and diaries. Although we can assert that the unit of analysis should not be the individual but the group, methodologies for analyzing the group are in their infancy. In the coming decades, new methods for facilitating and documenting the sociocultural influences on learning—in other words, distributed meaning-making—should yield ever better and more realistic views of free-choice learning in general and museum learning in particular. By contrast, the effect of physical context on museum learning, which we examine in the next chapter, is more fully understood.

KEY POINTS

- Sociocultural mediation, either direct or indirect, plays a critical role in personalizing the museum experience for visitors, facilitating their efforts to learn and find meaning. The sociocultural dimension of the museum experience is an important component of the "contextual stamp" that enhances people's ability to remember the experience and shapes subsequent experiences with the same objects, ideas, or events.

- At a fundamental level, museums support the participation of visitors in a wide range of learning communities. This participation can take many forms, including pursuing inquiries, making connections among various contexts, sharing interests with others, and learning how to learn and how to assist and collaborate with others. Most museum visitors arrive as part of a social group, each representing its own unique community of learners.

- Conversation is a primary mechanism of knowledge construction and distributed meaning-making. However, not all of the behaviors observed in these communities of learners are verbal. Group members observe each other to gain information, to figure out how to interact with exhibitions, and to learn effective ways to engage in inquiry. Modeling, also called observational or social learning, is a frequently observed social behavior both within and between groups.

- The museum represents a community of practice in which myriad communities of learners mingle and learn. Museum staff—volunteers, guides, explainers, demonstrators, and performers—positively influence the visitor experience, particularly when staff are skilled interpreters, helping to facilitate and make the experience meaningful for visitors.

NOTES

1. Falk and Dierking 1992; Rosenfeld 1979; Dierking and Martin 1997.

2. Throughout this book, when we refer to family, we mean an intergenerational group of adults and children who self-define themselves as a family (in other words, all members are not necessarily biologically related). We recognize that technically families can contain all-adult members and include couples with no children, but our research suggests that these constellations behave far more like all-adult groups and so are categorized that way in this book.

3. Benton 1979; Birney 1986; Diamond 1980, 1986; Dierking 1987, 1989; Dierking and Falk 1994; Falk and Balling 1982; Hilke and Balling 1985; Hilke 1989; Kropf 1989; McManus 1987; Rosenfeld 1979, 1980; Silverman 1990; Snow Dockser 1987a, 1987b, 1989; Taylor 1986; Tuckey 1992; Wolf and Tymitz 1979.

4. Silverman 1990.

5. Chase 1975; Diamond 1986; Dierking and Falk 1994.

6. Leinhardt 2000, 1.

7. Matusov and Rogoff 1995.

8. Chase 1975; Dierking 1987, 1989; Hilke and Balling 1985; Rosenfeld 1979; Taylor 1986; Lakota 1975.

9. Wolf and Tymitz 1979; Rosenfeld 1980; Hilke and Balling 1985.

10. Taylor 1986.

11. Leinhardt 2000; Rogoff 1990; Wertsch 1997.

12. Hensel 1987.

13. Taylor 1986.

14. Moll and Greenberg 1990; Greenberg 1989; Velez-Ibanez 1988.

15. McManus 1987, 1989.

16. Borun, Chambers, and Cleghorn 1996; Borun and Dritsas 1997; Borun et al. 1998.

17. Bandura and Walters 1963; Dierking 1987.

18. Dierking 1989.

19. Dierking 1989; Dierking and Falk 1994.

20. A. Santini 1988. Personal communication, 3 November.

21. Crowley and Callanan 1998; Crowley et al. 2000; Crowley et al. in review; Schauble and Gleason 2000.

22. Guberman et al. 1999.

23. Schauble and Gleason 2000.

24. Ash 2000.

25. Ellenbogen 2000.

26. Falk, Phillips, and Boxer Johnson 1993; Rosenfeld 1979.

27. Crowley and Callanan 1998.

28. Osberg 1998.

29. Lakota 1975; McManus 1987.

30. Silverman 1990, 1999. See also Rounds 1999.

31. Katz and Liebes 1986; Iser 1978.

32. Thelen 1989; Iser 1978; Katz and Liebes 1986; Silverman 1995; Custen 1980.

33. Gregg and Leinhardt 2000; Feinberg and Abu-Shumays 2000; Stainton 2000; Paris and Mercer 2000; Allen 2000.

34. Leinhardt and Tittle 2000.

35. Jean was part of the study we described in chapter 1. "Jean" is a pseudonym.

36. Sachatello-Sawyer and Fellenz 1999.

37. Balling, Falk, and Aronson 1980; Chi, deLeeuw, and LaVancher 1994; Crowley and Siegler in review.

38. Birney 1986.

39. Birney 1986.

40. Wolins, Jensen, and Ulzheimer 1992.

41. Azmitia 1996.

42. Tuckey 1992.

43. Tunnicliffe 1995, 1996.

44. Griffin and Symington 1997.

45. Anderson 1999; Anderson et al. in press.

46. Forman and Larreamendy-Joerns 1995; Scardamalia and Bereiter 1991; Wells 1992.

47. Baum, Hein, and Solvay n.d.; Maloney and Hughes 1999; Jackson 1998; Inverness Research Associates 1995; Cosmos Corporation 1998.

48. Rosenfeld 1980.

49. Koran et al. 1988.

50. Dierking 1987.

51. E.g., Sachatello-Sawyer and Fellenz 1999.

52. Gardner 1983.

53. Benton 1979; Diamond 1980; Hilke and Balling 1985; Rosenfeld 1980; Taylor 1986; Wolf and Tymitz 1979

54. Wolf and Tymitz 1979.

55. Koran et al. 1988.

56. Dierking 1990; Dierking and Falk 1998; Baum and Hughes 1999; Hughes 1988.

57. Dierking 1990; Dierking and Falk 1998; Baum and Hughes 1999; Hughes 1988.

58. Schauble, Leinhardt, and Martin 1998.

59. Bruner 1996; Feldman et al. 1995; Cortazzi 1993; Doering and Pekakirk 1996.

60. Roberts 1997, 137.

61. Davis 1997.

62. Martin and Leary 1996, 1997; Schauble, Leinhardt, and Martin 1998; Martin and Toon in review.

63. Rosenfeld 1980.

64. Taylor 1986.

65. Rogoff 1996.

7

A Place for Learning

We can experience any place because we've all received, as part of the
structure of our attention, a mechanism that drinks whatever it can
from our surroundings. . . . For this perception to emerge, we need a
place that seems safe, where the information presented to each sense
is complex but not overpowering.

—Tony Hiss,
The Experience of Place

As we have stated repeatedly, the dominant motivation for humans is
meaning-making; the need to make meaning is innate. Continuously
monitoring the environment, always measuring the new against the
expected, is an evolutionary strategy designed to help humans make
sense of what is happening in their world, to make meaning of the
world. This need plays out in museums in many ways—in the need for
visitors to orient themselves in space, to explore that which is novel, to
prepare themselves mentally for what is to come, and to make overall
sense of the museum environment. But much of a visitor's behavior in
a museum is reactive, unconsciously responding to space, color, shape,
form—in short, responding to design in general and the objects and settings in which they are displayed in particular. Finally, the physical
context of the museum is not limited to the narrowly defined confines
of the museum's interior space but extends into the larger world
beyond the museum's walls. The entire world of educational experience, the educational infrastructure, contributes to and reinforces learning from museums.

ORIENTATION AND ADVANCE ORGANIZERS

Curiosity and Novelty

The visitor walks through the front door and into the building. What do they see? What do they think? Most visitors, particularly first-time visitors, do not begin by looking at signage and maps; they look at the space. In a recent study investigating how visitors navigated through the new California Science Center, 85 percent of visitors reported, "I just found my way."[1] How does one "just find" one's way around a place one has never visited? Psychologists have determined that people construct mental, or cognitive, maps that allow them to know where they have been and, hopefully, predict where they are going. These mental maps are used to guide interactions with, and movements and decisions about, our surroundings. These maps are always being updated and modified as more information is gathered. Humans have the ability to learn almost instantly about space at a basic level: "I'm in a typical room with vertical walls and horizontal floors and ceilings and easy exit through that door over there." It is one of the few examples of "one-trial" learning—do it once and you know it. The moment people walk into a new room, just by gazing around they gain an almost instant sense of its layout, and at least some aspect of this cognitive map will stay with them permanently. These maps are crucial to the operation of a person's life. People constantly call upon past experience to verify the current perceptual information flooding into their senses, updating past maps in light of current information. These maps are always moderately flexible and open-ended. As long as the new information more or less squares with past information, a person feels comfortable and content. However, when the new information coming in from the senses is starkly at odds with past representations, the individual will feel great discomfort, anxiety, and a loss of control. Since survival depends upon knowing where one is in space and time, being lost or disoriented is very threatening. The need to remain oriented and safe in the environment is about as basic a need as exists, taking precedence over the need for food, sex, or self-actualization.[2] Thus, walking into a museum where you have never been before, especially if you have not been to many museums previously, can be tremendously stressful.

Mental mapping of the physical context is influenced by two important psychological processes, curiosity (novelty) and expectation,[3] both of which facilitate the process of meaning-making, and both of which are fundamental to learning.[4] Curiosity and expectation are psychological constructs or dimensions and are not absolute; they can only be determined relative to the individual, and both depend upon prior experience. For example, first-time visitors to a museum will find much to be curious about; everything will appear novel and new. However, for people who work at the museum every day, there will appear to be less to be curious about; the environment is no longer novel, and much is already known.

Humans are inordinately curious, and this curiosity is directly tied to learning. Curiosity and learning represent a feedback loop: curiosity evolved in order to facilitate learning, learning occurs in order to satisfy curiosity.[5] Like so much about learning, curiosity is not a uniquely human trait. As one psychologist put it, "Cats are reputedly killed by curiosity, dogs characteristically make a thorough search of their surroundings and monkeys and chimpanzees have always impressed observers as ceaseless investigators."[6] In a series of illuminating experiments, psychologist Harry Harlow and his coworkers in the 1950s showed that monkeys who were otherwise content (not hungry, thirsty, or otherwise driven by some kind of "primary" drive) tended to play with a puzzle of some complexity for no other apparent motive than the "privilege" of playing with it.[7] Curiosity, it seems, is driven by the need for stimulation. In the absence of stimulation, animals are driven to be curious, in other words, to seek stimulation. Mental stimulation appears to be a fundamental mammalian need. This desire for stimulation, the desire to promote then satisfy curiosity, aptly characterizes the motivation behind most free-choice learning. According to environmental psychologists Stephen and Rachael Kaplan, curiosity is a major factor in determining whether environments are appealing.[8] Environments that have "mystery," provide a moderate sense of the unknown, are complex, and invite exploration are far more desirable than those without these qualities.[9]

Directly related to curiosity is novelty. Novelty is how we describe unfamiliar environments, events, or objects; curiosity is how we respond to them.[10] Beginning in the 1970s, Falk and his colleagues began studying the impact of environmental novelty on learning in out-of-school settings.[11] They discovered that novel settings dramatically influenced learning. When settings were extremely novel, learning was depressed. Learning was also depressed in extremely familiar (i.e., boring) settings. However, if an optimum amount of novelty was introduced, learning was enhanced. These basic findings have been replicated by a range of investigators in a wide variety of other museum settings.[12]

A considerable amount of the learning that occurs in free-choice conditions is a result of novelty-seeking behavior. For example, when visitors to museums are specifically asked why they came, they tend to give a variety of answers, including that they wanted to see and do something that they had not seen or done before.[13] People self-select to put themselves in situations where learning will be optimized, hence they seek out moderately novel situations. Nobody wants to go someplace that is boring, nor does anyone want to go someplace that will be scary. Instead, they seek environments where the conditions will be "just right." Moderately novel settings are stimulating and exciting, and therefore fun. For some people museums fulfill this condition, for others it is sporting events, for others it is the shopping mall. In all these situations, though, people are seeking out opportunities to see and do things that they do not normally get to see or do. More and more people in their free time are actively choosing to engage in learning activities to satisfy their need for stimulation, and in the process they seek out moderately novel environments in which to learn. Thus, learning in a moderately novel environment is maximally satisfying. What is fascinating is that free-choice learners know beforehand that participating in their chosen activity will stimulate their curiosity. People like to be able to make meaningful predictions. This preference for situations in which prediction is possible turns out to be nontrivial.[14] In fact, it is the expectation of novelty, the prediction that curiosity will be piqued and satisfied, that motivates most, if not all, free-choice learning.

Humans expect the world to be a particular way because of the preliminary mental representations they form and their memories of similar environments or events. For example, we expect books to have printed words, movies to have moving images, and museums to possess objects and/or exhibitions. We guide our behavior by these expectations and keep checking their accuracy. The corollary is that anything interesting or different is immediately attended to until it is incorporated in the cognitive map or identified as unimportant.[15] Expectations of the physical world in a very real way shape our learning. For example, research on visitors to national forests revealed that the majority of the recreation-oriented people who visit them have an image of what they expect to see. Such a mental picture is generated by available information about a particular area and the person's experience with that or similar areas. According to the investigation, the image produced represented the knowledgeability, expectedness, romanticism, and emotionalism associated with features in the area. Obviously, several images may exist simultaneously, even within a single individual, and yet a particular geographic region tends to have an identifiable image.[16]

These expectations directly affected visitors' enjoyment of their forest experience. When the landscape unfolded the way they expected it to, visitors reported high levels of satisfaction and enjoyment. When expectations were not met, satisfaction and enjoyment were significantly diminished.[17] Similar findings apply to museums, zoos, and aquariums.[18] Expectations have also been found to affect learning. Children who knew what to expect to learn from a school field trip to a zoo learned significantly more than children who did not know what to expect. Children who knew what to expect both cognitively and spatially showed the greatest amount of learning.[19] This reality is true not only for children but also for adults.[20] Psychologists refer to this prior knowledge of what to expect as an *advance organizer*. In fact, the psychologist David Ausubel believed that the single most important thing one could do for learners is provide them with an advance organizer.[21] Advance organizers do in fact facilitate learning; this has been shown in studies of schoolchildren on field trips[22] and of advance organizers embedded in exhibitions.[23] For example, the new *World of Life* exhibition at the California Science Center contained a special exhibit element called the "Life Tunnel," which was intended to give visitors a conceptual overview of the exhibition. Approximately two-thirds of the visitors to the exhibition went through at least some part of the Life Tunnel. These visitors showed an improved ability to reasonably articulate the "big idea(s)" of the exhibition when compared with those who did not visit this space.[24]

Orientation, which is a kind of advance organizer, is another way of providing individuals with a conceptual and spatial preview of a space. Orientation helps visitors feel more comfortable and ensures greater learning. Visitors who were given an orientation of some sort prior to their visit were more likely to learn than were those who did not receive an orientation.[25] Most museums assume that their primary orientation responsibility is to provide visitors with a physical map, either on a stanchion or on paper, or both. Unfortunately, the majority of visitors neither use maps nor find them very usable.[26] Good signage and maps may facilitate navigation through the museum,[27] but they are limited in their ability to compensate for a disorienting building.[28] According to environmental psychologist Gary Evans, several physical features are known to support good orientation and navigation. These include interior settings that conform to relatively simple, overall geometric patterns; well-marked and bounded distinctive subsections or districts; interiors with views of the surrounding external environment; and spaces with interior grid patterns (i.e., parallel interior hallways and ninety-degree intersections) that indicate both direction of movement and extent of progress as the path is traversed. All of these attributes enhance visitors' ability to navigate easily through the building on their own.

How Visitors Make Sense of Museum Spaces

A search image is a general image that a person keeps in mind of what is being sought. Unlike the mental or cognitive maps described earlier, a search image is usually not about a space but about an object. In an art museum the search image may be general—for example, paintings and sculpture—or more specific, such as an impressionist painting; or even more specific, such as the works of a specific artist or even a single painting. Search images can even be abstract—for example, a visitor to a history museum may have a search image of items from the American Civil War. Such an image is specific not to an object but to a concept, in this case, things related to a particular historical period. Armed with such search images, visitors move through the museum. More experienced visitors have better museum search images than less experienced visitors, but virtually all visitors come with some sense of what they're looking for and a general sense of how to find it. At one time in this country large percentages of the population had never been to a museum before, and such is still the case in many other parts of the world. However, few American museum visitors today, even people visiting a particular institution for the first time, arrive without having had some museum experience. Thus, the public can be assumed to possess a generic museum-going strategy, albeit often poorly developed and lacking in specificity for either the subject or the institution. These expectations come from a variety of sources, especially friends and relatives who have previously visited the museum or earlier personal experience visiting the museum.[29] If these predetermined search images are particularly strong, visitors will walk past half the exhibits in the building in search of their goal.

The better the search image—the closer to reality and the more specific it is—the easier it is to utilize and satisfy.[30] Expectation strongly influences behavior and learning. If things are the way we expect them to be, we find this very reinforcing and continue. If there is a discrepancy, we may become curious and proceed, but more likely we will either ignore or skip over the inconsistency. Few things are more rewarding for the visitor than to have heard that there is a "really cool" exhibition in the museum, search for it, find it, and then agree that it is really cool. This confirmation of the expected is a very powerful feedback loop.[31] Advertisers use this type of anticipatory information to hype the release of many kinds of products and experiences, such as movies. As museums join the ranks of an increasingly market-driven world, museum visitors too can be expected to arrive more frequently with heightened and often very specific expectations. So despite the many choices the museum may afford the visitor, it is not surprising to discover that more and more visitors limit their choices to the well promoted and well advertised. This is not necessarily all bad, particularly given the almost overwhelming number of choices the average-sized museum offers.

The number of choices presented in most museums imposes an information-processing challenge for the brain. Too many choices and the brain goes into overload. Researchers have discovered that there is an upper limit to the amount of information the human brain can process at any given moment. Using the prevailing information-processing metric, the bit (binary digit), it has been determined that a simple display with two choices represents 1 bit of information to be processed. For example, if there is a display with two spoons, it takes 1 bit of information to decide which spoon to look at first. A display that requires four choices is the equivalent of 2 bits of information, and a display requiring eight choices requires 3 bits of processing information (2 x 2 x 2). What does this mean? Studies suggest that the brain is capable of handling about 7 bits, across all senses, at any given time.[32] Given that the brain can process several events in the same channel per second, it turns out that the brain, in theory, can process a maximum of 126 bits of information per second.[33] Although this capacity seems quite formidable, studies show that simply trying to understand someone who is speaking requires about 40 bits per second of processing, while ambient noise and sights also suck up bits. Thus it is relatively easy to see how a complex environment like a museum could easily overload the senses and create a situation where the visitor would be unable to detect appropriate information.[34] A clear and unambiguous search image helps, as does the ability to "chunk" information.

One of the most important discoveries of cognitive science was the observation and quantification of the fact that people do not perceive information comparably. Experienced visitors can look at a display and, quite literally, in a given amount of time see more and remember more than inexperienced visitors. This has nothing to do with intelligence and everything to do with experience and training. This ability to perceive more information per unit of time is what cognitive psychologists refer to as "chunking" information. In a classic paper, psychologist George Miller argued that the capacity of humans to recall information was limited by "the magic number seven plus or minus two."[35] The limit is not necessarily on the number of items that can be remembered but on the number of meaningful groupings, or chunks, of items. One person may look at a display case and see a spy glass, a map, and a pistol, but miss the pen-and-ink set and blotter, compass, telegram, tent, field table, and camp stool. A second person may look at the same display case and see a Civil War officer's field office and, without dwelling on the case, be able to reliably predict all of the things that should be there. The second person can recall seeing more things in the display, despite mentally listing only one thing. The degree of ability to chunk, which we all do, is one of the major differences between experts and novices in any given subject. The tremendous benefit that chunking permits (and chunking is learning) is that it enables humans to process orders of magnitude more information than would be possible if each item in the environment had to be individually, painstakingly itemized each time.

Accordingly, visitors with more subject matter and/or museum background experience the museum in qualitatively different ways than visitors with less background. Experienced visitors are able to take in more of the content of exhibitions and can readily see relationships and appreciate concepts because they chunk the contents in higher-order categories. Less experienced visitors see exhibitions with dozens of often seemingly unrelated objects. Even when they "see" all the objects, inexperience and the seven-plus-or-minus-two rule mitigate against their being able to process, remember, and make meaning of all the objects. In the end, they are less likely to have gleaned relationships, appreciated the conceptual underpinning of the exhibition, or personally connected with it. The experienced person's perceptual power in seeing and understanding a familiar environment is the result of an extensive process of progressive simplification, generated over time.[36] While experience does not occur instantaneously, design can facilitate conceptual organization. Design and text can be used to help create physical and intellectual groupings that assist an inexperienced visitor in making meaningful chunks of what would otherwise be random information within an exhibition. Over the last decade, a variety of studies have shown that exhibit location and arrangement directly affect concept development, although not always in the ways exhibition designers intend or hope.

In a series of studies, Falk and his associates showed that exhibitions located closest to the entrance of the museum attract more attention than do those farther away. This effect was independent of either the exhibition's design or its content.[37] In another study by Falk, a prototype of an exhibition at the Smithsonian's natural history museum was designed so that each of the elements was movable. The exhibition was set up in two different configurations. Research findings suggested that when visitors interacted with exactly the same exhibit elements, different learning resulted depending upon the arrangement with which they interacted.[38] One of the arrangements was linear, presenting concepts like chapters in a book. The other arrangement took advantage of natural clusters of content and did not assume that visitors would utilize it in a linear fashion. The less linear arrangement proved superior.

In a similar vein, psychologists Stephen Bitgood and Donald Patterson investigated the effects of specific exhibition elements on visitors.[39] The research was conducted in an Egyptian mummy exhibition at the Anniston Museum of Natural History (Anniston, Alabama). Bitgood and Patterson added exhibit labels to walls, changed the physical characteristics of these labels, and introduced a bronze bust reconstructed from a mummified person. The results demonstrated that several of the factors directly influenced whether visitors read labels and the extent to which they did so. For example, visitors were significantly more likely to read three 50-word labels than a single 150-word label containing the same text. The size of the letters on the labels and their location relative to the objects also influenced label reading. The more visitors read labels, the more likely they were to stop and look at the objects associated with them.

In another study, this one conducted at the California Museum of Science and Industry (currently California Science Center), Falk investigated the implications of exhibition clustering on visitor conceptual development.[40] One of the most common museum exhibition design practices is to cluster groups of conceptually related exhibits, on the assumption that the public implicitly understands that clustered exhibits communicate a single overarching concept. This is a good theory but one with little data to support its validity. Falk conducted an experiment using two exhibition clusters, one on how transportation in Los Angeles affects air pollution (*Transportation*) and one on the conception and early development of vertebrates (*Eggciting Beginnings*). The five *Transportation* cluster elements included simple manipulatives with accompanying text, an animated film loop, an "environment-style" video theater, and interactive computers. The four *Eggciting Beginnings* elements included a film loop of human conception and development, cut-away models, preserved specimens, and two live-animal habitats, one containing adult and juvenile bullfrogs and one with chicken eggs and chicks hatching. The two exhibition clusters were investigated under two treatments: with and without explicit labeling. The first treatment used the common museum practice of placing conceptually related exhibits near each other, as the exhibition was originally designed and currently installed at the museum. Other than an exhibit title placed at the "front" of the exhibition, the exhibits had no explicit signage or labeling informing visitors that they contained conceptually related content, nor was there any signage or labeling explicitly defining for the visitor the overarching concept the cluster was designed to communicate. In the second treatment, temporary labels were attached to each exhibit element. Each label contained a "headline" and a "subheadline." The headline briefly summarized the main message of the exhibition cluster; the identical headline was placed on each of the cluster elements. The subheadline provided a brief description of the main message of the individual exhibit element and was different for each element in the cluster. It was assumed that the presence of the headline labels would enable visitors to more readily identify the individual exhibit elements as part of a single related cluster.

Although most visitors derived some benefit from the two exhibition clusters under both treatments, the second treatment resulted in significantly more learning. Visitors in the second treatment not only learned more about the specific information and big ideas but also spent significantly more time in the exhibition. The study suggested that clusters of conceptually linked exhibits should be clearly and explicitly designated and delineated for visitors, lest they fail to perceive the connection themselves. The strategy of providing at *each* exhibit element labels that contained a headline and a subheadline as described above appeared to be a successful way to give visitors a sense of connection between the exhibit elements and also enhanced conceptual development. As is typical of museum visitor behavior, visitors in this study did not interact with the exhibit clusters in a linear or sequential manner, even in the very linear *Transportation* exhibition cluster. Thus the presence of consistent, reinforcing conceptual organizers on every element facilitated comprehension of the exhibit messages and compensated for the random pattern of visitor utilization.

As stated earlier, humans not only are good at perceiving order but actively seek order. Through judicious use of design and content, exhibitions, and in fact the entire museum experience, can be made to be powerful information-organizing experiences for people. Humans generally find viewing exhibitions, unlike reading large blocks of text or listening to a lecture, to be an easily comprehensible way to access information and make meaning. Easy should not be construed as limited. Good exhibitions organize information in ways that make it remarkably easy to chunk information. It is probably the ability of exhibitions to simplify, organize, and contextualize information that makes them such potent teaching tools. People respond powerfully to exhibitions. Exhibitions, like all successfully constructed images, can dramatically affect people.[41] They can make people feel good or bad, they can "elate and excite, arouse and satisfy, anger, shock and depress. Indeed [exhibitions] can play havoc with the emotions."[42] Successful museum exhibitions can move visitors to higher levels of understanding across a large range of topics.

HOW DESIGN AFFECTS VISITORS

Once oriented, the typical visitor will move to the first exhibition gallery, usually on the first floor and to the right, and begin the visit in earnest.[43] Once the visitor is in this first gallery, other parts of the physical design take precedence. According to designer Marjorie Elliott Bevlin, "Design is the organization of materials and forms in such a way as to fulfill a specific purpose."[44] In the case of museums, that purpose is to visually, and increasingly aurally and socially, attract and pull in the visitor. Good design draws the visitor in, engages all the senses, and compels the visitor to investigate the topic at hand. The visitor will usually begin the journey at the first exhibit element that they perceive, which may or may not be chronologically the first exhibit. What makes an exhibit attractive to a visitor? This is a very simple question with many complex dimensions. We will attempt to circle in on the answer, first through the vocabulary of design, then through the vocabulary of psychology. From a design standpoint, what makes something attractive is an appropriate blending of the basic design elements of space, shape, mass, color, texture, and pattern, as well as unity and variety; balance, emphasis, and rhythm; and proportion and scale.[45] In a museum context, we should also throw in sound, substrates, smells, potentially people, and of course text and objects. Let us explore each of these briefly.

Space

Museum exhibition designer Kathleen McLean says, "The exhibition space becomes the vessel in which objects, ideas, and people are brought together and transformed."[46] Space is more than a void. Designers know that in creating form, they must always manipulate space. There is the actual space that exists, whether two-dimensional as in a mural or graphic or three-dimensional within an exhibition or inside a building. There is also a more pictorial space: the illusions created by perspective in paintings or perception of depth by manipulation of color and shadow. Within the three-dimensional space of a museum, time, too, is an element of space. As a visitor moves through the museum, the space changes, either drawing the visitor in or not, challenging or comforting. Space is created, and in fact defined, by the design. At the level of the exhibit, at the level of the exhibition, and finally at the level of the building, the visitor's experience is influenced by the creation of space. Good design enables the visitor to navigate through all of these spaces without the help of a guide. A visitor's eyes or feet are guided through the exhibition through the placement of elements, by the creation of perspective, by the development of appropriate volumes and frames either through real constructs or through the use of implied space. (Implied space is a device that allows a designer to create an illusion of greater or lesser space by the way an object or view is framed for the visitor.)

Shape and Mass

The primary tools for creating space are what designers refer to as shape and mass. *Shape* refers to the general outlines of something; like the shape of a building, a book, a display case, or a room. *Mass* refers to the space that shape occupies in the three-dimensional world. Thinking back to high school geometry class: shapes are things like circles, squares, and triangles, while mass refers to the volumes occupied by spheres, boxes, and pyramids. Geometric shapes dominate the constructed environment. They appear in buildings, bridges, furniture, and machines of all kinds. For example, the right angles of floors, walls, and ceilings form a horizontal and vertical framework into which most museum exhibitions must fit. However, objects can and do assume an almost infinite variety of shapes and masses. Shape and mass can be manipulated to create stability or tension. Place a pyramidal shape on its base and it defines stability, place it on its apex and it creates immediate instability and tension. Not all shapes and masses are solid and permanent. A flag waving in the breeze, a wave in the water, people moving through an exhibition hall, all are examples of shape and mass in movement. In ways that have been understood aesthetically for centuries but are only beginning to be understood scientifically, shape and mass, as well as the other design elements described here, can be manipulated in ways that either promote exploration and curiosity, or do not.

Color

Color has long been considered a key element of exhibition design,[47] perhaps because it, more than any other design element, affects people emotionally. This is no doubt a function of the deep biological roots of our color vision, which evolved to enable us to distinguish edible from inedible, safe from hazardous. The fundamental link between color and survival makes us keenly aware of color. More poetically, color has been called the "music" of the visual arts.[48] Color brings a mood and a depth of experience that cannot be achieved in any other way. Like the notes of the basic scale when expanded into a symphony, color has seemingly unlimited variation and enormous capacity to manipulate our moods and feelings. Integral to color is light; in fact, without light there could be no color. Most people are aware that color is not absolute but is the way our brain perceives the reflection of different wavelengths of light. Similarly, we perceive black as the absence of all color or light, and white as the presence of all colors or light. Most authorities distinguish three properties of color: hue, value, and intensity. Hue is the basic state of a color, such as red or blue, without any white or black mixed in. Value refers to the relative lightness or darkness of a color—in other words, the amount of white or black mixed into the color. Finally, intensity, also known as chroma or saturation, indicates the relative purity of a color. Color can be expanded to include additional properties such as iridescence, luster, luminosity, and transparency. Color can make objects "pop" from the walls or cases, or it can make them disappear.

The aesthetics of color have changed historically. The Victorians would show pictures against deep red backgrounds, making their gold frames appear especially rich, while more recently gallery walls are painted stark white so as "not to interfere with the color values in the pictures, and [because white] reflects light around the exhibition space whilst absorbing ultra-violet radiation."[49] In previous periods, pastels were used. In many cases, darker colors are again finding their way into galleries, often to evoke period. But color's impact is more than aesthetic.

Color influences the visitor in many, often predictable, ways. For example, reds, oranges, and yellows give a sensation of warmth, while blues, greens, and violets evoke coldness. So strong is this effect that people in a blue room will set the thermostat four degrees higher than those in a red room.[50] "Warm" colors stimulate, "cool" colors relax, so that, for example, audiences hearing an identical lecture found the lecture boring in a blue hall and interesting in a red hall.[51] Warm colors make things look closer, cool colors make objects look farther away. Dark colors make a space seem smaller, light colors open up a space.[52] Noises sound louder in a white room than in a dark-colored room.[53] Dark colors even make objects feel heavier.[54]

Beyond these widely shared responses to color, there are cultural and even personal responses. In some cultures, such as India, red is a symbol of fertility, and increasingly in the United States and other Western countries, green has been used literally and figuratively as a symbol of "environment."[55] Thus, when placed in appropriate contexts, colors can elicit whole complexes of feelings and thoughts because of the long-term associations built up around them. This occurs at the level of the individual also. Each person brings to the perception of visual information a collection of experiences, associations, and memories that may be triggered by a given color.[56] Such associations may be evoked by seeing the color one's room was painted in childhood or the color of the sky on a special remembered day. Colors have the ability to evoke a response, positive or negative, a response that often the viewer only dimly understands.

Other Design Features

The designer's toolbox also includes texture and pattern, the look and feel of the surface of an object. Texture can vary physically, such that the surface is rough or smooth, hard or soft, bristly or velvety. It can also vary visually; through light and shadow, the appearance of the surface can undulate or shine or appear dappled. Texture thus blends into what we think of as pattern. To the extent a visual texture is repetitive, it becomes pattern. The human brain seems to be "wired" to see patterns. If the patterns are not already there, humans will impose them.[57] Textures and patterns, like colors, can evoke an emotional response. Rooms with smooth textures seem "cold," while rough textures such as those created by shag rugs, plush fabrics, and uneven wall surfaces contribute to a sense of "warmth" in interior spaces.[58] The power of this effect can be experienced by walking from the stark white walls and smooth marble floors of an art museum's galleries into the carpeted, wallpapered, plushly furnished interior of the donors' lounge; the galleries are cold, the lounge warm. Pattern can also create a sense of movement or even jar the eye and create a sense of disquiet. Texture and pattern, along with the tools of visual unity and variety, as well as emphasis, balance, and rhythm, allow designers to manipulate where the eye is drawn and how the visitor will respond to an exhibition.

An exhibit case with a total hodgepodge of objects with no obvious visual or informational relationship is unsettling. It will appear haphazard and chaotic to the visitor, while a display with row after row of seemingly identical objects, neatly laid out without variation, has a mind-numbing effect. Good design balances unity and variety to evoke relationships and forge visual and mental associations. Balance between unity and variety can be achieved through shape, texture, color, pattern, or informational content. Unity is essential to communicate information and provide context; variety is essential to maintain visitor interest and enjoyment. Similarly, the design principles of balance, emphasis, and rhythm relate to the designer's capacity to create a visual "feast" for the visitor that both attracts attention and facilitates intellectual engagement, allowing the visitor to engage in the whole and focus on the specific. When all of these aesthetic elements complement each other, an exhibit "works"; when they do not, neither does the exhibit.

Proportion and scale are also important design elements. Proportion usually refers to size relationships within a composition; scale indicates size in comparison to some constant, such as the size of the human body or the size something "ought to be."[59] People have an intuitive sense of proportion and scale, engendered by a lifetime of experience in the world. Bigger usually means stronger and heavier, smaller implies fragile and precious. Museums display and interpret objects, events, and even ideas, all of which must be presented within appropriate proportion and scale to each other and to the larger physical context in which they are embedded (i.e., the museum). People are attracted to very big things and to very small things.[60] By manipulating surrounding objects, designers can manipulate the apparent size of a given item. The large elephant in the rotunda of the Smithsonian Institution's National Museum of Natural History is accentuated by its isolation and its placement on a raised pedestal. The same elephant surrounded by similar specimens and placed at ground level would not engender the same awe. Sometimes to make the point that something is truly unique requires providing a context by displaying the special object surrounded by its inadequate rivals. Creating an appropriate juxtaposition enables the visitor to see how impressive the proportions of this special object are. Many visitors come to the museum in order to see the "biggest" and the "best." Design can be used to visually accentuate size and quality. For example, rather than burying a masterpiece among twenty other lesser works, enshrining the painting on a wall all by itself communicates to the visitor that this object is special and worth taking the time to contemplate. Sometimes the only way to show the real scale of the object is to provide photographs or pictures of the object in its natural setting and in this way create an appropriate context for understanding. Thus, proportion and scale are not only important design elements but also important communication elements.

Over the past few decades museum exhibition design has undergone a revolution in quality and complexity. The driving force in this change has been the move away from the concept of exhibitions as merely spaces for visually displaying objects to the view of exhibitions as environments in which visitors experience art, history, nature, or science. Exhibitions have come to envelop the visitor in visual, tactile, aural, and, increasingly, olfactory sensation. Aquariums today encircle the visitor in fish; tanks literally wrap around the space, from floor to ceiling. Zoos provide immersion experiences that mimic safaris and animal-watching blinds. Science centers create spaces where visitors can scale faux mountains, play virtu-al basketball, and sit in the cockpit of a plane or spacecraft and bring it down for a landing. History museums create living performances where actors portraying historical figures in period dress and speech engage the visitor in conversations and tasks appropriate to the time. Thus, the tra-ditional design toolbox of color and shape, materials and lighting has expanded to include sounds, substrates, smells, plants, animals, and even people.[61] For example, it is becoming increasingly common for designers to devise ways to incorporate the visitors into the exhibition, not only for themselves, but for other visitors as well. For example, at the Baltimore Museum of Industry, school groups are regularly invited to be part of an oyster-shucking assembly line, complete with conveyor belts and aprons; in the process, groups can both see and experience an assembly line in action. Balancing so many variables, though, makes design infinitely more complex than in the past. Although never simple, designing a Vic-torian era display case and situating objects within it was child's play compared with the creation of multidimensional environments with syn-chronized sounds and light that meaningfully involve visitors.

Finally, exhibitions are more than sensory experiences, they are also intellectual experiences. Many visitors consider the objects as the heart of the exhibition experience. The sensory components of an exhibition are vital to the success of the experience since they dictate whether or not vis-itors will initially attend to the exhibition and how engaged they will become. If a visitor is not attracted to an exhibition long enough to attend to it and remain engaged, little learning is likely to occur. But good design alone, even well-designed context, does not automatically yield an effec-tive exhibition. Good design can create a framework that encourages the visitor to look at an object or read a label, but in the end the topic, too, needs to appeal to the visitor. Quality design goes hand-in-hand with quality ideas.

BEYOND THE MUSEUM

Ironically, understanding learning in museums requires understanding not only what happens within the walls of the museum but also, and equally important, what happens beyond those walls. Subsequent experi-ences, some reinforcing and others not, dramatically contribute to what someone ultimately learns from the museum. It is only as events unfold for the individual after the museum visit that experiences that occurred inside the institution become relevant and useful. As we have discovered, if one attempts to talk to visitors as they are departing the museum to see what they learned, they often can only somewhat answer the question. It is not that they wish to withhold information, it is just that they really do not know. It is only after weeks and months, and sometimes years, that events unfold sufficiently so that visitors can appreciate the significance of those in-museum experiences.[62]

Thus, in order to fully understand the learning that occurs as a consequence of museum experiences, it is important to situate museums within a larger context; to appreciate that as educational institutions, museums are part of a larger educational infrastructure. Visitors, then, come into the museum with a wealth of prior experience and knowledge and leave with the seeds of knowledge and meaning that only subsequent experience can reveal and sustain. How do prior experiences and knowledge blend with the museum experience? To address this question, one must step back and realize that museums are part of a larger educational infrastructure.

THE EDUCATIONAL INFRASTRUCTURE

The educational infrastructure includes elementary, secondary, and postsecondary schools; libraries; print media such as newspapers, magazines, and books; broadcast media such as radio, television, film, and video; nonprofits with an educational mission, such as community-based organizations and government; museums of all types; and, increasingly, the Internet. According to museum researchers Mark St. John and Deborah Perry, who first proposed the idea of thinking of museums as part of the educational infrastructure, the word *infrastructure* refers to something that "lies below the surface and provides critically important support to a wide range of economic and social activities."[63] For example, the highway infrastructure facilitates transportation, and an infrastructure of community services such as fire and police departments and waste removal permits a community to support a growing population. Infrastructure investments help provide structures, create conditions, and develop capacities that are necessary to the functioning of daily life. Thus, museums can be seen as part of the educational infrastructure of the nation. St. John and Perry argue that just as the economic health of a nation depends on the strength of its transportation and utilities infrastructure, so too the educational health of the nation depends upon its educational infrastructure, including museums. This infrastructure supports the educational activities of the community and constitutes a network of resources, information, and learner support.

As part of a recent study, investigators John Falk, Pauline Brooks, and Rinoti Amin attempted to determine how the California Science Center was situated within the educational infrastructure of greater Los Angeles.[64] Based on both face-to-face interviews in shopping malls and libraries and a random telephone survey of over a thousand residents, the research revealed that the public does indeed piece together their understanding, in this case science understanding, from a wide range of resources. The study found that to stay current in science, the adults depended upon the following resources, in this order: books (not for school), television (public, commercial, and cable), newspapers and magazines, on-the-job experiences, museums, and, to a more limited degree, radio and the Internet. Museums were perceived by the public as an important, but "middle-tier," resource. More than two-thirds of the public claimed to have utilized some type of museum as a science resource, though most people did not depend upon museums as their primary mechanism for staying current in science. For most people, the motivation for going to museums was to learn about science, but to learn generally, not specifically. The decision to go to a museum was about education, but not solely about that. Museum-going was both an educational and a recreational activity, both a personally enriching experience and an opportunity for social interaction and bonding. Museum experiences were combined with other educational experiences to develop meaning about science; what understanding of science the public possessed was derived from many sources. In sum, learning does not respect institutional boundaries.

The Role of Subsequent Experiences

We can more specifically chart the role of subsequent experiences in museum learning by looking at several studies that have attempted to monitor what visitors retain and do after their visit to the museum. The first of these is a study conducted at the National Aquarium in Baltimore that concluded in 1999.[65] In addition to focusing on visitors' incoming knowledge (see chapter 5), the study also attempted to determine to what extent visitors retained and acted upon the conservation knowledge, attitudes, and beliefs developed during their visit. The study revealed that visitors exiting the aquarium had clearly absorbed the institution's fundamental conservation message. Visitors' descriptions of this main message were consistent with their incoming understanding of conservation as "preserving/protecting/saving" the environment and nature, but their understanding had clearly been extended and refined. The aquarium visit appeared to focus visitors' conservation-related thoughts while broadening and enriching their understanding of conservation. For instance, upon entering the aquarium, visitors talked about conservation in a variety of ways, but their descriptions lacked detail and emotion. Following their visit, they most commonly talked about conservation with great emotion and in terms of the complex interconnections between animals, people, and the environment. Visitors also talked about the need to balance the coexistence of people and nature.

These changes in visitors' conservation knowledge, understanding, and interests by and large persisted over several months. The data indicated that, overall, the aquarium visit effected positive short- and long-term change in visitors' understanding and awareness of conservation issues in their lives. The aquarium visit not only increased their general knowledge related to topics addressed at the aquarium but also provoked a greater sense of awareness and appreciation for conservation issues and the connections between their own lives and conservation issues. For instance, after six to eight weeks, more than two-thirds of visitors continued to discuss conservation in terms of complex interconnections and the need to balance the coexistence of people and nature. Even after several months, visitors were more likely than upon entering the aquarium to relate conservation issues to social/political/cultural/economic factors and root causes, such as overpopulation.

The National Aquarium experience also connected to visitors' lives in a variety of ways following their visit. Even within the brief time frame of two months, a quarter of the visitors specifically noted that their visit had inspired or motivated them to visit other aquariums, zoos, museums, and parks. These visitors talked about how things they had seen at these other institutions reminded them of things they had seen or heard at the National Aquarium. Visitors also made connections between their recent visit and their personal and family lives or things they had seen on TV or in the media. However, these personal connections rarely inspired conservation action. In fact, within the six to eight months that had elapsed since their aquarium visit, the general enthusiasm and emotional commitment for conservation that had been so notable immediately following their visit almost totally disappeared. It appeared that in the absence of reinforcing experiences, emotion and commitment had generally receded to the baseline levels observed when visitors entered the aquarium.

A growing number of studies have attempted to track visitor experiences over time.[66] In all of these, the majority of visitors showed persistence of knowledge and interest and a tendency to follow up experiences with learning from other settings, particularly television, other museum visits, and books. Also prevalent in all of these studies were self-reports of

conversations with family and friends, recommendations of the experience to friends and family, and just general reflection upon the experience.
However, also like the National Aquarium study, for many visitors there
were no subsequent reinforcing experiences. For most of these visitors,
the experience faded, and in some cases disappeared altogether. To what
would we attribute these differences in response? Perhaps it was the quality of the museum experience, or, equally likely, perhaps it had something
to do with incoming interest, knowledge, and motivation. At the moment
we cannot say. No study of which we are aware to date has attempted to
closely follow individual visitors over time to learn specifically what they
do or do not do after a visit. All of the studies mentioned here are heavily dependent upon self-report data and hence are potentially biased; visitors could be exaggerating, or neglecting to mention, their positive experiences. It will only be through a fine-grained, case study approach, where
individuals are tracked and interviewed frequently over many months
that we will learn how subsequent experience affects learning from museums. This kind of intensive study is needed for us to discover the factors
that lead some individuals to follow up and extend their museum learning experiences and others not to. Fortunately, Kirsten Ellenbogen is
attempting just such a study as part of her doctoral work at King's College, London. We look forward to her results.

Thus as we conclude this chapter, it is clear that much is known about
the specifics of how people learn from museums. We have also pointed out
huge gaps that remain in what we would consider fundamental pieces of
the story. Yet today, unlike as recently as five years ago, we understand a
tremendous amount about museum-based learning. We have a conceptual framework on which to hang our current understanding and a growing
empirical base from which to build future understanding. In the next three
chapters we will summarize this understanding and apply it to the important questions of what people learn from museums and how to make
museums better, more effective free-choice learning environments.

KEY POINTS

- The dominant motivation for humans is meaning-making. The need to
  make meaning of the physical setting is innate. This need plays out in
  museums in many ways—in the need for visitors to orient themselves
  in space, to explore that which is novel, to prepare themselves mentally for what is to come, and to make overall sense of the museum environment.

- Good design draws visitors in, engages all their senses, and compels them to investigate the topic at hand. It immerses visitors and enables them to navigate without the help of a guide. Finally, good design is increasingly moving away from the concept of exhibitions as spaces for visually displaying objects to the view of exhibitions as environments in which visitors experience art, history, nature, or science.

- Subsequent experiences, some reinforcing and others not, dramatically contribute to what an individual ultimately does or does not learn from the museum. It is only as events unfold for the individual after the museum visit that experiences that occurred inside the institution become relevant and useful.

NOTES

1. Falk and Amin 1999.
2. Maslow 1954.
3. Caine and Caine 1994.
4. O'Keefe and Nadel 1978.
5. Kaplan and Kaplan 1982.
6. White 1949.
7. Harlow 1954.
8. Kaplan and Kaplan 1982.
9. Kaplan and Kaplan 1982.
10. Berlyne 1950.
11. Falk, Martin, and Balling 1978, Martin, Falk, and Balling 1981; Falk and Balling 1982.
12. E.g., Kubota and Olstad 1991; Anderson and Lucas 1997.
13. Kimche 1978; Rosenfeld 1980; Falk, Balling, and Liversidge 1985; Balling and Cornell 1985; Adams 1989; Falk, Holland, and Dierking 1992; Falk 1993; Horn and Finney 1994; Borun, Cleghorn, and Garfield 1995.
14. Kaplan and Kaplan 1982.
15. Caine and Caine 1994.
16. Newby 1972.
17. Newby 1972.
18. Falk and Amin 1999.
19. Falk and Dierking 1992.
20. Screven 1986; Serrell 1996; Hein and Alexander 1998.
21. Ausubel, Novak, and Hanesian 1978.
22. Balling, Falk, and Aronson 1980; Kubota and Olstad 1991; Anderson and Lucas 1997.
23. Screven 1986; Amin and Falk 1998; Anderson 1999.
24. Amin and Falk 1998.

25. Serrell 1996.
26. Cf. Falk and Dierking 1992.
27. Cf. Cohen et al. 1977; Hayward and Brydon-Miller 1984; Serrell and Jennings 1985; Bitgood and Richardson 1987; Talbot et al. 1993.
28. Talbot et al. 1993; Passini 1984.
29. Falk and Dierking 1992.
30. Hedge 1995.
31. Neisser 1976.
32. Hedge 1995.
33. Csikszentmihalyi 1990a.
34. Hedge 1995.
35. Miller 1956.
36. Kaplan 1977; Kaplan et al. 1989.
37. Cf. Falk and Dierking 1992; Falk 1993.
38. Falk 1993.
39. Bitgood and Patterson 1993, 1995.
40. Falk 1997a.
41. Freeberg 1989.
42. Belcher 1991, 41.
43. Cf. Melton 1972; Falk and Dierking 1992; Serrell 1998
44. Bevlin 1977, 10.
45. Bevlin 1977.
46. McLean 1993, 115.
47. Belcher, 1991.
48. Bevlin 1977.
49. Belcher 1991, 129.
50. Porter and Mikellides 1976.
51. Porter and Mikellides 1976.
52. Bevlin 1977.
53. Porter and Mikellides 1976.
54. Porter and Mikellides 1976.
55. McLean 1993.
56. Bevlin 1977.
57. Broudy 1987.
58. Bevlin 1977.
59. Bevlin 1977.
60. Bitgood and Patterson 1993.
61. Coe 1985; Ogden, Lindburg, and Maple 1993.
62. Falk 1997b; Spock and Leichter 1999.
63. St. John and Perry 1993, 60.
64. Falk, Brooks, and Amin in press.
65. McKelvey et al. 1999.
66. Falk and Holland 1991; Holland and Falk 1994; Falk, Luke, and Abrams 1996; Bielick and Karns 1998; Luke et al. 1999.

8

The Contextual Model
of Learning

Analysis breaks down when we are dealing with complex systems
with many interactive loops. In such systems, you cannot just isolate
the parts and put them back together, because in isolating the parts
you change the system. The system has to be considered as a whole.
So we try to use conceptual models, which are a sort of hypothesis of
what may be happening.

—Edward de Bono, *Sur/Petition*

It is human nature to want simple explanations for complex reality. For
example, in a book we recently read, a physician described how during
his days in medical school he was constantly overwhelmed with the
quantity of information. He said some teachers could package the information
very simply: "Here, this is what you need to know." Medical students
loved those teachers, he said. But there were other teachers who
always offered two or more (often contradictory) perspectives on things.
This the students hated. "It involved more work on our part," said the
doctor. "Who wants to be told that some people think this, and some people
think that? It was so much easier just to be told what is what." But,
he said, as the years went by and he became more and more experienced
as a doctor, he realized that the concise, neatly packaged views were
wrong. The teachers had chopped off all the rough edges that didn't fit
into the system. In the end, the simplest solutions were not always the
best.

For better or for worse, we believe, learning is a phenomenon of such
complexity that a truly simple model or definition will not result in a

135

sufficiently realistic and generalizable model. The complexities of learning can only be simplified so much before they become less than useful. Consequently, what we are proposing is not really a definition of learning but a model for thinking about learning that allows for the systematic understanding and organization of complexity. The Contextual Model of Learning is an effort to simultaneously provide a holistic picture of learning and accommodate the myriad specifics and details that give richness and authenticity to the learning process.

In this book we have focused on the learning that occurs from museums, since this focus has permitted us to make concrete and tangible that which is inherently abstract and intangible. As we have repeatedly stressed, the where and why of learning does make a difference. Although it is probably true that at some fundamental, neurological level, learning is learning, the best available evidence indicates that at the level of individuals within the real world, learning does functionally differ depending upon the conditions under which it occurs. Hence, learning in museums is different from learning in any other setting by virtue of the unique nature of the museum context. Although the overall framework we provide should work equally well across a wide range of learning situations, compulsory as well as free-choice, the specifics apply only to museums. In the final analysis, to truly understand how, why, and what people learn, specificity is essential. There is no simple, stripped-down, acontextual framework for understanding learning. Learning is situated.

Learning is a dialogue between the individual and his or her environment through time. Learning can be conceptualized as a contextually driven effort to make meaning in order to survive and prosper within the world. We have chosen to portray this contextually driven dialogue as the process/product of the interactions between an individual's personal, sociocultural, and physical contexts. As we have stated repeatedly, none of these three contexts is ever stable; all are changing.

EIGHT KEY FACTORS THAT INFLUENCE LEARNING

The Contextual Model of Learning provides the large-scale framework within which to organize information on learning; inside the framework hang myriad details. The factors that directly and indirectly influence learning from museums probably number in the hundreds, if not thousands. Some of these factors are apparent and have been described in this book. Many other factors are either not apparent or are currently perceived by us to be less important and have not been described. However, after considering the findings from the hundreds of research studies reviewed for this book, we found that eight key factors, or more accurately suites of factors, emerged as particularly fundamental to museum learning experiences:

Personal Context

1. Motivation and expectations

2. Prior knowledge, interests, and beliefs

3. Choice and control

Sociocultural Context

4. Within-group sociocultural mediation

5. Facilitated mediation by others

Physical Context

6. Advance organizers and orientation

7. Design

8. Reinforcing events and experiences outside the museum

Individually and collectively, these eight factors significantly contribute to the quality of a museum experience. When any of these eight is absent, meaning-making is more difficult. Each of these factors, examined in detail in the preceding chapters, is summarized here.

Motivation and Expectations

People go to museums for many reasons and have predetermined expectations for their visit. These motivations and expectations directly affect what people do and learn. Usually the public's agendas are closely matched to the realities of the museum experience, but not always. When expectations are fulfilled, learning is facilitated. When expectations are unmet, learning suffers. Intrinsically motivated learners tend to be more successful learners than those who learn because they feel they have to. Museums succeed best when they attract and reinforce intrinsically motivated individuals.

Prior Knowledge, Interests, and Beliefs

Prior knowledge, interests, and beliefs play a tremendous role in all learning; this is particularly the case in museums. By virtue of prior knowledge, interests, and beliefs, learners actively self-select whether to go to a museum or not, which type of institution to visit, what exhibitions to view or programs to participate in, and which aspects of these experiences to attend to. The meaning that is made of museum experiences is framed within, and constrained by, prior knowledge, interests, and beliefs. At a very fundamental level, in the absence of appropriate prior knowledge, interests, and beliefs, no one would ever go to museums and no one would ever learn anything there even if they did. Because of the constructed nature of learning and the heterogeneous nature of museum-visiting populations, the prior knowledge, interests, and beliefs of museum visitors vary widely across, and even within, museums. For all these reasons, learning in museums is always highly personal.

Choice and Control

Learning is at its peak when individuals can exercise choice over what and when they learn and feel that they control their own learning. Because museums are quintessential free-choice learning settings, they more often than not afford visitors abundant opportunity for both choice and control. When museums try too hard to mimic compulsory education or force specific learning agendas on the public, they undermine their own success and value as learning institutions.

Within-Group Sociocultural Mediation

The vast majority of visitors go to museums as part of social groups—groups with histories, groups that separately and collectively form communities of learners. Parents help children understand and make meaning from their experiences. Children provide a way for parents to see the world with "new" eyes. Peers build social bonds through shared experiences and knowledge. All social groups in museums utilize each other as vehicles for deciphering information, for reinforcing shared beliefs, for making meaning. Museums create unique milieus for such collaborative learning.

Facilitated Mediation by Others

Socially mediated learning in museums does not only occur within an individual's own social group; powerful socially mediated learning can occur with strangers perceived to be knowledgeable. Such learning has long evolutionary and cultural antecedents, and few other museum experiences afford as much potential for significantly affecting visitor learning. Many such interactions occur with museum explainers, docents, guides, and performers, and they can either enhance or inhibit visitor learning experiences. When skillful, the staff of a museum can significantly facilitate visitor learning.

Orientation and Advance Organizers

Study after study has shown that people learn better when they feel secure in their surroundings and know what is expected of them. Museums tend to be large, visually and aurally novel settings. When people feel disoriented, it directly affects their ability to focus on anything else; when they feel oriented in museum spaces, the novelty enhances learning. Similarly, providing conceptual advance organizers significantly improves people's ability to construct meaning from experiences.

Design

Whether the medium is exhibitions, programs, or web sites, learning is influenced by design. Exhibitions, in particular, are design-rich educational experiences. People go to museums to see and experience real objects, placed within appropriate environments. Two-dimensional media they can see elsewhere, computer terminals they can find elsewhere, text they can read elsewhere. Not so authentic, real "stuff" in meaningful settings. Appropriately designed exhibitions are compelling learning tools, arguably one of the best educational mediums ever devised for facilitating concrete understanding of the world.

Reinforcing Events and Experiences outside the Museum

Learning does not respect institutional boundaries. People learn by accumulating understanding over time, from many sources in many different ways. Learning from museums is no exception. The public comes to museums with understanding, leaves (hopefully) with more, and then makes sense of this understanding as events in the world facilitate and demand. In a very real sense, the knowledge and experience gained from museums is incomplete; it requires enabling contexts to become whole. More often than not, these enabling contexts occur outside the museum walls weeks, months, and often years later. These subsequent reinforcing events and experiences outside the museum are as critical to learning from museums as are the events inside the museum.

UTILIZING THE CONTEXTUAL MODEL OF LEARNING: THE CASE OF BENJAMIN

The following is an example of how this framework allows us to think about the learning that might occur for an individual visiting a museum. By necessity, our example will need to be a specific individual at a specific museum, in this case Benjamin Winthrop,[2] a bright, engaging seven-year-old we had the pleasure of following during his visit to the Smithsonian's Natural History Museum on September 27, 1994.

Personal Context

Benjamin seems a bright enough child. His mother, Sophia, and sister, Jasmin, sometimes just shake their heads at the questions he comes up with. Still, it is not as if he is some kind of "genius," they say, just a very curious and outspoken little boy. Benjamin's classmates at Martin Luther King Jr. Elementary School in Atlanta also find him to be pretty normal, even if he does ask a lot of questions in class. He enjoys playing kickball, basketball, racquetball, and baseball, gymnastics, and reading. He collects Goosebumps books and has eight or ten of them. He also likes to watch TV; his favorite shows include everything from *Magic School Bus* to *The X Files*. He also enjoys learning about dinosaurs. He owns a number of books on dinosaurs and has watched several videos on them, including *Land before Time*. Even in a brief conversation, it was clear that Benjamin already knew quite a bit about dinosaurs, throwing around names like *Apatosaurus, Ankylosaurus, Tyrannosaurus, Miasaurus,* and *Stegosaurus*.

This was Benjamin and Jasmin's second visit to the museum. The first time they came, the children were two and three years old. Benjamin claimed that he remembered his previous visit. According to

Sophia, they had often talked as a family about this previous visit, but this time the children would be able to enjoy the museum much more because they were older. Sophia said she believed that there were a lot of interesting things for the kids to see—animals, insects, and dinosaurs, to name a few. According to Benjamin, it was strictly his mother's choice to visit the Museum of Natural History. However, he said he was really looking forward to his visit because his mother had told him there were a lot of "really cool" dinosaurs exhibited there.

Sociocultural Context

Benjamin entered the museum accompanied by his mother and his eight-year-old sister. As they traversed the museum, the family pretty much stuck together. Occasionally, one of the children got ahead of the others, but he or she always waited for the others to catch up.

As they walked through the museum, Benjamin mostly, but occasionally Jasmin, asked questions of their mother. The museum seemed to stimulate lots of questions for Benjamin about practically every exhibition he saw, and he directed the questions to his mother. He appeared to be on a very serious quest to soak up every detail. Sophia tried her best to answer all of Benjamin's questions. She scanned the labels for information and pulled from her own repository of knowledge. Sometimes her answers satisfied Benjamin, sometimes they just prompted more questions. He never seemed unhappy or frustrated with his mother, just very curious. One was left with the impression that this seven-year-old was trying hard to make sense of the complex information he encountered as he walked around the museum.

A significant amount of conversation and discussion ensued when the children were in the *Discovery Room*. Sophia would check out a discovery box, and the family would follow the directions and investigate the items. Sophia would not only follow the discovery box script but also would frequently interject her own questions. She regularly attempted to relate the contents of boxes to issues and questions specific to the family's personal experiences and interests. Benjamin's sister, Jasmin, took a much more active role in these activities than did Benjamin. While in the *Discovery Room*, Benjamin asked fewer questions and did less talking than while in the rest of the museum.

The museum was only moderately crowded that day, although it was a weekend. The threesome had relatively little difficulty avoiding crowds and navigated from exhibit element to exhibit element pretty much as their interest and time permitted. Although it was difficult to say for sure,

Benjamin and his family appeared to be oblivious to the other people in the museum. Once or twice, Benjamin seemed to watch other visitors, but more often the focus of his attention was on exhibitions.

Twice during the visit they stopped to ask a guard a question. Once it was to find out where the *Discovery Room* was located and once it was to ask where the rest rooms were. Each time the guard, first a man and then a woman, was polite and helpful, smiling and pointing out the pathway. In the *Insect Zoo* a volunteer was conducting a demonstration. He had large hissing cockroaches in his hands and allowed visitors to handle them. Benjamin got to hold one of the cockroaches. There was also a staff person in the *Discovery Room* who checked out boxes. Benjamin did not interact with this woman, but his mother did. Other than these few occasions and of course the initial conversation with us, Benjamin interacted only with his own family and seemed quite content to do so.

Physical Context

It was a beautiful fall morning the day Benjamin, Sophia, and Jasmin walked off the Washington Mall, up the granite stairs, and through the main entrance of the Museum of Natural History. Once inside, they paused as they stared at the high-ceilinged rotunda and then ahead to the large elephant. First stop was the elephant, but only briefly. Sophia then led the children over to the information kiosk, where she picked up a map. Then, guided by the map and Sophia, Benjamin and Jasmin were directed off to the right and into the *Hall of Paleontology*.

Thus began a very thorough, three-hour-and-forty-minute visit to the museum. By the time it was completed, the family had visited almost every gallery. In the *Hall of Paleontology* the family moved very slowly and carefully from one exhibit to the next, stopping to look, read labels, point, and ask questions. This pattern persisted throughout the visit to the museum, though never as much so as in the area with the dinosaurs. After paleontology they visited the *Ice Age Mammals Hall* then the *Africa Hall*. They wandered back through the cultural halls to the front of the building where they visited *Mammals, Life in the Sea, Birds,* the temporary exhibition *Ocean Planet*, and the *North American Indian Halls*. After asking a guard for directions, Sophia led Benjamin and his sister back to the *Discovery Room*. They spent half an hour in that area alone. Sophia literally had to tear the kids away. After another orientation check with a guard, the family had a rest room break and a brief lunch in the cafeteria. The family then traveled up to the second floor of the museum. On the second floor they visited the *Osteology Hall*, the *Insect Zoo*, the *Geology, Gems and*

Minerals Hall, and the area containing South American mummies. This area, too, seemed to hold great fascination for Benjamin. After this, they traveled into the farthest reaches of the museum, into the *Western Cultures Hall*. The final stop for the family was on the ground floor for the new temporary exhibition on spiders. Benjamin, and to a lesser extent Jasmin and Sophia, seemed to possess boundless energy as they gleefully visited one exhibition after the next. Finally, fatigue set in, and the family mutually decided that it was time to quit and go back to their hotel.

What Benjamin Learned: The Data

As they were getting ready to leave the museum, we intercepted Benjamin and his family and conducted a brief interview. We asked Benjamin to tell us about his museum experience. We prompted him to talk to us about what he enjoyed seeing and doing and what new ideas or thoughts, if any, he had gained from his visit.

Benjamin said his favorite parts of the museum were the dinosaurs and mummies, and both he and his sister agreed that they loved the *Discovery Room*. Benjamin singled out for comment most of the interactive elements of the museum, for example, the *Discovery Room*, the *Spiders* exhibition, the *Insect Zoo*, and a video in the *Western Cultures* area that allowed him to choose what to see.

When asked what new ideas or things he had discovered, Benjamin talked briefly about the *Triceratops* skeleton, especially the fact that the head bones were thicker than he thought they would be. He also liked some of the other dinosaur skeletons, such as the *Apatosauraus* and the *Edmondasaurus.*

He mentioned how "cool" the mummy was, "all brown and creepy looking." He said he liked all the gems in the *Geology, Gems and Minerals Hall*, especially the big crystals. He particularly liked one of the large quartz crystals; he said he really liked crystals. He also said that he thought the hissing cockroaches in the *Insect Zoo* "were really cool." He said it was fun to be able to hold one. "But watching the black widow spider eating crickets was even more cool." And then he stopped. It was clear Benjamin and Sophia were really tired. So we thanked them all, ended the interview, and let them go on their way.

Four months later, we telephoned the family at home in Atlanta and again interviewed Benjamin. Benjamin said that he and his family had not been to any museums as a family since their visit to the Museum of Natural History but that they had talked periodically about their visit. For example, Benjamin had studied dinosaurs in school and told his mom

how he remembered the skeletons he had seen at the museum. In particular, he mentioned the *Triceratops* and *Apatosaurus* skeletons. He went on
to say that sometimes he and his mom had talked about stuff in the *Discovery Room* and how they got to touch and hold neat things like arrow-
heads and animal skulls. Benjamin told us he also remembered thinking
about the *Insect Zoo*, specifically the beehive and the interactive exhibit
that showed where in a house insects hide.

Benjamin described how, when the family went to see *The Lion King* for
the second time, he remembered the stuffed lions at the museum. He said
he was struck by the fact that the lions in the movie did not look like the
real lions he had seen at the museum. He said the movie lions "were
fakey, they didn't have big enough teeth and stuff."

As we continued talking to Benjamin, he said he remembered the
dinosaur bones, "whales that were back in time," and the live black
widow spider that he saw: "It was gross. It was eating crickets, four or
five of them. The crickets were dead, frozen in position about to hop." He
remembered the cafeteria and the "jewels, I mean rocks, crystals and stuff
. . . Indian bow and arrows, a caveman, a cave boy that was dead and
being buried. . . . He was curled up." At the museum, Benjamin said, he
learned that "when a girl black widow [spider] gets married, she kills [the
male] and eats him." When we asked him how he learned this fact, Benjamin said his mom had told him that while they were watching the spider eat.

Benjamin told us he had gone to a natural history museum in Atlanta
(Fernbank Science Center) with his class two weeks earlier. So we asked
him about that trip. He said he learned about crocodiles (alligators) there
that were "from eleven inches long." Without pausing, he went on to say
he recently he saw a television show about snakes on Nickelodeon. Benjamin proceeded to describe in detail how a man extracted a yellowish-
green venom from the snake's fangs, dropping it into a glass. He added
that he had also seen snakes at the Smithsonian. He said that he had read
a book about sea turtles since his visit to the Smithsonian and thought that
reptiles were pretty cool animals.

We said it sounded like his museum visit had made him think of quite
a lot of things. He replied that, yes, since the visit he had thought about a
number of things related to it. One of them was that he realized "why a *T.
rex* has teeth shaped like a finger bending; because he doesn't chew . . . he
just rips and swallows." He said he learned that during the field trip to
the Fernbank museum but remembered wondering about it at the Smithsonian. At the Smithsonian natural history museum he had wanted to see
sharks and also dinosaurs. He said he did not see any sharks, nor for that

matter did he see a *T. rex.* "Do you have one?" he asked.

Once Benjamin got warmed up, his questions kept coming. He fired question after question at us: "How do they get elephants' tusks off? How do they make gold into jewelry? How do they put diamonds into gold? Isn't gold bumpy when they find it? How does it become smooth? How do horns grow out of a *Triceratops*'s nose? When an *Ankylosaurus* is about to be killed by a *T. rex*, does he flop down on the ground? Does *T. rex* get hurt when an *Ankylosaurus* fights back?" We did our best to provide some answers. The entire telephone conversation lasted about thirty-five minutes.

What Benjamin Learned: Our Analysis

Finally, we can ask, What did Benjamin learn from his museum experiences? At the very least, it is clear that this brief experience resulted in demonstrable, albeit modest, changes in Benjamin's knowledge and thinking. As a direct consequence of his three-hour-plus experience at the museum Benjamin could discuss changes in interest, understanding, and knowledge; he could describe facts and ideas he experienced and relate them to pieces of knowledge gleaned from other sources. There was clear evidence that the events Benjamin experienced and the information he perceived during his Smithsonian museum visit were not only stored in memory but also retrievable, utilized, and extended subsequent to his visit. In other words, Benjamin demonstrated clear evidence of having learned.

There were aspects of Benjamin's learning that were predictable, based upon what we knew about his expectations and interests and what was available at the museum for him to see, but much of what he seemed to take away from the experience was highly unique and extremely personal. The serendipity of what was happening at the museum that day—the hissing cockroach demonstration, a feeding black widow spider, the particular combination of exhibits he saw, and the order in which he saw them—combined with the social interaction engaged in by his mother, sister, and the *Insect Zoo* volunteer to become the specifics of Benjamin's set of meanings and constructed knowledge.

He showed a preference for those exhibits that he was interested in and about which he possessed prior knowledge and experience. He particularly liked parts of the museum that enabled him to control the outcomes—for example, the interactives in the *Spiders* and *Western Civilization* halls. But Benjamin did not only respond to what he already knew. At various points in the visit he was captivated by the wonder of real objects presented within an appropriate setting. The mummies, insects, prepared specimens, and gems created vivid, concrete images. Particularly memorable were more environmental exhibitions, the Neanderthal cave-boy burial, and the re-created house where insects hide. Throughout his visit, Benjamin was skillfully guided by his mother, who, armed with knowledge from a previous visit to the museum and a map, was able to find her way through the space. And when her sense of direction and map failed, there were helpful guards who cheerfully pointed the way. The result was an experience heightened by newness rather than blunted by strangeness.

Obviously, Benjamin's curiosity and interest were very much central traits, as much a part of self for him as his eye color or height. A museum like the National Museum of Natural History is a veritable mother lode for the curious. The outpouring of questions four months after the experience was testimony to how rich Benjamin's museum experience was. Without hyperbole, we can imagine him mining this experience for years to come. From his museum experience Benjamin already has constructed, and will continue to construct, concrete images about such things as the real size and shape of a lion (as compared with the animated exaggerations depicted in *The Lion King*), the image of a real black widow spider feeding, the size and shape of a raw gold nugget as compared with the size and shape of a piece of gold jewelry, and how a real elephant tusk fits into the head of a real elephant. These visual images were richly bound to conceptual ideas, thanks in large part to his mother.

Sophia mediated Benjamin's observations with information and ways of thinking that enabled Benjamin to develop intellectual meanings greater than any he would have been able to construct alone. For example, concepts about the mating behavior of black widow spiders became connected to the size, shape, and behavior of an actual black widow spider. In the *Discovery Room*, Sophia, again aided by the structure of the discovery boxes, guided Benjamin's inquiry. One can only infer that the interesting exchange of roles between Benjamin and Jasmin in the *Discovery Room* (Jasmin now taking the lead) perhaps resulted from longstanding family history as well as the different learning styles of the two children. Finally, although not anticipated, the interaction with a staff person in the *Insect Zoo* proved both memorable and educational for Benjamin. Being singled out by an important adult and allowed to hold a precious living creature left a long-lasting impression.

By taking them there in the first place, Sophia was also modeling for both Benjamin and Jasmin the role that museums can play in their lives as places for learning. Clearly she recognized this, having taken both of the children when they were far younger. Through this experience, Benjamin was learning a great deal about how to use museums to satisfy his many curiosities, an activity that he can enjoy throughout his life.

Benjamin did not totally rely on his mother for his learning; he also demonstrated an ability to guide his own inquiry and make his own inferences. A good example related to investigation into the growth and functioning of a *Triceratops* horn, based upon his careful examination of an actual fossilized *Triceratops* skull. Benjamin was clearly a special child, but he was not unique. He demonstrated a keen eye, an acute curiosity, and a consistent desire to make connections between things he read and heard about and the things he saw with his own eyes, connections between ideas and objects. Museums happen to be particularly good places for this activity.

Also evident from this example was the seamless, continuous nature of learning. For Benjamin, the museum experience was part of a larger continuum of experience— conversations with family, visits to other museums, television specials, books read, and classroom experiences. What Benjamin learned in one place was part of what he learned in some other place; all were intertwined—so intertwined that they challenge our abilities to reliably extract from his memories what was attributable to the museum experience and what was more appropriately attributable to some other, related experience. This is not a flaw in our approach but rather a reflection of the realities of learning.

In conclusion, the framework provided by the Contextual Model of Learning did not simplify the task of understanding what Benjamin learned, but it did provide a road map for our inquiry. The model permitted a thoughtful and reliable approach to considering the complexity and richness of the learning process without significantly compromising either precision or generalizability. It helped us focus our attention on salient parts of the data, such as the eight key factors of prior knowledge, interest, and experience; motivation and expectations; choice and control; family sociocultural mediation; the role of museum staff as facilitators of learning; orientation and advance organizers; the importance of real objects and appropriate contexts; and finally the larger community and society-wide context. In short, the model reduced the major issues to a manageable number, within a comprehensible framework, without losing sight of the inherently holistic and synergistic nature of learning. By no means complete, the three contexts we have proposed provided a starting point from which to think about how to understand free-choice learning. As this example demonstrates, museums emerge as particularly effective learning environments because they enable people to explore cultural, aesthetic, and scientific issues perceived as important within a socially supportive, intellectually comprehensible, and contextually appropriate environment. Utilizing the Contextual Model of Learning allows us to better understand, and ultimately influence, learning in these rich environments.

KEY POINTS

Eight Key Factors That Influence Learning

Personal Context

1. Motivation and expectations

2. Prior knowledge, interests, and beliefs

3. Choice and control

Sociocultural Context

4. Within-group sociocultural mediation

5. Facilitated mediation by others

Physical Context

6. Advance organizers and orientation

7. Design

8. Reinforcing events and experiences outside the museum

NOTES

1. Hagen 1997, 1–2.
2. Benjamin's family participated in the 1994 study at the National Museum of Natural History described in chapter 1. His name is fictitious.

9

Documenting Learning from Museums

We teach people what they almost already know.
—Tom Krakauer, "It's Fun, but Can It Really Be Science?"

That people learn in museums is easy to state, harder to prove. Learning is such a common concept in our society that it would seem that it should be reasonably straightforward to document. However, as the preceding chapters have attempted to make clear, learning is *common* but definitely not *straightforward*, particularly if one is trying to understand and document free-choice learning. The framework provided by the Contextual Model of Learning certainly gets us closer to being able to document learning from museums by providing insights into the factors that affect the nature of such learning. In other words, it helps us know where and how to look for learning. However, it is important to appreciate that what these eight factors help us know more about is *how* visitors learn; they tell us relatively little about *what* visitors learn. It is like learning that a pregnant woman needs to have a healthy, balanced diet in order to nurture the fetus and deliver a healthy baby, truly an important and useful piece of knowledge. However, knowing that a woman had a healthy diet during pregnancy does not tell us what her infant will look like, only that her baby will more likely be born healthy. In a somewhat analogous fashion, we know that the eight factors we have described are essential for "healthy" museum learning, but they are insufficient to predict the exact "outcomes" of that learning.

Additional challenges have made it difficult to provide compelling evidence for learning from museums as well, not because the evidence does

not exist, but because museum learning researchers, museum professionals, and the public alike have historically not asked the right questions.
The result has been a search for inappropriate evidence of learning using
flawed methodologies.

A variety of efforts have been made to document learning in free-
choice settings, particularly in museums. The overwhelming majority of
the investigations, including a number by us, have been predicated on
historical views of learning, which are basically thinly veiled Behaviorist,
stimulus-response models. In the most common of these traditional
views, what psychologists call the absorption–transmission model, individuals are assessed to determine whether they have learned *specific, predetermined* information.[1] This model can be characterized as follows:

> Topic X is presented to a learner either in the form of an exhibition,
> demonstration, lecture, text, program, film, or immersive experi-
> ence. Learning is determined by measuring the positive change in
> the amount of topic X the individual absorbs.

This is the model of learning all of us grew up with. It is simple and
straightforward and seems on the surface totally reasonable. However, as
we have noted throughout this book, this model makes a number of leaps
of faith, particularly within the context of museum learning. Just to name
a few, it assumes that the learner is predisposed intellectually, emotionally, and motivationally to learn topic X; it assumes that the individual actually attended to topic X (which in a museum is a huge assumption); it
assumes that topic X was presented in a form that was commensurate
with learning within the limited time and attention constraints of a typical museum experience; and it assumes that change in understanding is
always measurable as a quantitative addition of information.

As the epigraph at the beginning of this chapter suggests, most of the
time what we learn about are things that we *almost* already know; this is
particularly true of the things we learn from museums. In the previous
chapter we provided an example of seven-year-old Benjamin's visit to the
National Museum of Natural History. If prior to the visit we had asked
Benjamin to describe a *Triceratops*, without a doubt he would have been
able to do so. Thus, it could not be said that he learned what a *Triceratops*
was as a consequence of his visit to the museum. But it could be said that
now he *really* knows how big they were, how thick their bones were, and
how their horns were placed on their skull. In this case, Benjamin learned
about things that he *almost* already knew. We have observed this recon-
textualization process over and over again in our studies, as have others.
For example, during a recent summative evaluation of the *Aliens* exhibi-

tion at Pacific Science Center in Seattle, in which clever interactives and elegant visuals communicated principles of size and scale to visitors in new ways, one man summarized this very common phenomenon when he said, "I always knew Jupiter was bigger than the Earth, I just never realized how big!"[2]

Another problem that has affected hundreds of investigations of museum learning flows from the historical use of the traditional absorption–transmission model. For lack of a better way to describe it, we will refer to it as a problem of focus. Deriving from experiences with learning in school contexts, investigations have traditionally focused on the learning of specific, often very narrowly defined, concepts or even facts. In school, it is common to define the objectives of a lesson as the communication of a few specific ideas, such as the conservation of momentum, the color theory of art, or the impact of the intermarriage of royals on European history during the nineteenth century. This focused level of teaching and assessment works reasonably well within learning contexts in which, by and large, the prior knowledge of learners is relatively homogeneous, learners are constrained to attend to a limited number of things, and learners are exposed to the lesson for relatively long periods of time— anywhere from an hour to dozens of hours over many months. In museums, none of these assumptions hold completely, and the validity of utilizing this type of focused learning objective is questionable. Instead, museum learning is likely to occur at a different scale. Typically, museum learning occurs at both a large-scale, very generalized level of knowledge (e.g., Van Gogh used a lot of bright colors, heavily applied) and at the very smallest scale, a sampling of bits and pieces of very specific information (e.g., that shark over there has a funny humped back). Less frequently do visitors concentrate on one or two key ideas. Thus, our search for learning, when driven by a desire to find evidence of these one or two key ideas, has led many investigators astray. It is as if a bird were sitting on a branch above you and you tried to see it by using a telescope and all you saw was a blur, or perhaps nothing at all. Selecting an even better, more powerful telescope is not going to help. After looking for hours through the telescope and seeing nothing, should you conclude that there was no bird there? No, it merely means you were not using the correct instrument to see it; a pair of binoculars might have served the purpose better. The key to finding something is knowing both what you are looking for and how to look for it.

Only recently, and only in the most limited way, have investigators attempted to understand museum learning using more robust models of learning such as the Contextual Model of Learning described in this book.

We would assert that if an investigator is armed with this more appropriate and accurate search image, finding and documenting how museums facilitate learning should be possible. Specifically, the search image for museum learning described here suggests that one should expect visitor learning to be contextually driven, to be affected by an interaction between the personal, sociocultural, and physical contexts of the experience. One should expect learning to be:

- scaled to the realities of an individual's motivations and expectations, which in the case of museums normally involve a brief, usually leisure-oriented, culturally defined experience.

- highly personal and strongly influenced by an individual's past knowledge, interests, and beliefs.

- influenced by an individual's desire to both select and control his/her own learning.

- socioculturally influenced, both by interactions and collaborations within the visitor's own social group and potentially by interactions with others outside the visitor's group, for example, museum explainers, guides, demonstrators, performers, or other visitors.

One should expect visitors to react to exhibitions, programs, and web sites in a voluntary, nonsequential manner, as informed by orientation and organizational cues provided by the setting. One should expect that myriad design factors, including lighting, crowding, presentation, context, and the quantity and quality of the information presented, will affect the nature of the learning that goes on. Finally, one should expect that most learning will be the confirmation and enrichment of previously known constructs and that subsequent experiences will play a large role in what is ultimately remembered and utilized.

A key understanding that flows from this perspective is an appreciation that finding and documenting learning from museums requires setting aside the expectation that all learning will necessarily follow a totally prescribed and predictable course. It is important to appreciate that well-thought-out exhibitions and programs can and often do facilitate visitor learning along predetermined pathways, but the learners themselves need to be given an opportunity to help reveal the nature and character of their own learning. Methodologically, this means that expectations that individuals will only learn a specific concept or idea need to be tempered; individuals may learn specific concepts and ideas, or they may not—but invariably they will learn something. More typically, visitor learning follows two parallel pathways: the learning of global ideas (e.g., that history or science is fun); and the learning of very specific, usually idiosyncratic facts and concepts (e.g., George Washington had funny teeth, or, moving your arms and legs in and out in a gyroscope chair affects how fast you spin). The learning of concepts and overarching principles does occur, but seemingly less frequently. Determining the depth and breadth of visitor learning becomes the challenge to the investigator. Everyone in the process needs to understand and respect that, in the end, what individuals learn depends upon their prior knowledge, experience, and interest; what they actually see, do, and talk and think about during the experience; and equally important, what happens subsequently in their lives that relates to these initial experiences. More so than we have historically believed, all of these factors matter tremendously, and all are different for each person.

What follows is a range of examples, taken from a sampling of studies that, in our opinion, provide unequivocal evidence of the role museums play in facilitating visitor learning. Up to this point we have relied heavily on research studies to understand learning from museums. However, as we switch gears from examining *how* people learn from museums to *what* people learn from museums, we will be relying more on evaluation studies because so few research studies documenting this broad notion of learning exist. The examples we present are also drawn disproportionately from exhibition evaluations, although we have included data from a program evaluation that documented long-term learning and a research study describing learning resulting from a science center visit and a related postvisit classroom activity. The data was gathered in a variety of institutions including a history museum, science centers, an art museum, and a zoo.

Learning was documented in a variety of ways in these studies, primarily through in-depth, open-ended interviews, but all of the studies employed additional methods, including observations, tracking, and, in a few cases, paper-and-pencil questionnaires, all in an effort to accommodate the highly personal and sometimes idiosyncratic nature of museum learning. Some new approaches to measuring learning were utilized in the studies we describe, but by and large, the tools used were the standard tools of present-day museum learning documentation. We do not cite these studies as paragons of research; in fact, virtually all suffer from some flaws, and none completely accommodates the framework and philosophy espoused in this book since those studies are only currently being designed. The first two studies (*Think Tank* and *World of Life*) represent efforts to document specific learning outcomes, and the other four studies (*Points in Time, What About AIDS?, Art Around the Corner,* and a dissertation study at the Queensland Sciencecentre) document learning more broadly. In that respect, they collectively do a good job of documenting the range and extent of learning from museums.

THINK TANK AT THE NATIONAL ZOOLOGICAL PARK

A study at the National Zoo in Washington, conducted by Stacey Bielick and David Karns, attempted to determine the long-term impact of the Zoo's *Think Tank* exhibition on visitors.[3] *Think Tank,* a permanent exhibition exploring the concept of cognition and thinking in animals, opened at the National Zoo in 1995. The exhibition includes demonstrations, texts, graphics, several interactive components, and the opportunity to observe live animals. The exhibition introduces visitors to the concept of animal thinking by presenting three factors necessary to establish the existence of thought: image, intention, and flexibility. The exhibition allows visitors to explore three areas of animal thinking—tools, language, and social behavior—by addressing the questions: What is a tool? Are animals capable of language? Does social behavior require thinking? The assessment of *Think Tank* investigated how well three key educational goals were met by asking: (1) Did the experience increase the visitor's expressed interest in science? (2) Did the exhibition add to the visitor's scientific knowledge? and (3) Did the experience increase the visitor's respect for animals?

Personal interviews were conducted with two large, systematically determined samples, one with visitors entering the *Think Tank* building and one with visitors exiting the building. Visitors to the exhibition were surveyed before and immediately after their visit and were found to have gained a significantly improved understanding of animal thinking behavior, as well as significantly greater respect for animals. For example, when visitors were asked to give examples of animal thinking before experiencing the exhibition, their answers were vague and generally inaccurate. After the exhibition experience, the most frequent response was something about tool use or social behavior, both prime responses. Only moderate improvements in science interest were noted.

Thirteen months later, roughly half of these visitors were contacted by telephone and resurveyed. The evidence for learning in this group of visitors remained essentially unchanged, even after more than a year. Almost a quarter of those interviewed reported having been back to the National

Zoo and *Think Tank* at least once over the thirteen-month period; one in ten reported returning two or three times. The individuals interviewed had no difficulty recalling what they did during their visit to the exhibition and freely discussed such things as watching animals, using specific interactive displays, and watching demonstrations. Although only four of five visitors said they thought about *Think Tank* in the ensuing year, more than half claimed to have recommended the exhibition to someone else.

Among those indicating that they had thought about *Think Tank* since their visit, the four most frequently mentioned contexts for these subsequent thoughts were:

- "A related television program stimulated thoughts about *Think Tank.*"

- "It came up in conversation with other people."

- "Just thought, out of the blue, about something in the exhibition."

- "Thought about *Think Tank* during a visit to another zoo."

Thirteen months after the visit to *Think Tank*, significant evidence for learning was still evident. In fact, there was no appreciable decline in the percentage of visitors able to provide reasonable answers to questions about animal learning. The percentage of visitors who reported that the exhibition had influenced their thoughts about animals was only slightly lower than in the original exit survey; this percentage increases if visitors who had thought about or recommended *Think Tank* during the thirteen-month period are included. Examples of responses included:

"It was another addition to the information I already know about animals." (Female, thirties)

"Brain size isn't what really matters, it just matters what type of thinking it does." (Male, fourteen)

"I got a more realistic approach of their everyday living as opposed to what I see on TV." (Female, thirties with seven-year-old daughter)

Not only was there evidence for learning from the exhibition, but also over half the visitors in the call-back group self-reported that the exhibition had influenced their attitudes toward animals, and half indicated that it influenced their behavior with respect to animals. For example, some individuals said that the zoo experience prompted them to watch relevant television shows, others said they were inspired to read books on the subject, and still others said the exhibition caused them to engage in conversations on the topic of animal learning with friends and/or family. All in all, the data provided evidence that a slight majority of visitors experiencing the *Think Tank* exhibition had improved understanding, changed attitudes, and even changed behaviors relative to animals and the ways they think.

WORLD OF LIFE AT THE CALIFORNIA SCIENCE CENTER

In February 1998, the California Museum of Science and Industry reopened as the California Science Center, featuring two brand-new major exhibitions, *World of Life* and *Creative World*. These two exhibitions were designed to fulfill very specific conceptual goals. The *World of Life* was designed to communicate a single large, overall message that all living things have many characteristics in common. In addition, the exhibition was intended to show that all living things, including humans, carry out five basic life processes: they take in energy; take in supplies and get rid of wastes; react to the world around them; defend themselves; and reproduce and pass on genetic information to their offspring. A complete summative evaluation was conducted by Rinoti Amin and John Falk to determine how successfully these messages were conveyed.[4]

A large sample of visitors to the exhibition was tracked, observed and interviewed. Visitors were asked a series of questions related to their understanding of life processes and the relationship of humans to other life forms. For example, visitors were asked in an open-ended way to describe similarities between humans and other organisms and encouraged to generate as many examples as they could. These lists were then classified into the five categories of similarities presented in the *World of Life* exhibition. Not surprisingly, many visitors entered the exhibition aware of many of the life processes all living systems share. In particular, a majority of visitors entered the exhibition aware of the similarities between humans and other organisms in the areas of food intake/digestion, reproduction, and circulation/supply-network types of functions. After completing their visit, visitors of all ages demonstrated a significantly greater understanding of the multiple life processes that all living systems share. Statistically significant increases were seen in four of the five life processes areas described in the exhibition: food intake/energy factory, reproduction, defending life, and control/reaction. Only the area of circulation/supply network showed no significant change in frequency of responses as a function of visiting the museum. The greatest growth for young children was in the areas of control/reaction and reproduction; for teens, defending and control/reaction; and for adults, control/reaction, food intake/energy factory, and defending. Not only did the quantity of responses increase after viewing the exhibition, so too did the quality of many visitors' responses, as indicated by several of the examples presented below:

Pre: "We all have babies, eat, breathe."
Post: "We all reproduce, digest food, expend energy." (Male, in twelve-to-fifteen age group)

Pre: "We need to eat, and we have eyes, ears, and nose."
Post: ". . . take in energy and have similar senses." (Male, in eight-to-eleven age group)

Pre: "Reproduction and digestion."
Post: "Passing on genetic material through reproduction, digestion, elimination of waste, defending." (Female, in thirty-to-fifty age group)

Pre: "We are all similar in the things we do to stay alive."
Post: "Similar chemical and biological processes like reproduction and other intercellular processes." (Male, in thirty-to-fifty age group)

Pre: "We all eat, run, walk, have arms and babies."
Post: "All living things see, have brains and nerves, defend, reproduce." (Female, in eight-to-eleven age group)

Pre: ". . . have similar senses and processes."
Post: ". . . react to the environment, reproduction, digestion." (Male, in thirty-to-fifty age group)

Pre: ". . . eat food, drink, breathe, run."
Post: ". . . digestion, circulation, maintain balance in the body." (Male, in thirty-to-fifty age group)

Pre: "Digestion, reproduction, breathing, excretion."
Post: "Reproduction, digestion, circulation, defense (like camouflage), communicating." (Male, in twelve-to-fifteen age group)

In general, there was evidence that there was an increase in sophistication of both concepts and vocabulary used by visitors as a consequence of experiencing the *World of Life* exhibition. Particularly notable was the increase in length and richness of children's explanations. Most children's previsit descriptions were short and unsophisticated; postvisit explanations were consistently longer and more sophisticated.

Overall, results revealed that most visitors to the *World of Life* exhibition spent a great deal of time in the exhibition (roughly one hour) and used, at some minimal level, all parts of the exhibition. All of the major sections of the exhibition were visited by virtually every visitor for at least some minimal amount of time. Visitors did not utilize the exhibition in any obvious order or pattern. In fact, there was little behavioral evidence to suggest that visitors recognized, or at least respected, the conceptual organization of the exhibition. Patterns of use seemed to be driven more by practical (exhibit availability) and social (interests and needs of children) realities than by intellectual desires (the conceptual organization of the exhibition). The presence of live animals and real specimens in the exhibition significantly contributed to the public's enjoyment and, by inference, learning. These elements appeared to have enhanced the public's visit by making the exhibits "more real." Visitors stated that they found the real specimens to be great learning tools and felt that the specimens made the learning more fun and interesting.

The exhibition met its overarching goal of facilitating the public's understanding of the similarities and interrelatedness of all living organisms. Visitors entered the exhibition already aware of many of the life processes that all living systems share. However, there was strong evidence that visitors exited with significant gains in their understanding that all living things must solve similar problems in order to stay alive. This message appeared to be successfully communicated by four of the exhibition's five topic areas—energy factory, life source, defense line, and control center. Supply network was the only area of the exhibition that did not appear to successfully communicate this message. The most impressive gains were seen in children, who initially could provide only the most rudimentary explanations of life processes and, after going through the *World of Life*, were able to provide significantly better definitions and more detailed responses.

POINTS IN TIME AT THE SENATOR JOHN HEINZ PITTSBURGH REGIONAL HISTORY CENTER

In a summative evaluation of the *Points in Time* exhibition at the Senator John Heinz Pittsburgh Regional History Center, researchers Courtney

Abrams, Dale Jones, and John Falk were asked to determine generally what visitors experienced and learned while visiting the exhibition, which presents a rich, lively depiction of the region's history utilizing a number of artifacts, photographs, period rooms and spaces, live theater, and multimedia components.[5] Face-to-face qualitative interviews were conducted with visitors as they exited the exhibition; no specific effort was made to collect data on prior knowledge and experience, though this information emerged in the course of postvisit interviews. Efforts were made to correlate visitors' exit interviews with in-museum behaviors. Questions focused on the elements of the exhibition; their usefulness and significance; what visitors learned from them; visitors' overall thoughts, opinions, and expectations; and their thoughts on the exhibition's highlights and main messages.

Interviews revealed that, for the most part, visitors were very pleased with their visit to *Points in Time*. They felt it provided ample, interesting information about a wealth of topics related to regional history, and they were able to find aspects of the exhibition that spoke to their personal interests. Many visitors commented that the exhibition had "a lot to see," and, as one man said, "It kept my interest. Just as you thought you would be bored, it went on to a new topic."

Visitors said that they appreciated the opportunities provided throughout the exhibition to learn in different ways and to engage many of their senses. The multimedia served to animate the exhibition and make it seem more current. Interestingly, observational data suggested that visitors were spending the majority of their time looking at the more traditional museum items, such as artifacts, photographs, and labels. Visitors especially appreciated the artifacts and photographs when they were displayed in context in the many period rooms and spaces that were a part of the exhibition.

The artifacts and photographs made the greatest impact on visitors. All of the visitors used these items to learn about the region's history, and their comments demonstrated that these items had helped them to visualize the different people who had lived in the region in the past. In particular, the period rooms and spaces were an excellent way to display the items and photographs and to communicate their uses within the appropriate context. Nearly half of the visitors interviewed made a point of saying how much they liked these spaces, without being prompted. Though the more elaborate spaces like the 1910 home and the 1950s home seemed to be focal points for visitors, even smaller-scale re-creations prompted comments from visitors about real-life experiences. In particular, visitors commented on the religious displays and the steel mill washroom.

Although they could not enter these spaces physically, the display of objects in an appropriate context and with accompanying audio was enough to allow visitors to enter the spaces mentally. The following comments are examples of how visitors used artifacts, photographs and period rooms to visualize the past:

> "It was interesting to see how the immigrants lived, in the old photos. What's in the background was fun to look at also. . . . It seems like a lot [of the exhibit] is the reality of life stuff." (Female, twenties)

> "I loved the insides of the different churches, the synagogues, the school. I didn't have an opportunity as a child to enter those places. Growing up Roman Catholic, God forbid you ever stepped foot in another's place of worship." (Female, seventies, who lived entire life in Pittsburgh)

> "I really liked all the photos. You can see the people and the city in the past as it really was." (Male, fifties)

> "The family homes and kitchens made you part of the era." (Female, thirties)

People often commented about the things within the exhibition that they could relate to personally—for most it was the 1950s house. In other cases, their experience in the exhibition reaffirmed their part in Pittsburgh's history:

> "I like how new the exhibit is, that there are modern things in it. It makes me feel like I'm getting older, like things in my life are worth talking about. Things from my lifetime are here." (Female, twenties)

> "I'm amazed how close, if you stop and think. It's the same kind of life we live today, living in the city. [Especially with] the one with the clothesline between the houses, the one where they were cleaning the clothes with the washboard." (Female, fifties)

> "I liked stuff I could remember, like the kitchen and living room from the mid-1900's." (Female, forties)

> "I used it to see about coal mining in McKeesport, my hometown." (Male, thirties)

After the 1950s home, visitors most enjoyed the information about the steel mills. Most of these people had either worked at a steel mill themselves or had parents who had. Visitors delighted in sharing their own stories and in reminiscing about the mills:

"I always knew it was a dangerous job coal mining when I grew up, because that was big in my area [West Virginia]. Here, it was steel. I didn't realize how dangerous that was, but it was really clear in the exhibit." (Female, twenties)

"I used to work in J and L steel works. The exhibit was excellent because it was so real, especially the washroom at the steel mill. It brought home my youth. For my wife, it was the kitchen." (Male, sixties)

"[The best part was] the rooms, like the steel workers' room, you hear the voice-overs and think about what life might have been like." (Male, forties)

Visitors not only enjoyed *Points in Time*, but many also indicated that they had learned something new. Although the learning described was very personal, most visitors mentioned either empathizing with others' experiences (such as those visitors who said they had thought about what it felt like to live in other times) or related some fact or detail about a specific topic of interest. There were no real patterns in what visitors said they had learned, or even in what type of information was shared; learning was very idiosyncratic.

Researchers did not ask people directly what they felt they had learned. That is a method we do not recommend, because it is a difficult question for visitors to deal with owing to their own stereotypical views of what learning is (e.g., "I didn't have time to read so I didn't learn much") and the fact that it can be difficult to assess what one has learned right at the moment. Rather, researchers asked visitors what they thought, in their own words, was the main point of the exhibition. Answers were very unified, with the vast majority feeling that the exhibition was a historical account of Pittsburgh's development. In addition, a third of visitors thought the exhibition focused on the diversity and life experiences of the people who had settled in Pittsburgh and contributed to its history.

Within the framework of learning about the history of the region or its people, visitors gleaned a variety of facts or ideas that were new to them. Some of these had to do with learning generally about other lifestyles, such as one man's comment that "I found out how hard everybody worked in the past," or a woman's comment that "I didn't know Pennsylvania was so rich in history. It had lots of culture, lots of immigrants, and lots of history." A few visitors also appreciated that the exhibition focused on "points in time" not of the elite but of the general public: "I like that [it seems to be focused on the working class]. It shows most people's experience. I guess it's Pittsburgh's reputation as blue collar" (male, thirties).

Visitors did learn facts and ideas specifically related to a display or an object in *Points in Time*. However, most of these were historical details about a topic the visitor had a prior interest in, such as World War II or politics:

> "I liked World War II, the Arsenal of Democracy, about the mills, what they made. It was so cool how Heinz switched from pickles to planes and ketchup to . . . whatever." (Male, twenties)

> "I was amazed about the early leaders, the Mellon and Frick families. I've known about them since I was a kid but it really reinforced how much they did for the country and the city." (Female, fifties)

> "I learned a lot about the former businesses that were important." (Female, teens)

Other facts that visitors learned related to their own experiences with Pittsburgh:

> "It gave me a lot of historical insight. Especially because it showed so many turning points in my younger life that I didn't [appreciate] at the time. I knew of them but didn't realize the magnitude." (Female, sixties)

> "I've lived here since '85. I went to school here. [The exhibition] gave me a better idea of the communities. I know they are very divided. We have Polish Hill and stuff, and now I saw how they were settled and it gave me a better idea. I was surprised Indians settled here. I didn't know the Hill District was settled by Italians as well as African Americans; I thought it was just African Americans. I was surprised." (Female, twenties)

There was also some evidence that the exhibition was promoting further learning beyond the immediate museum experience: "The computer [program] said you had no pictures of Carnegie. My dad was a steel worker. We're going home to look for pictures of the steel mill, of Carnegie" (male, forties).

Because this exhibition was so experiential, allowing visitors to visualize and think concretely about living in the past, this was the primary way that visitors expressed their learning from *Points in Time*. Although few visitors said, "I learned what a suburban house looked like in the 1950s," probably all visitors could now describe a 1950s suburban home better than they could before visiting. The *Points in Time* experience was about reconfirming, expanding, and visualizing time periods in Pittsburgh's regional history. As a result, visitors left the exhibition with an enriched understanding of the human experience in Pittsburgh's past. The perspective of the entire exhibition helped visitors visualize the past. They noticed and appreciated that the history was told from some real person's viewpoint and that the people were average citizens, not just the rich and elite. This allowed them to relate to and compare the experience with their own lives, to see through others' eyes, and to empathize.

WHAT ABOUT AIDS? TRAVELING EXHIBITION

Several years ago, with support from the U.S. Centers for Disease Control, a consortium of prominent American science museums developed a traveling exhibition on HIV/AIDS, *What About AIDS?*[6] When the exhibition was being developed in the early 1990s, awareness and concern about the disease were very high. Although opinions differed widely on a number of HIV/AIDS-related issues, most Americans felt a strong need to learn more about the subject. Thus, although the exhibition was potentially controversial, at the time of its development it was clear that an exhibition on this topic was going to be widely perceived by the public as interesting and timely. Front-end evaluation had revealed that most Americans possessed both a high degree of awareness about the HIV/AIDS epidemic and a reasonably high knowledge of basic "facts" related to the disease; however, most Americans lacked detailed knowledge of the science underlying AIDS.[7]

A series of evaluations conducted by Dana Holland and John Falk revealed that, by all measures, this exhibition (described in more detail in chapter 10) was a successful learning experience for most visitors.[8] Although not every visitor walked out of the exhibition knowing at least one predetermined specific new fact or concept about HIV/AIDS, the exhibition afforded every visitor the opportunity to connect to the topic and learn something that was personally relevant; the data suggested that this learning was highly variable and often very personal. Visitors found the exhibition exceedingly accessible in a number of ways, with information presented from a variety of perspectives. At a variety of points within the exhibition, observation data collected during the summative evaluation of the exhibition revealed that visitors had taken advantage of the choices offered. The developers appreciated that visitors entered and exited the exhibition with differing learning agendas and purposes and strove to accommodate these differences. The result was an exhibition that permitted—in fact encouraged—visitors to bring their own experiences and interests to this one single exhibition.

In-depth, open-ended interviews with people after they completed their visit to the *What About AIDS?* exhibition revealed just how personally constructed each visitor's learning was:

> "They [in the exhibit] were talking about coming in contact with people who have AIDS and they were saying that you are more . . . of a threat to them than they are to you. You know, because the virus, uh, something about how the viruses can't be treated with antibiotics, but bacteria can. I saw that on one of the things, and I said, that's very interesting because everyone is so scared of the person with AIDS, but the person with AIDS should be scared of you." (Female, teens)

> "I like the beginning to the end, the history of what started, where it started, and where it's gone through until now." (Male, fifties)

> "It made you aware, it made you really realize that it can happen to anybody, you know. And I think it also puts, for people who don't know it, the three main things how you can get it." (Male, twenties)

Although the specifics of what was learned were sometimes hard to predict, the relationship of that learning to the individual was predictable. More often than not, a visit to the exhibition significantly strengthened visitors' prior understanding of the subject; only occasionally did they exit with a significantly new understanding. Very few of the visitors interviewed upon exiting *What About AIDS?* showed evidence of a radically new view of the epidemic. Most people made statements like, "I learned a few new things, but mostly the exhibit helped me better understand stuff that I already knew." If someone walked into the exhibition believing that you can get HIV/AIDS from touching someone or from mosquitoes, she was likely to walk out of the exhibition still holding these views. If someone believed prior to viewing the exhibition that birth control was immoral, he was almost certain to still hold this view after seeing the exhibition, even if he learned that use of condoms could help reduce the spread of HIV/AIDS. Rather than indicating that significant learning was not going on, these outcomes confirmed that learning was mostly building upon the base of what people already knew and understood.

Finally, follow-up data revealed that the effects of the HIV/AIDS exhibit extended far beyond the brief time visitors were within it. Three months after seeing the exhibition, two-thirds of visitors claimed to have thought about the exhibition since their visit:

"I found myself still thinking about some of the things in the exhibit even weeks later. For example, I hate to say it, but the dice exhibit [probability of getting AIDS interactive] really made me think about who I go out with these days." (Female, twenties)

"Just the other day, I saw this piece on TV about AIDS and I was able to understand what they were talking about, the immune system [and] all, because of that exhibit." (Male, thirties)

ART AROUND THE CORNER MULTIPLE SCHOOL VISIT PROGRAM OF THE NATIONAL GALLERY OF ART

In the spring of 1993 the National Gallery of Art pilot-tested a multiple-visit program for fifth- and sixth-grade students from three Washington, D.C., inner-city elementary schools. The program, called *Art Around the Corner*, reflected the National Gallery's desire to increase involvement with the D.C. schools, include its collections in the public school curriculum, and enhance students' art-related enjoyment and learning. A National Gallery docent made a previsit trip to each class, and two museum visits were planned and conducted to incorporate writing activities and interdisciplinary approaches to teaching. The success of the pilot program resulted in an expansion in both scale and content of the program; now more students are involved, and students visit the gallery six times during the year and receive a sequence of lessons from a docent. The lessons introduce students to the sensory, technical, and expressive properties of art. The program culminates in "Docent for a Day," when each student chooses a work of art on display at the gallery to present to his or her family and friends.

The main goals of *Art Around the Corner*, as identified by National Gallery of Art staff, included having students look forward to coming to the gallery and developing in students a positive attitude toward art museums in general; developing in students an appreciation of, and love for, art; and developing students' ability to talk before an audience about a work of art using criteria such as the elements of art (line, shape, color, space, texture).

Over a several-year period, Courtney Abrams, Jessica Luke, Marianna

Adams, and John Falk assessed the impact of this program on student participants.[9] Qualitative interviews were conducted with approximately fifteen program graduates and fifteen children who did not participate in the program (matched by age, gender, academic ability, race/ethnicity, and socioeconomic background) in each of the first three years of the assessment. Students were asked open-ended questions relating to their relationships with art museums and works of art and were shown a number of reproductions that they were asked to discuss. Findings from this series of studies suggested that program graduates had positive attitudes toward art museums and art in general. *Art Around the Corner* graduates, but not the control students, expressed a genuine appreciation of and love for works of art and demonstrated enhanced abilities to articulate their responses to art. Graduates were consistently better able than were the control students to discuss a work of art using vocabulary and skills taught in *Art Around the Corner.*

A subsequent study attempted to complement these primarily qualitative findings with a quantitative study exploring the long-term impact of the program on a larger number of graduates. This study was designed to determine the extent to which the *Art Around the Corner* program produced a lasting effect on students' knowledge of, and attitudes toward, works of art and art museums. Finding evidence of a causal relationship between the *Art Around the Corner* program and students' ability to discuss and interpret a work of art represented a particularly challenging problem, given the myriad variables that could affect students' lives and the inherently highly subjective nature of responses to art the experience of looking at and appreciating art.

With the cooperation of the D.C. public schools, students who had participated in *Art Around the Corner* from one to three years previously were identified and located in twenty classes across grades 7, 8, and 9. Students who had not participated in the program, or control students, were also included in the sample for comparison purposes. Students were shown a reproduction of a painting by the American artist Edward Hopper and asked to respond with a written interpretation. In addition to the written component, a subset of both *Art Around the Corner* and control students was selected from the larger sample and given an opportunity to talk about art in a small informal group discussion. The students' responses were scored using a variation on a new constructivist-based assessment tool called Personal Meaning Mapping.[10] Personal Meaning Mapping measures learning as a result of a particular concept or experience along a series of semi-independent dimensions; scoring follows prescribed valid and reliable rubrics for each of the dimensions. Personal Meaning Mapping is not a test; it does not assume or require that an individual produce a right or wrong answer, let alone a *single* right answer, in order to demonstrate learning. Instead, Personal Meaning Mapping starts from an individual's own ideas and perceptions about a concept or experience and measures differences in the quantity, breadth, depth, and quality of responses, either before and after an experience or, as in the current case, between two groups of individuals.

One to three years after graduating from the *Art Around the Corner* program, students were given a reproduction of Hopper's *Cape Cod Evening* and asked to respond to it. Specifically, students were asked to write what they saw, what they thought or felt about the painting, and what evidence from the painting supported their claims. Students' written responses were analyzed along four dimensions: (1) vocabulary used to describe the painting; (2) interpretive devices used to analyze the painting; (3) support for the interpretive devices used; and (4) overall response to the painting. Students who participated in *Art Around the Corner* provided, on average, significantly lengthier descriptions of the painting than did students who did not participate in the program. In addition, *Art Around the Corner* graduates tended to qualify their descriptors with richer, more detailed vocabulary. They gave responses such as:

"I see a brown and white collie and two dreary-looking people standing in front of a classic-looking country house outside beside the dark woods." (Female, grade 8)

"[I see] a chubby woman with a blue-green dress [and] a red-necked man with a white undershirt and black pants." (Male, grade 8)

Other phrases used by program graduates included "sunburned man," "trees that look dark and shadowy," "big fancy house," and "bright yellow grain [of] grass." Overall, control students tended to use fewer descriptors and fewer qualifiers. They made observations such as "I see a woman with a green dress [and] a man with a red face" (female, grade 7) and "[I see] brown grass and blue trees" (female, grade 9). Only a few of the students in the study used vocabulary indicative of art training; those who did were *Art Around the Corner* graduates.

The effects of the *Art Around the Corner* program on students' descriptions of a work of art appeared to be long-lasting. The impact of the program was equally expressed in students graduating one, two, and three years earlier. There were no significant differences between students as a function of grade level.

Students were also assessed on how well they developed their explanations, and, again, significant differences existed between *Art Around the Corner* graduates and control students. Students who participated in the program were much more likely than nonparticipating students to support their interpretations with evidence from the painting. Examples of this richness were:

"It isn't night time right now because if it was, the colors would be darker on the ground and on the house." (Male, grade 7)

"I feel kind of lonely. Nobody's there except for the dog, man, and woman. I also don't see any other houses in the picture." (Female, grade 7)

"I see sadness . . . because the artist used a color that makes the trees look dead and the back is full of darkness in the forest." (Male, grade 9)

"The trees [are] at an angle because of the wind blowing, and the green and white grass [is at an angle] too." (Male, grade 9)

Control students tended to give vague or general support for their interpretations:

"I feel sad because to me he [the man] looks sad, and if I look at something that looks sad, it generally makes me react in a sort of irritable manner." (Male, grade 8)

"I feel scared because the people in the painting look very mean and I hate dogs." (Female, grade 8)

"I think the lady is angry or in deep thought because her face looks kind of scrunched up." (Female, grade 7)

Again, the effects of the program appeared to be long-lasting, and grade level did not influence students' development of their interpretations.

Finally, students were also given a holistic score based on their overall response to the painting. This measure attempted to compensate for those students who lacked verbal fluency but overall may have provided a quality response. Students who participated in *Art Around the Corner* gave higher-quality responses overall than did students who had not participated in the program.

It would appear that *Art Around the Corner* had a significant and long-lasting impact on students. First, the program made a difference in their ability to describe a work of art. Students who participated in the program used rich and detailed vocabulary to describe the painting and often talked about the artist's intentions, while nonparticipating students were much less descriptive and rarely attempted to describe the artist's intentions. Second, and more important, the program had a substantial effect on students' ability to support their interpretations of a work of art. While both program graduates and comparison students gave similar interpretations of the painting, *Art Around the Corner* graduates connected with the painting on a higher level than did comparison students. Program graduates supported their interpretations with clear, thoughtful evidence from the painting, focused on thinking about what the artist meant to convey or was trying to communicate. Comparison students, on the other hand, gave vague or general support for their interpretations that oftentimes did not relate to the painting at all. The *Art Around the Corner* graduates and comparison-student groups came from the same population of students and were highly comparable in both their attitudes toward, and their experiences with, art and art museums outside of the *Art Around the Corner* program. Consequently, the enhanced ability of program graduates to describe and interpret a work of art can best be attributed to participation in the National Gallery of Art's *Art Around the Corner* program.

SCHOOL FIELD TRIP RESEARCH STUDY AT QUEENSLAND SCIENCENTRE

Our final example is David Anderson's recent doctoral dissertation study at Queensland University of Technology.[11] His approach affords us an opportunity to look in detail at the learning experiences of a few people, rather than the more general learning of many. Anderson documented the learning that can occur as a result of a school visit to a science center, exploring the role that a postvisit activity designed to reinforce the experience can play in the learning process.

Twelve students were investigated, and in-depth case studies were developed for five of them, documenting their understandings of electricity and magnetism prior to a visit to the Queensland Sciencentre. Anderson trained students in the creation of concept maps, a device developed by science educators to elucidate an individual's underlying cognitive structure for a concept or an idea. Prior to the visit, each of the students created a concept map detailing what they knew about electricity and magnetism, and an in-depth interview was conducted using their map as a discussion point. They then visited the science center and were interviewed again in an in-depth manner shortly after the visit; once again their maps were used as a probing tool; students could modify their map or make a new one. After participating in postvisit activities back in the classroom that were designed to reinforce and extend the museum experience, students were again administered an in-depth interview using their own concept maps as a probing device.

The results of this study strongly support the role that a science center experience can play in a person's understanding of particular topics. The unprecedented depth and focus of the study enables a rare glimpse into the very specific connections these children made as a result of their experience at the science center and participation in the subsequent postvisit classroom activities. All the students constructed knowledge about magnetism and electricity as a result of the Sciencentre experience and the classroom-based postvisit activity, but this knowledge construction was revealed to be exceedingly personal and inextricably connected to the prior knowledge and understandings they brought to these two experiences.

The learning observed varied in its form; in some instances it was a subtle change, much of it was recontextualizing or strengthening something that a child already knew, and in a few cases the experience fostered personal theory building. These variations in learning seemed to depend upon students' prior knowledge and experience, but they also embodied the students' personal approach to learning. For example, the personal theory builders had a great deal of prior knowledge and experience with the concepts, which facilitated their ability to take this more abstract approach and construct a personal theory, but they also seemed to be the kind of learners who would pursue theory building anyway. This was confirmed by their teacher. Interestingly, even among the theory builders, each student's knowledge developed in ways that were at times consistent with current notions of science and at other times resulted in the entrenchment of existing alternative conceptions or in the development of new alternative conceptions. Regardless of the scientific acceptability of each student's knowledge, individual understandings were seen to change and develop in ways that demonstrated increased levels of personal meaning.

The other fascinating aspect of learning that this study elucidated is that each student's knowledge was clearly constructed and developed from a rich variety of related learning experiences that included interactions with parents and others in enrichment and extracurricular activities. These experiences included activities at home such as reading books, watching television, and playing with and disassembling electric and motor-driven toys, as well as school- and museum-based experiences. For example, one student described in great detail how to make a simple compass by magnetizing a pin and placing it in a cork floating in a cup of water. He had learned this at home by reading a book and conducting a scientific experiment facilitated by his mother:

> D I like this . . . [Researcher points to the link between "compasses" and "magnetism" on Andrew's previsit concept map] Can you tell me how it was that you knew that compasses were magnetized?
> A Because when I was little at home I had—I was reading this book about electricity and magnetism we had, and after I'd—well, I was not reading it, I was too young then. But I was looking at the pictures, and I saw that they had a little cork with a needle, and my mum showed me how to do it.
> D She actually made it?
> A She cut the cork and showed me how to magnetize the needle and stuff.
> D She did it by stroking it with a magnet?
> A Yeah. And you put it in a cup and you point . . .

At the Sciencentre, students interacted alone and with peers at the interactive exhibits and also watched a live, facilitator-led science demonstration. There was evidence that students learned from the live demonstration, which followed students' free-choice interaction at the exhibits, as well as from interactions with specific exhibit elements, such as the *Electric Generator* exhibit component. Students seemed to be able to describe their understandings in much more explicit ways after the experience at the science center and after participating in the postvisit activities in the classroom, as evidenced by changes in their interviews from previsit to postvisit to postactivity. Students were also able to articulate the sources of their learning, as shown in the following excerpt from a transcript:

Post-Activity Interview
> D I'd like to just take you through an exercise where you describe to me how you think your knowledge has changed as a result of these experiences. Let's start with these two maps.
> A Well, before we went to the centre, yeah, I didn't really know that much about the um . . . the—um, the . . . the—I've forgotten the word, . . . the um dynamo sort of thing.
> D Generators?
> A Generator, yeah, because after we went to the Sciencentre, I turned that handle on their generator and saw that show.
> D You didn't [put] the dynamo in [this previsit map] but you had it here [researcher pointing to postvisit map]. So did you pick that up from the Sciencentre?

A Yep.

D From that generator electricity exhibit?

A Yeah.

D You didn't know anything about that before?

A Not much, no. I knew that dynamos made electricity, [but] I wasn't sure how they did it.

Although learning was uniquely personal, there were similarities in learning from person to person, as evidenced by another student's interests in the *Electric Generator* exhibit:

D What did you like seeing at the Sciencentre?

R . . . And I also liked seeing the—the generators. Yeah. That—when I got home my dad told me how they worked.

D Oh. Tell me about that.

R Well, he said that um . . . I already knew that when you turned the handle and copper wire went either through some magnets or went um around with the magnets either side of it. That would generate electricity, like dad explained it.

D Right. So in the Generator exhibit—I'll get the photograph of it— what's actually going on?

Perhaps you can point to some of those bits in there.

R Um, well, what that's doing is you turn the handle and that turns a piece of rubber um and that turns a wheel which turns some copper wire inside some magnets and that generates electricity.

D You didn't know that before you went to the Sciencentre?

R I'd heard about it but I hadn't actually seen it before.

D And dad explained it to you that night?

R Yeah.

In the two excerpts presented above about the *Electric Generator* exhibit, students had some sense of how generators worked prior to visiting the science center, but the experience provided a concrete and appropriate setting in which to test and contextualize their knowledge ("I knew that dynamos made electricity, [but] I wasn't sure how they did it"; "I'd heard about it but I hadn't actually seen it before").

The interactive nature of learning; the notion that it continues beyond the museum experience; and the fact that because it is personally constructed, it resembles a series of related, overlapping experiences, were observed in all five students. In one situation the student had further refined his interpretation of the operation of the *Hand Battery* exhibit in the time between the postvisit and postactivity interview by reading a science textbook in preparation for his personally selected school science project. All students indicated that they had talked about their museum experience with people after their field trip, primarily parents. In many cases, the experiences had been followed up at home by doing an experiment or reading further. Although the example cited here involved a class science fair project, students also were choosing to investigate these ideas further on their own. In summary, the evidence for learning in museums was consistent and compelling, though variable, even across five children from the same class provided with the same experiences, in arguably a very similar context.

CONCLUSION

We selected only a handful of museum studies to feature, although we could have picked any of perhaps a hundred or more recent assessments of museum learning. These studies have been done by us and by a growing number of researchers and evaluators worldwide. It is worth reiterating that the examples chosen are neither the best nor necessarily the most compelling, but they admirably illustrate the depth and breadth of learning that occurs as a consequence of a visit to a museum, whether as a casual visitor or as part of an organized school field trip.

Unlike earlier learning studies that showed that museums only occasionally facilitate learning, the research presented here strongly supports the premise that museum learning experiences facilitate some degree of learning in virtually all participants, although not necessarily exactly the learning an educator or developer would predict, or even necessarily hope for. However, armed with an appropriate search image and set of assessment tools, researchers consistently found evidence of learning from museums. The specifics of what visitors learned, however, were more variable. Visitors could be expected to learn broad generalizations and show generalized increases in understanding and interest, but the specifics of what they learned were normally highly personal and unique. Although this was not the way we were taught to think about learning, it is in fact the nature of all learning, particularly the learning that occurs from museums.

Museums support rich and consistent learning, learning that allows individuals to construct personal meaning about the world that persists over long periods of time. Visitors learn in all kinds of museums about all facets of human knowledge, including history, science, and art. Because learning is always strongly influenced by the physical context, the content and design of exhibitions and programs in the museum strongly affect what visitors learn. However, the specifics of what is learned varies from person to person, depending upon the individual's unique personal and sociocultural contexts. This understanding can and must be applied to designing ever more effective assessment strategies. It also can be applied to planning and designing better, more effective museum learning experiences to meet the needs of an increasingly diverse and demanding constituency.

KEY POINTS

- Over the years providing compelling evidence for learning from museums has proved challenging. This is not because the evidence did not exist, but rather because museum learning researchers, museum professionals, and the public alike historically asked the wrong questions and searched for evidence of learning using flawed methodologies.

- Recent research using an appropriate search image and set of assessment tools strongly supports the premise that museum learning experiences facilitate some degree of learning in virtually all participants.

- Visitors learn in all kinds of museums about all facets of human knowledge, including history, science, and art. Visitors learn broad generalizations and show generalized increases in understanding and interest; however, the specifics of what they learn are normally highly personal and unique.

NOTES

1. Roschelle 1995; Hein 1998.
2. Dierking 1999.
3. Bielick and Karns 1998.
4. Amin and Falk 1998.
5. Abrams, Jones, and Falk 1997.
6. Members of the National AIDS Exhibit Consortium were National Museum of Health and Medicine, the Franklin Institute Science Museum, Maryland Science Center, Exploratorium, Museum of Science and Industry (Chicago), California Museum of Science and Industry, and Museum of Science (Boston) (cf. Aprison 1993).
7. Falk 1991.
8. Falk and Holland 1993; Holland and Falk 1994.

9. Abrams and Falk 1995, 1996; Abrams, Falk, and Adams 1997; Luke et al. 1998.

10. Falk, Moussouri, and Coulson 1998.

11. Anderson 1999.

10

Making Museums Better Learning Experiences

There is nothing as practical as a good theory.
—Eric Sotto, *When Teaching Becomes Learning*

Staging experiences is not about entertaining customers; it's about engaging them. . . .
Experiences are events that engage individuals in a personal way.
—B. Joseph Pine II and James H. Gilmore,
The Experience Economy

As stated numerous times in this book, people learn all the time, and much of the learning is casual and unplanned. However, a significant percentage of all free-choice learning occurs in situations where learning is anticipated. Museums are free-choice learning settings in which learning is an outcome that is often *expected* both by the people who visit them and the people who design them. Professionals in these settings are tremendously successful at this educational function. However museums would probably be even more effective if staff better understood the nature of learning, the reasons people seek out and use museums as places for personal learning, and how contextual factors can be used to facilitate learning.

One advantage that their rich resources give museums as free-choice learning settings is their ability to create memorable, meaningful, and highly contextualized experiences. We have emphasized in this book the reasons that such settings, when designed thoughtfully and well, facilitate learning. Pine and Gilmore claim that we are entering a new economic era in which successful companies will be in the business of designing memorable events for customers who will pay for the experience.[1] Certainly,

177

museums have a tremendous "experience" advantage right now; museum-going is one of the most popular experiences one can currently participate in. However, if Pine and Gilmore are correct, museums need to be positioning themselves even more firmly in the experience economy than they are now. In other words, they need to figure out how to design ever better, ever more successful experiences.

We will utilize the Contextual Model of Learning laid out in this book to make a number of specific suggestions about how to make museum experiences better learning experiences, ultimately facilitating free-choice learning in general and learning from museums in particular. However, as we have suggested, it is important to appreciate that the three contexts—personal, sociocultural, and physical—are not in any way contradictory or mutually exclusive. The physical space strongly influences social interactions, and both the physical and sociocultural contexts are filtered through the lens of prior experience and knowledge; we appreciate that reality is far more integrated than the treatment in this chapter (or the book, for that matter) would suggest. In fact, we would argue it is the interactive and overlapping nature of these contexts that constitutes the experience we call learning.

In chapter 8 we summarized the Contextual Model of Learning and teased out eight key factors that influence learning in museums:

Personal Context

1. Motivation and expectations

2. Prior knowledge, interests, and beliefs

3. Choice and control

Sociocultural Context

4. Within-group sociocultural mediation

5. Facilitated mediation by others

Physical Context

6. Advance organizers and orientation

7. Design

8. Reinforcing events and experiences outside the museum

If these eight suites of factors are truly key influences upon museum learning, then it stands to reason that museum practitioners will benefit by focusing on them. We believe that they are and that museum practitioners can work proactively to maximize their positive influence on visitor experiences.

USING WHAT IS KNOWN ABOUT
THE PERSONAL NATURE OF LEARNING

As we have argued throughout the book, all learning is contextual. Arguably, at the center is the context of the learner himself the personal context. The makeup of each individual's brain, his preferred learning style and modality, motivations, expectations, prior experiences, knowledge, interests, and beliefs form the foundation upon which all future events and experiences are constructed. The educator's first important task is communication with the audience, but where should this communication begin? Must it wait until the visitor enters the building? The visitor's learning certainly does not begin there!

Motivation and Expectations

Visitors come to museums with a wide range of motivations and expectations that can and do affect learning. In fact, in many ways, by the time a visitor arrives at the front door, the nature and quality of the visitor experience have already been determined to a large degree. However, museums need not passively accept whatever attitudes the visitor comes with. Instead, we advocate actively seeking to frame appropriate expectations and motivations for visitors prior to their arrival. Arguably, one of the worst expectations an individual can have about a museum is "This place is not for me," and one of the worst motivations is a lack of motivation to visit. Questions of who does and does not visit and what visitor attitudes are prior to the visit fall within the jurisdiction of marketing. Marketing is equally about getting people in the front door and about bringing people in the front door with an appropriate mind-set and readiness for the realities of the museum experience. It is about positively priming the pump.

Several excellent examples of the positive use of marketing can be found in the range of projects supported over the past decade by the Lila Wallace Reader's Digest Fund, under its Museum Accessibility Initiative. This initiative has supported a wide range of museums, primarily art museums, in efforts to provide access to their collections to a larger and more diverse audience. The effort with which we are most familiar was at the Virginia Museum of Fine Arts (VMFA) in Richmond. Richmond has a large African American community, which historically eschewed visiting the museum. The reasons for not visiting were many, including, at worst, racism and, at best, benign neglect. The situation was compounded by the fact that the museum was located within an area of town historically unwelcoming to blacks. For all these reasons, African Americans were significantly underrepresented at the museum. Although more than half of the residents of Richmond and surrounding communities were African American, prior to the start of the project African Americans represented only 7 percent of the museum's visitors.[2]

The major focus of the project was to expand the overall audience of the Virginia Museum of Fine Arts; in particular, the museum wished to attract new visitors and expand its existing base of African American visitors. The primary vehicle for this effort was the *Spirit of the Motherland* project, a reconceptualization and reinstallation of the VMFA's extensive African art collection, a series of associated programs, and a gallery guide designed specifically for families.

Throughout the course of the *Spirit of the Motherland* project, the VMFA employed a variety of marketing strategies and program initiatives designed to appeal to a larger percentage of African Americans in the community than traditionally had visited the museum. Efforts were made to promote the initiative using a range of methods not previously implemented, including an appealing logo and signature photo, banners outside the museum, advertisements on the sides of buses, and flyers distributed through African American churches and businesses such as barber shops and beauty parlors. The exhibition and associated programs were also advertised on African American radio and television stations. The major message communicated was that the VMFA was a great place to bring children for positive family experiences and interactions. During the opening-day celebration, schoolchildren who had learned African dancing and drumming from an African master who had visited schools for several weeks before the opening performed with him, and many families came to proudly watch their children perform.

The museum was successful in increasing African American attendance during the course of the *Spirit of the Motherland* exhibition and associated programs. Evidence suggests that a new Caucasian audience was also attracted by the exhibition and programs. From the base of 7 percent, the percentage of African American visitors rose dramatically following the opening of the exhibition. On the day of the exhibition's opening celebration, 42 percent of those attending were African American, and during the first few months of the exhibition African Americans accounted for 21 percent of the VMFA's visitors. During the last months of the exhibition the percentage of African American visitors was 12 percent. Immediately after the exhibition closed, the percentage of visitors who were African American dropped back to the preexhibition level of 7 percent. On the surface, these data suggest that the initiative was successful at reaching African Americans but not in increasing their long-term commitment to the museum. However, reality turns out to be a little more complex.[3] It is important to remember that percentage breakdowns for visitation are always relative to the total population of visitors. Since the visitor survey was a random sample, those data can be used to make inferences about the total number of visitors who entered the museum. According to the counts, the number of visitors to the museum substantially increased during the run of the *Spirit of the Motherland* exhibition and programs; in fact, there were 70 percent more visitors than typically visited. Even after the close of the exhibition and programs, numbers stayed well above preexhibition counts. This means that although the absolute percentage of African American visitors dropped to preexhibition levels after the exhibition closed, there were actually more African American visitors at the museum; 7 percent of a big number is more than 7 percent of a small number. Overall, the data indicate that after the conclusion of the *Spirit of the Motherland* exhibition there was a roughly 20 percent increase in the number of African Americans visiting the VMFA. There was good evidence to suggest that the reason for this increase was the *Spirit of the Motherland* initiative, and the data strongly suggested that it was the effective and sensitive marketing and community collaboration efforts that were primarily responsible. Not only did the exhibition attract a record number of African Americans to the museum in the short term, but there appeared to be a long-term positive effect as well.

Tapping into people's personal history, creating personal connections with the institution, and facilitating positive family experiences and interactions are all ways to build positive expectations and enhance motivations for visiting; they are also excellent ways to facilitate learning. However, attracting visitors to the museum and providing them with appropriate expectations and motivations for the visit is only the first step. This is only the promise of a quality museum experience. The experience itself must fulfill these expectations and must directly connect with the unique perspectives, motivations, prior experiences, interests, and beliefs of the learner for the promise to be fulfilled. Every learner brings to the visit a wealth of prior experiences. Even a young child brings years of experience to a new learning situation. The challenge is connecting with and building upon that experience.

Prior Knowledge, Interests, and Beliefs

Learning experiences successfully take into account the factor of prior knowledge, interests, and beliefs when they provide "hooks," or entry points, that enable learners to relate their previous experiences to this new one, be it new information being presented in an exhibition or program or an aesthetic connection being made through a special art gallery performance. Learners want to be able to "see themselves" within an exhibition, program, even a web site. Either consciously or unconsciously, they are seeking ways to connect this particular exhibition, program, or web site to who they are and what they need and/or are curious about. In order for this to occur, at some level learners have to understand why this particular experience is relevant to them and, if they attend to it or participate in it, how the experience and information contained within it will enhance their life. At some basic level, every museum learner is seeking to be made happier, healthier, wiser, or in some way enriched or transformed. What makes this task inherently challenging is that every personal context, every person's store of knowledge, interests, and beliefs, is different.

Creating a learning experience for a single individual, someone you know relatively well, such as a friend or family member, is relatively easy. Given that there is only one person to design for, the content and presentation can be customized for that individual. However, if the learning experience you are trying to create needs to serve hundreds, perhaps even millions, of other people, it is not so straightforward. How do you design a learning experience for a mass market that simultaneously accommodates the unique prior experiences and interests of all potential users?

The simple answer is that you cannot. It is not possible to design an exhibition, program, web site, or any other learning experience that equally accommodates the specific beliefs, interests, and knowledge of millions of people. Remarkably, though, it is possible to come close; the key ingredients are making an effort to connect the learning experience to what people already know and are interested in and building into the design opportunities for choice. One exhibition project illustrates this approach well. In the previous chapter, we described a summative evaluation for the *What About AIDS?* exhibition that suggested that the exhibit had been a highly successful learning experience for visitors.[4] Why was this the case?

As noted in the previous chapter, the exhibition was developed in the early 1990s, when the vast majority of Americans had not only heard about HIV/AIDS but were also deeply concerned about, and interested in, the topic. Although opinions differed widely on a number of HIV/AIDS-related issues—for example, who should take responsibility for prevention and treatment, and whether it was ethical to widely distribute condoms to teenagers or to distribute clean needles to IV-drug users—many, if not most, Americans felt a strong need to know more about the subject. Thus, at the time of its development it was clear that an exhibition on this topic, although potentially controversial, would be widely perceived by the public as interesting and timely. Through front-end evaluation (evaluation designed to assess what people knew about or were interested in knowing about the topic conducted at the beginning of the exhibition development process), it was also determined that most Americans possessed both a high degree of awareness about the HIV/AIDS epidemic and a reasonably high knowledge of basic "facts" related to HIV/AIDS. However, most Americans lacked detailed knowledge of the science underlying HIV/AIDS—for example, the nature of viruses and the workings of the human immune system—and most were totally unaware of the various permutations of prevention strategies.[5]

Using this information about potential visitors, it was possible to devise a strategy for how to present the topic of HIV/AIDS in an exhibition that would accommodate the interests and prior understanding of the vast majority of the public likely to encounter the exhibition. At least briefly, this was a case where most people shared a common interest, a common level of awareness, and, in general, a common range of understanding, though not a common set of beliefs. Thus, a single exhibition had a reasonable chance of meeting the needs and interests of a diverse public by connecting what was familiar and known about HIV/AIDS to some of the new information exhibit developers hoped to convey. Several years later, public interest, awareness, and knowledge have shifted considerably in the area of HIV/AIDS; consequently, this same exhibition, although still a good one, may not be as effective.

However, despite this rare confluence of *general* interest, awareness, and knowledge in the early 1990s, the *What About AIDS?* exhibition would not have been successful if it had been designed in a linear fashion, with a single entry and exit point. Although the public shared a general interest, awareness, and knowledge about HIV/AIDS, they did not share a *specific* interest, awareness, and knowledge about the topic. Although two individuals may have been generally interested in HIV/AIDS and had roughly comparable awareness and knowledge, individual A, who was married, monogamous, and sixty-seven years old, might have been primarily interested in learning about how the epidemic might influence the health care system and the economy, while individual B, who was nineteen years old and single, might have been primarily concerned with her chances of getting HIV/AIDS over the next few years.

A major element in the success of this exhibition was the incorporation of choice. Visitors could select between three general topics—biology of HIV/AIDS, HIV/AIDS as epidemic, and HIV/AIDS prevention—and then could also select from a multitude of specific topics—for example, what is a virus? how does the immune system work? what does the worldwide spread of HIV/AIDS look like? and what are the relative advantages and disadvantages for HIV/AIDS prevention of different birth-control methods? There were also choices for different learning modalities; for example, visitors could read, watch video, manipulate hands-on interactives, use computer programs, and/or listen to audiotapes. Visitors also could choose between a variety of approaches to the topic of HIV/AIDS; for example, they could learn about it through presentations of scientific facts and concepts; they could examine epidemiological charts and graphs; there were tapes and photographs detailing firsthand accounts of individuals with HIV/AIDS; and there were even opportunities for visitors to share their own personal stories about HIV/AIDS. As a consequence, a wide range of visitors with diverse interests and knowledge could select how and what they chose to learn about the topic. Unlike many museum exhibitions, *What About AIDS?* afforded very personal experiences. A family group could enter the exhibition, split up, and use separate parts of the exhibition, occasionally coming together to share notes and suggest parts of the exhibition for others to see. In large part because of the subject matter, but also by design, this exhibition not only permitted but also encouraged individual exploration.

As we suggested in the previous chapter, the evidence for the success of this exhibition was not that every visitor walked out of it knowing at least one specific, predetermined new fact or concept about HIV/AIDS but rather that the exhibition afforded every visitor the opportunity to connect and learn at least one new thing that was personally relevant. The developers appreciated that visitors were entering and exiting the exhibition with different learning agendas and purposes, and they strove to accommodate these differences. The result was an exhibition that permitted—in fact, encouraged—visitors to bring their own understandings and interests to the experience, which yielded a wide diversity of learning outcomes.

When designing free-choice learning experiences, this should be the norm rather than the exception. Unlike compulsory education, where it is assumed that everyone will attend to a single lesson with a single purpose in mind, resulting in only a few, predetermined outcomes, everyone learning that single lesson, free-choice learning cannot assume any of these things. Learning is always going to be diverse in a free-choice context, because what people attend to, and why, will vary.

The emotional component of this exhibition was also important to its success. As outlined in chapter 2, emotion is a vital aspect of learning and problem solving and, consequently, is an important dimension of many successful learning experiences. Compared with the subjects of most exhibitions, HIV/AIDS is strongly infused with emotion and controversy, an aspect of the exhibition that caused some administrators and boards of directors great angst. The emotional and controversial aspects of the *What About AIDS?* exhibition may have been a political negative in some communities, but these factors contributed to its being a very successful exhibition for personal learning. Capitalizing on emotion is an important key to successful educational programming. Fun, excitement, joy, mystery, sadness, surprise, pathos, anticipation, and empathy are all emotional experiences that can and should be considered fundamental constituents of learning. As we suggested previously, education and entertainment are not opposite ends of a continuum, they are separate and complementary, and in the museum context they combine to become the museum experience. Arguably, the essence of this experience is choice in what and when to learn—personal control over learning.

Choice and Control

All museums to some degree afford visitors the opportunity to choose where to go, what to attend to, what to learn. After all, it is inherent in the free-choice nature of museums. Controlling one's learning can take many forms, both passive and active. Interactive experiences in museums allow more autonomy, but even traditional presentations permit the visitor a degree of control. What would be an exemplary model of a museum that facilitates choice and control? In this case we diverged from the pattern of singling out a single institution, exhibition or program, and opted to discuss a whole class of institutions. In our opinion, no group of museums better embodies the celebration of choice and control than children's museums. Children's museums allow children, particularly young children, an unrivaled opportunity to navigate through a world made to their specifications, in which they have the opportunity to choose what, when, and how to learn. Perhaps most important, they place the young child in a position to be much more in control. Here we give only a few examples of how these events play out in the real world. Although intended to be generic, our comments are heavily influenced by the many weekends spent watching our own children and others in these settings.

One of the things that one immediately notices upon entering the typical children's museum is the scale of the furnishings and exhibitions.

Children are running, climbing, and sitting everywhere, and everything is built to their dimensions. It is a world designed to accommodate the small of frame, the small of hand. And despite the apparent pandemonium, there is no sense of danger in the air. Despite the considerable exuberance of lots of young children, it is apparent that great thought has gone into the design of the space to ensure that the museum is a safe place in which to play and learn. It is not only adults who pick up on these vibes; so do children. Watching children enter the space, particularly for the first time, one is struck by the recognition that comes over their face when they realize that this place was built for them. This whole amazing place, just for them! This feeling creeps into the children's very being, the sense of ownership and empowerment that comes from being in a place, unlike anywhere else in their world, that is exclusively designed for them. Preschools and elementary schools have scaled furniture, but clearly those are not places where children feel in control. Many children come from homes where, even if they do not have their own room, they have their own toys and perhaps a special chair, but few children believe that their home environment is designed totally and exclusively for them. For better or worse, children live in an adult-centered world. When they enter a magical world where this is not the case, it is a truly energizing experience.

Children in children's museums get to choose which hat to try on, which rope to pull on, which blocks to play with, and what roles to select in the child-sized stores. And children take these roles very seriously. For example, once as we entered one such "grocery store," a little girl looked at us and said, "I want to check these out," pointing to the groceries in her miniature cart. It took a second to realize that we had entered her imaginary world and we were expected to play a role also. She was in charge; it was her world we were entering, not the other way around. So, of course, we walked behind the register and checked her out!

Children love to dress up, they love to role-play and pretend, they love to build, they love to climb and explore. Children's museums provide opportunities for children not only to choose between all these sensory and intellectual treats but also to decide which aspects they will engage in. They have permission to start what they want and stop when they want. In the "real" world, other people are always telling them what to do and when to do it. In the children's-museum world, they are in charge. In fact, they are even in charge of their adult companions. In the real world, adults tell children what and how to do this and when to do that. In the children's museum, roles are frequently reversed, and children tell adults how to do this and when to do that. What an amazing experience! Imagine being five years old and for this brief moment being in charge of your parents! It is a truly memorable and thrilling experience. Perhaps it is one of the reasons that there is one other thing that immediately strikes one upon entering a typical children's museum—the ever present feeling of childlike glee that hangs in the air. All of us in the museum world have much to learn from children's museums, perhaps most notably a willingness to let the learners have more autonomy and control over their own learning, to let them be in charge. And as we suggested in chapter 6, this does not preclude efforts to encourage collaborative learning between adults and children in children's museums; however, it does mean that any efforts designed to facilitate collaborative learning should still allow the child considerable autonomy and, hopefully, the opportunity to be the facilitator.

You may not be ready to turn the operation of your museum entirely over to the children, but it is possible to explore these ideas in the most traditional kinds of museums. A history colleague at the National Museum of American History, curator Steven Lubar, said that when he was a child, he loved to go to the Franklin Institute in Philadelphia, much less interactive then than it is today, and climb aboard the train. It was possible to sit at the controls in the cabin, and the train even moved very slightly from time to time. For years, Steve thought that he was actually controlling the train, and he is convinced this is one of the reasons he became a museum historian.

For nearly a generation, research on the role of prior knowledge and the personal construction of knowledge and meaning has dominated investigations in both school and laboratory settings. For whatever reasons, similar efforts have been almost totally lacking within the museum context. It is striking how little we currently understand about the role of prior knowledge, interests, and beliefs in museum behavior and learning, how little investigation has been conducted on the effects of enhanced choice and control. Our hope is that a new generation of researchers will soon address these shortcomings. Better understanding of how the personal context directly affects learning from museums will lead to better practice.

Recommendations for Maximizing the Personal Nature of Learning

Thus far, we have touched on just three of the important considerations for designing quality educational experiences from the perspective of the personal context. Summarizing these and adding a few others, we suggest that educators:

- Reach out to the public; start the museum experience before people arrive.

- Use marketing to provide meaningful connections with the institution, to build a positive motivation for a visit.

- Ensure that people's expectations for visiting the museum square with the realities they will actually encounter there.

- Provide opportunities for people to construct connections between museum experiences and their lives, both before and after the museum experience.

- Design experiences that allow people to personalize the information presented; this will encourage ownership of information and ensure that learners make the learning experience their own.

- Acknowledge that different learners prefer different types of learning strategies/styles, and offer learners clear choices.

- Provide a variety of entry and exit points ("hooks") that permit free-choice learners to pick the point that best meets their personal needs at the time and that acknowledge the varying reasons they want knowledge.

- Attempt to layer the complexity of the experience so that learners can self-select the complexity and depth of information they need and desire at the time.

- Always set as the goal to reinforce prior understandings and, occasionally, to help reshape understandings, attitudes, and behaviors.

- Work to effect both short-term and long-term changes in understanding, attitudes, and behaviors.

- Build emotion into the learning experience (e.g., humor, discrepant events, uncertain endings, human interactions).

- Make experiences enjoyable and entertaining; fun and learning are not mutually exclusive. Doing so is not only possible but essential to quality museum experiences.

- Work to ensure that what is to be learned clearly relates to the needs and interests of the learner. From the beginning, it should be made clear that participating in the learning experience will enhance the learner's sense of self-worth, self-awareness, and self-respect. The personal value and benefits of participating in the learning experience should always be apparent to the learner, as should the requirements for participation.

• Scale the challenge and rewards to the self-defined abilities of the learner. Quality learning experiences are open-ended; they possess multiple entry and exit points.

• Develop museum learning experiences that provide choices and put the learners squarely in control of their own learning.

USING WHAT IS KNOWN ABOUT THE SOCIOCULTURAL DIMENSION OF LEARNING

As we have stressed throughout this book, particularly in chapters 3 and 6, humans learn socioculturally. Even when they seem to be learning alone, people are learning socially. When a person looks at an exhibition, watches a video, or sits in front of a computer screen, he or she is participating in an effort by one person or a group of people to communicate information, to facilitate learning. All educational media are forms of socially mediated learning. Both the individuals within a visitor's group and the people encountered outside that group directly, and often profoundly, affect learning.

Within-Group Sociocultural Mediation

How can museums better facilitate learning experiences that capitalize on the sociocultural nature of learning, given that such mediation plays a critical role in personalizing museum experiences and in the case of some groups, like families, is the critical filter through which group members learn? One clearly successful strategy has been the development of exhibition spaces designed specifically and exclusively for small groups to work and interact together outside the flow of the larger museum. These spaces have come to be known variously as "discovery rooms" or "family learning rooms." One particularly exemplary space of this kind is the *Hands on History Room* at the Smithsonian Institution's National Museum of American History (NMAH). The *Hands on History Room,* designed by a team under the direction of Nancy McCoy, Director, Education and Visitor Services, NMAH, sets out to provide museum visitors with an opportunity to gain a deeper understanding of American history by offering them direct experiences with primary source materials, including opportunities to touch and examine objects and documents. In the process, history comes alive for visitors and allows them to create historical meaning for themselves. A key feature of the *Hands on History Room* is that it encourages and facilitates family and small-group interactions.

Located on the second floor of the museum, the two-thousand-square-foot space is warmly lit and comfortable. There are places to sit, tables to work at, and opportunities to explore objects and documents at a leisurely pace. Entrance is controlled so that the space, though always busy, is never overcrowded. Watching visitors in the space reveals not just families but all kinds of groups working together, interacting, sharing stories, and generally engaging in inquiry and conversation. Although by design all the activities involve learning by doing, the modes of interaction encouraged in the space range from active, physical involvement, such as riding an old highwheeler or caning a chair, to the more contemplative activity of leafing through old picture albums, diaries, and copies of letters from people who lived in the past. Supporting each of the activities in the *Hands on History Room* are written materials that ask questions and structure inquiry. These materials are designed to "pique visitors' interest and focus their attention on figuring out what something is, how it was used or worked, and what meaning it had for someone in the past."[6] Some of the materials take the form of instructional booklets; other materials are merely sets of questions to guide the examination of objects or documents. All materials are written in a conversational tone, and all are designed to help visitors step into the shoes of people who lived in the past.

Clearly, design can facilitate social interaction within groups; settings that facilitate collaborative learning can be created within museums. However, are there guidelines one can follow that permit all exhibitions, not just special rooms, to be designed to promote social interaction and collaborative learning? Guidance comes from Minda Borun and her colleagues working on the Philadelphia–Camden Informal Science Education Collaborative (PISEC), a National Science Foundation–funded initiative that investigated family learning in museums. The PISEC group identified seven characteristics of family-friendly exhibits that support collaborative learning. They are (1) being multisided so that a family can cluster around, (2) being multiuser so that several hands or bodies can interact comfortably, (3) being accessible so that children and adults can use them comfortably, (4) being multi-outcome so that results are varied and complex enough to foster group discussion, (5) being multimodal so that the exhibit appeals to different learning styles and levels of knowledge, (6) being readable in such a way that text is arranged in easily understood segments, and (7) being relevant so that the material provides links to visitors' prior knowledge and experience.[7] Although these characteristics were derived with families in mind, as we suggested in chapter 6, encouraging social interaction among all groups visiting museums is important. It is highly likely that these seven characteristics apply equally to other visiting groups such as all-adult groups and school groups.

One other important point regarding the sociocultural nature of learning: museums often make erroneous assumptions about social interaction (or the lack of it) in the development of technology-based experiences. As of this writing, very little is understood about how people actually use computers and the Internet, but preliminary research of a museum web site by John Chadwick revealed that fully a third of all users were groups, many of them family groups or small groups of children who went on line in their free time.[8] Despite these findings, most of the offerings on the Net reflect the inherently solitary nature of the medium's original creators. In all of these situations, significant improvements in educational effectiveness could be accomplished by designing the experience so that it permitted, perhaps even encouraged, collaborative learning. In a museum context, this might mean making the area around a computer in an exhibition large enough to accommodate several people, providing several stools in front of computer workstations to foster interaction, and designing computer experiences that require the participation of more than one person.

Facilitated Mediation by Others

As previously stated, individuals outside the social group also influence visitor learning, and none so profoundly as museum staff. Museum theater represents one particularly powerful, and often underappreciated, way to utilize staff to facilitate learning. Everyone loves a performance. As was suggested in chapters 3 and 6, there are good reasons for this. Fortunately, many museums are exploring how to use the narrative form more effectively in exhibitions, programs, and even on line. An excellent example of the power and potential of museum theater was the program *Heroes Just Like You: Careers in Science and Technology,* created by Dale Jones, at the time director of interpretation for the Baltimore City Life Museums. This program was originally developed in response to the Greater Baltimore Committee's challenge to Baltimore cultural institutions to support efforts that encouraged students to consider careers in the life sciences. Although it was not immediately clear what a history museum could do to meet this challenge, the museum staff set about working on the problem. Since many students make course decisions in late middle or early high school years, the museum felt that they should target this age. Since 80 percent of the Baltimore City students were African American, the museum decided to focus specifically on this target audience.

The museum opted to respond by creating a history-oriented theater piece that explored the employment of African Americans in three time periods—the 1890s, the 1940s, and the 1990s—and examined their decisions around turning points in their careers. Being good historians, the museum staff began by collecting data. They interviewed scientists and technicians who had overcome some obstacle—racial or gender discrimination, poverty, drug dependency, lack of parental support—to reach their careers. They found that, indeed, people did have turning points—not necessarily a discrete event, but more of a long-term change that usually involved changing peer group and friends and seeking out education. They also interviewed both black and white women who were secretaries in the 1940s and conducted research about employment of African Americans in the 1890s. In addition, Jones researched contemporary sociological and psychological studies of peer-group pressure among African American youth.

The result was a play infused with local African American history that attempted to help students understand that there can be turning points in people's lives and to realize and experience, through theater, the negative effects of peer-group pressure. The play also attempted to encourage students to consider the potential intellectual excitement, passion, and financial rewards of careers in science and technology, without disparaging other types of work.

From his extensive theater experience, Jones knew the value of audience interaction with staff members, but he did not want to incorporate it in such a way that it disrupted the dramatic flow of the piece. He also realized that in order to use audience interaction successfully, you could not present a play and expect students to have a worthwhile discussion about it unless they had been "prepped" for it. To get them to talk at the end, you needed to give them opportunities to talk in the beginning. Thus was born the idea of an *Our Town*–type narrator who would talk to the audience before the play and establish a rapport that he could build on throughout the show. Also, since the narrator would play several characters during the play, the audience would experience the immediacy of the performance and the fascination of watching the transformation as the actor became the narrator again. It was also important to the audience that the dramatic structure of a scene not be broken. The resulting structure looked like this:

The narrator greets the group and provides an introduction to the experience. The audience walks into a small space and takes their seats. Before them is the scene of an affluent home in 1890; an actress is already in the scene in the role of a servant. The narrator dons costume parts and enters as an 1890 character, the servant's husband. At the end of the scene, the actress exits; the actor breaks character and asks the audience, "What would you do if you were her?" "What are her choices?" "What limits her choices?" The scene is about twelve minutes long; the questions, about five minutes. The actor then leads the audience to another space which is the next scene, a 1940s office scene.

In this scene the actress plays a secretary. The actor dons a different costume and enters. At the end of the scene (again about twelve minutes) the actress leaves, the actor breaks character and becomes the narrator again and questions the audience. "What would you do in her situation?" "What has changed in the fifty years since the last scene?" The actor helps the audience identify the character's goals, turning points, and obstacles. The actor then invites the audience to move fifty years ahead in time to the next scene, a 1990s science research lab.

In this final scene the actress is a research chemist (like the other characters, this character was based on oral interviews). The actor enters, and the scene unfolds. At the end of the scene both actors leave and then re-enter, both breaking character and talking to the audience about what they have seen, the various characters' goals, and the obstacles and turning points in their lives. The discussion then moves into a discussion of the audience members' goals and the obstacles and potential turning points they might face.

The production was an overwhelming success. The performers were wonderful—young, "cool" African Americans who developed tremendous rapport with the students and showed obvious interest and concern for the educational well-being of the hundreds of young students with whom they interacted. Not only did middle- and early-high-school-aged African American students enjoy the performance, but also evaluation revealed a statistically significant change in attitudes about science among both black and white students, males and females. In short, the *Heroes Just Like You* museum theater piece provided an immediate and powerful vehicle both for presenting the history of Baltimore and for communicating important present-day information about careers and values. The feeling was that the program worked because it was based on solid oral-history research, which resulted in a series of stories that resonated well with the target audience. The design of the play also broke with tradition by creating opportunities for purposeful pauses that included dialogue between the actors and the audience. Since the balance in using theater is always trying to overcome the potentially "passive" nature of the medium, the skillful way in which this experience created opportunities for the audience to become meaningfully involved in the scenarios was key.

The need to capitalize upon the sociocultural context of groups suggests the importance of strategies that facilitate a sense of a community of learners among visitors. Such strategies require rethinking roles for docents or floor staff as facilitators of experiences rather than disseminators of information, and making such a commitment requires changes in the training and mentoring of staff and volunteers. But research suggests that efforts to facilitate interactions between visitors, whether school, family, or tour groups, and staff for the purpose of sharing and building upon each other's knowledge can be rewarding both personally and intellectually for visitors.

Currently one of the most active areas in museum learning research is investigation of the influence of the sociocultural context. More than a dozen serious investigators are exploring this topic across a wide range of institutions. Our hope is that this research will further strengthen the field's understanding of the important role that social interaction plays in the learning process. Armed with knowledge like this, museum professionals should be in a position to create better interactive visitor experiences that encourage and foster meaningful interaction, resulting in both enjoyment and long-term learning.

Recommendations for Facilitating the Social Dimension of Learning

Earlier we touched on just a few of the important considerations for designing quality educational experiences. Summarizing these and adding a few others, we suggest that educators:

- At the most basic level, design experiences and programs that permit more than one person to share the experience socially and physically.

- Reward and foster social interaction rather than penalize and inhibit it.

- Invest in people; there are few more successful devices for facilitating learning than a quality human facilitator. Good facilitators require training, not just in the content, but also, and most important, in the art of communication. Good communication starts with good listening.

* Create opportunities for group dialogue that extends beyond the temporal limits of the initial experience. Why not develop lists of questions that can be used as conversation aids at the dinner table or during the drive home?

* Create situations where motivated novices can work alongside knowledgeable mentors in an atmosphere of collaboration and shared goals.

* Utilize stories, songs, poems, dance, and/or music that help to string together information for the learner in a profoundly human context.

* Be sensitive in educational programs to the cultural specificity of language, gesture, and narrative and avoid the use of linguistic idioms and culture-specific humor.

* Recognize and build upon the diverse norms and values of many cultures.

* Finally, remember that the best learning experiences create multiple opportunities for diverse populations to "see themselves" and others like themselves within an exhibition, program, or web site and to assess their relative status from these experiences.

USING WHAT IS KNOWN ABOUT
THE PHYSICAL DIMENSION OF LEARNING

Learning is not all in our heads. Learning is a dialogue, a coming together of internal and external reality. As we have described in considerable detail, learning is not only facilitated by design and appropriate contexts, learning *requires* thoughtful design and appropriate contexts. When designed carefully and thoughtfully, places like museums (including zoos, aquariums, arboreta, and historical parks and homes) are the quintessential "appropriate" physical settings for learning and thus have unprecedented opportunities to facilitate long-term, meaningful learning. Immersing learners within a context that enables them literally to see how things are connected, to understand visually, aurally, and even through smell and touch what something looks and feels like, is a tremendous learning tool. To enable a child to actually see what people looked like and how they lived and even to hear how they might have talked in the past is to open up a window to history that no amount of text in a book can ever duplicate. For an individual not only to see how a wing is shaped but also to be able to put on wings and stand in a wind tunnel and feel lift is an unparalleled learning opportunity. Museums have the ability to present reality simply, dramatically, and, more than anything, authentically.

Not only does physical setting create a context in which learning can occur, but it also has the potential to create a desire to learn. In the right setting, real or imagined, the learner is surrounded by sights, sounds, and textures that foster curiosity and encourage exploration. So motivated, learning proceeds effortlessly and intrinsically; there is no need to force, prompt, or bribe. Regardless of the medium, the best free-choice learning occurs in such physically rich and appropriate settings.

The essence of the museum experience is the ability for an individual to experience real things, and under the best of circumstances, within real, meaningfully designed physical contexts. We are in the experience business. Three keys to facilitating these experiences are using advance organizers and orientation, creating well-designed educational experiences, and fostering meaningful, reinforcing subsequent experiences.

Advance Organizers and Orientation

The vast majority of museums that provide school field trips also provide schools with some sort of pretrip materials. And virtually every museum provides visitors with some sort of map or orientation sheet that describes the general floor plan and contents of the museum. But many of these efforts fall far short of the ideal, primarily because maps are difficult for many visitors to use and the techniques are not well integrated into the museum experience itself. Recently a number of institutions have explored efforts to make orientation a serious and central part of the museum experience, in our opinion, none more compellingly than Illinois's Cahokia Mounds State Historic Park.

The historic park is the site of the largest prehistoric Native American city north of Mexico. According to the article on Cahokia in the *Encarta 98 Encyclopedia*, this city, covering 16 square kilometers (6 square miles), may have been inhabited by as many as fifty thousand people of the Mississippian culture between 1050 and 1250. In addition to developing a complex agricultural system, the inhabitants moved more than 1.4 million cubic meters (50 million cubic feet) of earth to create their ceremonial mounds. Visitors to this modest-sized museum across the Mississippi River from St. Louis enter the museum and are strongly encouraged to begin their museum experience by watching a short introductory film. The film, presented in a comfortable but fairly typical auditorium, is a well-produced description of the mysteries surrounding the Indian groups who built large mounds up and down the Mississippi Valley some one thousand years ago. These were successful and prosperous people, who mysteriously disappeared, leaving behind their mounds and myriad questions. The film talks about what is known, and not known, about these peoples—their customs, lifestyles, and of course, possible reasons for building mounds. However, the magic of the orientation is not so much the film as the ending. At the conclusion, the narrator invites the audience to visit the museum's re-creation of a Cahokia Indian village. As the film ends, the screen turns from opaque to translucent, and through the screen the audience can see the activity and hear the sounds of an ancient Indian village. For that magic moment, as the screen rises and visitors are invited to walk under the screen and into the village, it seems like that ancient Indian village has actually come alive again, filled with appropriate sights, sounds, and activities.

In fact, the sounds of Indians at work and play are piped in, and the movement of people within the village is a powerful illusion created by the movement of other visitors exploring the museum—the theater is actually in the middle of the space. However, the net effect is a compelling orientation and invitation to explore the village and interact with a series of hands-on exhibits displayed around the perimeter of the village. As a visitor you feel truly ready to begin a meaningful exploration of the museum. As you continue to walk around the museum, examining artifacts, learning about the people and the archaeological dig being conducted on the site, you can still see and hear the sights and sounds of the village, which provide an appropriate context for the entire experience.

This Cahokia experience was an introduction and orientation to the entire visitor experience within the visitor center, but museum professionals, particularly designers, also spend a lot of time thinking about introduction spaces within individual exhibitions, certainly another technique for providing advance organizers. A great deal of this effort has concentrated on the entryway to exhibitions and has resulted in much disappointment for museum staff when visitors do not linger to read long introductory panels or watch introductory videos. Our suggestion is to decentralize the introduction and ensure that the major idea or ideas are repeated, clearly and explicitly, throughout the exhibition. An introduction of some kind at the entryway (some visitors do like and need this) is probably still desirable, but it need not be long and involved. Incorporating advance organizers into the entire design frees up space at the entrance to make an inviting threshold, a contextualizing portal into the real "stuff" people came to see.

Design

We believe strongly that there are few educational media as effective as quality, well-designed exhibitions and programs. The immediacy of real things, set in well-designed, appropriate contexts, provides tangible and readily accessible images that enrich and extend meaning. Increasingly, museums maximize the use of design through the creation of immersion experiences. Few museum experiences are more compelling to visitors than such experiences, which envelop the visitor in the sounds, smells, sights, textures, and even tastes of a place or event. Immersion experiences take many forms depending upon the nature of the site and its collections. One can walk through a rain forest in a natural history museum, experience living history with costumed characters at a historic site, participate in a fiesta with clothes to don and food to eat at a children's museum, enter a semidark jungle animal-viewing blind at a zoo, or participate in the re-creation of an artist's salon in an art museum; these are all examples of efforts to contextualize the ideas being presented and create meaningful and appropriate experiences for visitors.

For nearly twenty years museums have been working to build better, more immersive exhibition spaces. *Sound to Mountain* at the Seattle Aquarium offers an example of an immersion experience that, through its design alone, conveys a general sense of the exhibition's main idea even to those visitors who read little of the exhibition copy, while also providing a variety of experiences, such as interaction with computers and a play area for families with young children. *Sound to Mountain* is the last exhibition visitors encounter during their visit to the aquarium. The exhibition examines the watershed in the Seattle region by taking visitors on a journey from Puget Sound to the Cascade Mountains, where the water flowing into the sound originates.

The experience is a linear one, progressing from the sound to the mountains. The exhibition is partially exposed to the outside where sections of walls on the right have been removed. As a result, sunlight filters in, as does wind and, at times, rain. As you approach the end of the exhibition, you hear the sound of water rushing and can even see steam rising. At the very end is a re-created section of a mountain stream and waterfall, complete with thunderous cascading water and an ever present mist created by the stream and waterfall. At the base of the waterfall are several pools where the resident sea otters play and entertain visitors with a variety of routines. As visitors move through the exhibition, the effect of the ever increasing sound of water falling and the partial exposure to the elements conveys, without words, an appreciation and awareness of the exhibition's message. The general ambiance of *Sound to Mountain* with its "outdoorsy feel" of trees, rocks, rising steam, and the sounds of cascading water creates a multifaceted sensory experience for the visitor. The design helps to convey notions of the outdoors, water, and animals and seems to help many visitors think about the themes of watershed, water systems, the local environment, and conservation.

The summative evaluation found that visitors enjoyed the *Sound to Mountain* exhibition very much. They indicated especially liking the live displays of otters and fish; the exhibition's themes on the watershed and people's effects on it; the variety of experiences offered, such as interactives, the children's play area, the use of computers; and the general ambiance of the exhibition. Even visitors who said they did not have time to read labels or focus much on the exhibition because of young children or being tired after visiting other parts of the aquarium still felt positive about *Sound to Mountain*. Many said that if they had had more time, they would have done more reading and interacting with the exhibition. No one was neutral or appeared to dislike the exhibition.

The exhibition included spaces for children, experiences and information for adults, environmental treatments and computer interactives, live animals and objects with graphic panels—something for everyone—but each element worked with, rather than competed against, others. This exhibition is evidence that what we have learned about museums in the past couple of decades can be seamlessly combined into a successful exhibition. Interviews with visitors revealed an appreciation for the many facets of the design of the exhibition; some visitors mentioned specific sections that their children liked, and others mentioned more adult-centered parts of the exhibition. For example, visitors both directly and indirectly referred to the lifts, faucet, erosion, computer (at the beginning of the exhibition), and the marsh that provided an unsupervised play area for children when giving examples of what they liked or learned. Others talked about the otters and interactive games, and still others referred to the waterfall and streams and the ability to see and experience Puget Sound directly. Regardless of their varying experiences, visitors collectively indicated that experiencing the exhibition resulted in an increased understanding of, and appreciation for, watersheds and a desire to conserve them—the educational goals of the exhibition. But what happened to visitors after they left this exhibition? Will they, like the visitors to the National Aquarium described in chapter 7, find their enthusiasm and commitment waning over time in the absence of reinforcing events or additional experiences?

Reinforcing Events and Experiences

It is essential that museums think about their programs, exhibitions, even web sites as existing within a larger arena of learning, not in a vacuum. Sometimes exhibitions and programs are developed as if no other medium at any other place or time has ever presented this information before or will ever present it again. If this were true, it is unlikely that anyone would partake in the programming. It is because the topics presented in museums relate to events outside the museum that visitors come and show interest. It is because the public is acutely interested in the art of Vincent van Gogh that they flock to a show of his works. It is because of the film *Titanic* that the public developed a heightened interest in events surrounding the sinking of the *Titanic* and this period in history. To ignore these realities, or even worse to disdain them as trappings of popular culture, is to severely limit the learning opportunities afforded by the museum. Learning is a continuous process that begins before the visitor arrives at the museum door and continues long after. The extent to which a museum facilitates connections between prior and subsequent experiences and encourages utilization of other learning resources in the community is the extent to which the museum experience will be a totally successful learning experience.

Museums can certainly play a more active role in creating their own meaningful subsequent experiences. One such effort was recently completed at the National Museum of Natural History. The museum collaborated with IMAX on the creation of a large-format film about the Galapagos Islands, *Galapagos in 3D*. One component of this project, funded by the National Science Foundation, was an interactive family guide. The guides, sold in museum shops where the film is being shown, were designed to furnish the public with additional information about biodiversity and evolution, providing families a series of hands-on activities they can use to explore these ideas more deeply. Because the guide was designed to extend and reinforce the IMAX experience, it was important that it build on the narrative of the film and that it be a colorful, visual piece, similar to the IMAX medium. The Institute for Learning Innovation developed the guide, working in collaboration with an advisory group of scientists at the museum. It was graphically designed by 818 Studios in

Annapolis, Maryland.[9] The guide has three goals: (1) to provide clear and concise information about biodiversity and evolution for older children and adults, information that was difficult to convey in the medium of the film; (2) to allow families to explore some of these ideas in active, fun ways back at home; and (3) to encourage and facilitate collaborative learning within the family. The resulting family guide features many images from the film and allows families to learn more about the research of Dr. Carole Baldwin, the featured scientist, including a puzzle game that helps readers better understand the research she conducts. One of the Smithsonian scientists had taken his family to the Galapagos three years earlier, and the guide allows readers to see the Galapagos through their eyes, appropriate for a guide designed for families. Journal entries from one of the girls in the family, along with entries from Dr. Baldwin and Charles Darwin, model how scientists record their observations and experiences. There was a deliberate effort to build in a variety of activities to meet the learning needs of different types of families, so the guide also includes a board game, a role-playing game, and a web-based activity. A series of hands-on activities, focusing on ideas such as adaptation and natural selection, is designed so that each family member, even young children, has an important task to contribute to the collaborative effort. All of the activities were field-tested with families to ensure that the information made sense and that families knew what to do and why they were doing it. By spearheading the development of this guide, the National Museum of Natural History is proactively trying to extend the experience of families with their institution, encouraging further collaborative learning back at home.

In addition to activity guides designed to extend and reinforce the museum experience, many museums have another tool that can serve this role as well: their web site. Although many museums have been creative in their use of web sites as an advance organizer for a visit, there is no reason why web sites could not also serve postvisit purposes, for example, by providing opportunities for visitors to get more in-depth information, further explore a topic of interest, or engage in some related activity.

Clearly, the core of the museum experience is the ability for an individual to see and experience real things within meaningful physical contexts. By developing creative advance organizers and orientation, immersive environments, and meaningful and reinforcing subsequent experiences, museums can maximize the use of their rich physical contexts. In addition, a wealth of research on the physical qualities of the museum context currently exists. There is absolutely no reason to reinvent the wheel or, even worse, pretend that reinvention is required. Designers and developers should read the literature and benefit from the collective wisdom gained from three-quarters of a century of research on the physical context of museums.

Recommendations for Facilitating the Physical Dimension of Learning

In designing the physical context for an educational experience, we suggest that educators:

- Strive to frame the learner's experiences within richly described or appointed, relevant, and appropriately complex environments. Successful educational developers appreciate that effort invested in creating an appropriate setting is a waste of neither time nor money but is essential to the learning process.

- Design the learning environment to help the learner navigate from one experience to the next, in the absence of overt directions or instructions. Within an appropriate context, the setting itself helps to direct and motivate the learning.

- Have clear goals and appropriate rules and make them explicit. Learners should always know what is expected of them and how well they are doing. This implies providing visitors with appropriate advance organizers and building into all experiences continual, unambiguous feedback to let learners know whether they are successful at gaining the intended information, skill, or perspective.

- Design experiences so that they have appropriate levels of challenge and the opportunities for action and thought are always balanced by the skills and knowledge of the learner.

- Attempt to make learning experiences boundless; in other words, the experience should continue from learners' innate interests and experiences and enable them to continue or extend the learning beyond the temporal and physical confines of a single experience. A museum exhibition, should provide the visitor with concrete references to past experiences and suggestions for experiences that will extend and expand upon the learning experience provided in the museum. For example, provide visitors with lists of relevant and appropriate television shows, web sites, books, and magazines that can be accessed after leaving the museum.

- Bear in mind that the most compelling learning experiences are all-encompassing. All of an individual's sensory channels become engaged in the experience, reducing competing information without reducing complexity. Such all-encompassing experiences provide a sharper focus and a more memorable experience. This is why multi-channel/multimodal learning works; it is learning through all the senses.

- Pay attention to cleanliness, comfort, and security. In the same way that learning experiences can be enhanced by creative use of the physical context, they can be affected by poor ambiance. It is critical that the museum be perceived as a clean, comfortable, and safe environment.

- Use all of the museum to enhance learning. Learning experiences can and should happen throughout every part of the museum. Creatively use restaurants, rest rooms, coatrooms, parking lots, grounds, and gift shops as physical extensions of museum exhibitions and programs. Think of the entire museum as a stage, a setting for transforming learning experiences.

- Finally, use evaluation—front-end, formative, remedial, and summative—to help build better, more cost-effective, more learner-centered museum experiences.[10] Although evaluation adds time and money to the development process, it is rarely too much to pay for quality feedback from the public.

We hope that by following these suggestions, institutions will be able to offer ever better free-choice learning experiences to their visitors, because much of what people know is constructed from such experiences. It is our belief that this has always been the case but that it will become ever more apparent as America and the rest of the world fully transition into the knowledge economy, as we truly become a Learning Society. From this perspective, understanding free-choice learning is fundamental to the new Learning Society. Savvy museum professionals recognize that museum learning does not occur merely within the limited temporal and physical envelope of the museum. Chapter 11 explores learning from museums within this larger leisure-learning context, and chapter 12 discusses how museums can prepare for the coming Learning Society.

KEY POINTS

- Museums could be made even more effective free-choice learning settings if staff better understood the nature of learning, the reasons people seek out and use museums as places for personal learning, and how contextual factors can be used to facilitate learning.

- The Contextual Model of Learning laid out in this book can be used as a framework for making museum experiences better learning experiences. Specifically, museum practitioners should proactively ensure that the eight suites of factors that dramatically influence museum learning are always working positively for visitors.

NOTES

1. Pine and Gilmore 1999.
2. Dierking and Adams 1996.
3. The issue of changing visitors' museum-going behavior or encouraging someone to become a museum visitor is always complex. John Falk has adapted from the public health field a model for change created by James Prochaska and his colleague (Falk 1998; Prochaska and DiClemente 1986). The basic idea is that messages aimed at changing ideas and behaviors generally only work when an individual is ready to be influenced. Prochaska and DiClemente discovered that there are discrete stages of awareness of, and receptivity to, any behavioral change: precontemplation (the individual is not seriously considering change in the next six months); contemplation (the individual is seriously considering change); action (the person is actually involved in the change); and maintenance (this stage involves continued upkeep of the behavior). People at each of these stages require different marketing messages.
4. Holland and Falk 1994.
5. Falk and Holland 1993.
6. McCoy 1993, 3.
7. Borun et al. 1998.
8. Chadwick 1998.
9. The idea of developing an associated family guide was conceived of by Laura McKie, Director of Education at the National Museum of Natural History. Associates Shannon Quesada, Kathryn Foat, and Lynn Dierking, with assistance from John Falk and Leslie McKelvey Adelman, developed the guide.
10. For information on evaluation, see Taylor 1991; Dierking and Pollock 1998; Loomis 1987; Screven 1990; and Diamond 1999.

11

Museums in
the Larger Society

There is no place left on earth where one can plan one's destiny with-
out taking into account what happens in the rest of the world.
—Mihaly Csikszentmihalyi,
The Evolving Self

Boom times for museums, the articles in the *New York Times,* the *Washington Post,* and *Museum News* proclaim.[1] Boom times indeed! The museum community is experiencing unprecedented growth in the number of
museums, growth in the size of museums, and growth in museums' popularity. Every year, the statistics on how many people visit museums
seem to climb. Although there have been a few valleys and plateaus, the
overall trend is clearly up. Why are so many people flooding to museums? Certainly some of the popularity can and should be attributed to
the almost revolutionary change in museum culture in the last twenty-
five years, change that has seen the importance of visitors and the visitor
experience achieve ascendancy over the single-minded pursuit of the collection and preservation of the object.[2] And yet the kind of explosive
growth we are witnessing, as exemplified by statistics cited in other parts
of this book, cannot be explained merely by changes in museum practice.
For when all is said and done, to the uninitiated, museums still look and
feel remarkably similar to the way they looked and felt twenty or thirty
years ago. So to what can we attribute this remarkable growth in museum popularity, and how does it relate to museum learning? Arguably, the
answers lie in changes in the leisure behaviors and patterns of Americans,
in the very essence of what it means to be a citizen in the twenty-first

century, and, perhaps most important, in the fundamental role museums seem to play in American society as a whole.

As described in the previous chapters, many factors potentially influence the decision about whether or not to visit a museum. Word of mouth from family and friends, past leisure experiences, and personal interests and values all play major roles in this decision-making process. However, the choice of whether to go or not to go to a museum cannot be totally understood at the level of the individual. Museum-going also needs to be considered in a broader context, at the level of the society. Just as each individual within a society lives by the values and beliefs of that society and, in turn, reflects those values and beliefs, the institutions within that society also are affected by and reflect societal values and beliefs. Museums are no exception. Museums explicitly and implicitly communicate many things to the public. For example, museums explicitly communicate that they are about such things as objects, history, science, culture, and learning. But as a number of other investigators have suggested, museums also implicitly communicate messages about authority, power, and the values of the dominant culture.[3] This latter type of analysis is described by museum researcher Eileen Hooper-Greenhill:

> As socio-cultural institutions, museums, in common with other socio-cultural institutions such as schools, the cinema or the mass media, are susceptible to analysis through the "semiology of signification." The semiology of signification analyses messages that are often, but not always, unintentioned. This form of analysis generally searches for the hidden, ideological messages.[4]

While acknowledging the important role unintentioned messages play in the public's use and perceptions of museums, we leave that analysis to others. Instead, we will focus on the level of intentioned messages, those overt, more concrete messages that museums regularly communicate, especially the messages of education and entertainment. Museums do not exist in isolation. Rather, they can usefully be categorized as part of several overlapping communities of organizations. For example, most museums belong to the community of nonprofit organizations, and in many communities museums are part of a family of organizations that fall under the general heading of government. However, there are two other communities, or infrastructures, to which museums belong that are particularly relevant to the issue of learning in museums. Museums are one of a collection of institutions that provide the public with educational experiences, and they are also part of the collection of institutions that provide the public with leisure experiences. To fully understand the learning that occurs as a consequence of museum experiences, it is important to appreciate that museums reside at the intersection of two important infrastructures, education and leisure. In chapter 7 we talked about the American educational infrastructure; now let us explore more fully leisure in America.

MUSEUMS AND LEISURE EXPERIENCES

Leisure is not only big business; it is becoming the biggest business. Tourism is the single largest industry in the world, and the American public now spends more time on recreation than any other part of the household economy, including food and housing.[5] As is widely appreciated today, museums are competing for a piece of the public's leisure time along with an ever growing number of competitors. Competitors arise even among similar nonprofit institutions such as other museums, parks, and libraries, and also from a growing cadre of for-profit entities including shopping malls (many with interactive "learning" sites of their own), theme parks, sporting events, fairs, and myriad other "attractions." So many choices, so little time! If we are to better understand how people make choices within the increasingly crowded leisure landscape, we must first have an appreciation for the nature of leisure time itself.

Leisure Time

Over the past generation, the portion of our lives devoted to both paid work and housework has decreased.[6] Both men and women now average about forty hours of free time per week.[7] Although there are still disparities across the population, with the wealthy having more leisure time than the poor, all sectors of the population have gained free time. The main gain in free time occurred between 1965 and 1975, with only small gains since 1975.[8] However, most Americans feel that they have less, not more, leisure time.

According to leisure researcher Geoffrey Godbey, we perceive that we have less leisure time because perception of leisure time is not a function just of absolute number of hours but equally, if not more, how those hours are distributed. Godbey and his colleague John Robinson have documented that while free time has increased across the workweek, most free time—twenty-five of forty hours—now occurs during weekdays, not the weekend. Unfortunately, free time during the week generally has more limited value in terms of its possibility for leisure. With a whole day of free time, a broader range of activities is possible, such as taking a trip or visiting a museum. These activities are very difficult to squeeze into the forty-five minutes per day gained on workdays.

Not surprisingly, people generally report they would rather have their increases in free time in the form of three-day weekends or larger blocks of time, particularly since the chores of weekdays appear to be expanding into the weekend. As work has spilled into the weekend and free time has seeped into weekdays, changes appear to be taking place in people's use of free time. One reason for this may be that the many short segments of free time do not provide a psychological escape from necessity. People do not feel the transition from a rushed work pace to relaxed and tranquil leisure. Indeed, large segments of the public feel rushed both at work and during their free time, which helps account for perceptions of decreased leisure time. Americans believe they are in the midst of an unprecedented "time-famine," a phenomenon originally identified by a Swedish economist named Staffan Linder. Linder realized as early as 1970 that many people, particularly in highly developed countries, were bumping up against significant time-scarcity problems.[9] In time-famine cultures such as the United States, the balance between accomplishment in work and leisure has been destroyed as worker productivity has accelerated, increasing the yield on an hour of work. As work time became more economically valuable, it was thought of as scarcer, as would be the case with any commodity whose relative value had increased.

While the effects of increased productivity on hours of work are complex, its effect on our psychological perception of time is unambiguous: time becomes perceived as scarce as its economic value increases. Leisure is an inherently time-intensive, and thus "expensive," activity. Some leisure experiences require less time than others. Museum-going probably falls in the middle to longer end of the continuum, requiring more time commitment than reading the newspaper but less than traveling to a foreign country. Most museums require anywhere from a half to a whole day, neither of which is likely to be accommodated on a weekday; and even on a weekend, a visit requires advance planning.

Given the increasing "cost" of time, Americans have explored a variety of strategies to "stretch" or otherwise modify time. The trend is toward trying to increase the yield on leisure time, in the process transforming leisure into a frantic race to get as much as possible out of every minute spent. To do this, goods are combined with activities in a variety of ways. According to Godbey, strategies fall into three general categories: escalated consumption, simultaneous consumption, and faster consumption. Escalated consumption is driven by a need to make the most of the moment: "If we have to spend the time, we might as well make the most of it." One form of this is the increasingly common effort to combine what were previously disparate activities—for example, combining eating, shopping, and museum-going into a single experience.[10]

However, perhaps the most insidious trend is what Godbey describes as the development of "time deepening" skills[11] or, in the current vernacular, "multi-tasking."[12] Time deepening means that some people develop higher rates of "doing" than others. Rather than thinking of time as an either-or proposition—"I can either read the newspaper or watch television or eat dinner"—people develop the ability to do all three simultaneously through time-deepening techniques. Time, in effect, becomes transformed from a fixed commodity to one that can be stretched almost infinitely. What used to be either-or time-use decisions are now often "more, more" decisions. People who work longer hours, for instance, also engage in more forms of active recreation than those who work shorter hours.[13] Increasingly, people, especially Americans, attempt to "do" more and more within the same time and space. In multinational time-diary studies, Americans were more likely than people from any other nation to record multiple activities in their diaries.[14]

Time saving thus becomes a component of all behavioral decisions, particularly for the individuals who feel most rushed. A pervasive example is found in modern child-rearing, where a new term has crept into our vocabulary: "quality time." Quality time with a child first and foremost takes for granted that less time will be spent. In effect, being with the child, which is viewed as a means to an end, can be made more efficient so that more positive things can be accomplished.[15] Museum-going is frequently considered a quality-time activity, particularly for weekend dads. Anecdotal evidence suggests that the number of single dads taking children to museums on weekends is at an all-time high.

Historically, leisure was associated with voluntary activity, which implied a choice between alternatives. Today, through time deepening, many people seem to be more nearly able to avoid the sacrifice of one activity for another, seeking instead to do it all and see it all, and do it and see it now. We walk for fitness, play golf for contacts, and go to museums to improve our mind. Passing the time in activities that are pleasurable in and of themselves is almost a foreign notion. Efficiency rules our work and our leisure. Speed and brevity are ever more widely admired, whether in serving food, the length of magazine articles, conversations, or museum labels. The emphasis is on cramming more (information, quality, enjoyment, etc.) into less time. Arguably, time is replacing money as the most valued resource—the one for which demand has increased the most relative to supply. Museum-going has always been about time rather than money. For most visitors to museums, the decision whether or not to attend invariably comes down to time.[16]

There are only so many free weekends, only so many free blocks of time available that can be invested in what amounts to the commitment of the better part of a day. Most leisure time in America is spent at home, and the bulk of that is spent watching television. Currently, TV viewing overwhelms all other uses of free time, accounting for nearly half of all free time.[17] Outside-the-home activities represent only about a third of leisure time use. This time is divided between activities like sports, socializing with friends, going to museums, other similar short-term "trips," and going on longer trips as part of vacation. In this respect, museum-going decision making is about the investment in time for a trip, whether a short trip to the downtown to visit a museum or shop or a long trip as part of a tourist-type experience. Very similar decision-making strategies surround both types of trips. Interestingly, both museum-going and tourism fall at the intersection of the leisure and education infrastructures, and the two activities are becoming almost inextricably bound today in the minds of both the public and policymakers. A large part of what one does while touring a new city or country is visit museums, and increasingly even the trip to the local museum has become like a mini–tourist experience within a center city area.[18] In both cases, Godbey notes, the public is seeking multiple experiences—quality time with children and education, a cultural experience and a good opportunity to shop and eat, new and fun experiences and convenience.

Museums and Tourism

Writing about the museum and the visitor experience over 20 years ago, anthropologist Nelson Graburn also saw the connections between museums and tourism.[19] Graburn felt that museums were inextricably related to tourism in many ways. Both are relatively modern phenomena that were once the exclusive province of the rich and powerful but developed in the modern era into activities for the ordinary citizen. Both are public in that they are mass phenomena that take place away from the private home, and both involve the magic of a trip, an out-of-the-ordinary experience. Graburn believed that museum-going had become part of the postindustrial reorientation to leisure and work. In this view, "leisure is displacing work from the center of modern social arrangements."[20] A corollary to this thesis is that "work should have other than economic rewards and leisure should be productive."[21] Graburn believed that leisure has become a central part of our culture; considered a necessary and fundamental aspect of life. Reinforcing this belief is the fact that over the past 150 years, work has taken a smaller and smaller fraction of the hours of one's life. For example, in Britain it has been determined that the average career length has remained remarkably constant over these many years—around 40 years. What has changed drastically is the total hours worked over this 40-year period. In 1856 the average Briton labored on the order of 124,000 hours; by 1983 that number had shrunk to 69,000 hours. The fraction of waking lifetime hours spent working declined from 50 percent to 20 percent.[22] Even if we have not achieved a society of leisure, we have gained free time, not only on a daily basis but as a percentage of our total lives.

Thus, everyone is supposed to have both productive work and productive leisure time. However, according to Graburn, "the meaning of life is to be found less in one's occupation, and more in one's leisure or life style."[23] In this view, museum-going and tourism are part of the modern search for authenticity, a search that is increasingly being conducted in the nonmundane and nonordinary. For many, home and work can no longer provide a totally satisfactory life. Life requires a greater search for meaning that can only come from experiencing events, places, peoples, and knowledge outside the normal realm. Social pressures impel us all to be aware of and to understand all parts of this complicated world, to become "well informed" and "with it." Museums are part of this process of continual experiencing and learning that is thrust upon all of us, a process that is satisfied by neither traditional passive entertainment nor schooling. More than twenty years ago Graburn was anticipating events that were only beginning to be apparent. Today, evidence of these trends is everywhere. Daily we are witnessing the transformation of the United States into a Learning Society.[24]

THE LEARNING SOCIETY

Our society is in the midst of changes as great as any in its history, changes that are affecting everyone. These changes, which are directly influencing museums, are tied to the shifting of the American economy from one that is industrially based to one that is information and knowledge based.[25] The transition of America from a goods-based to a knowledge-based economy was first noted by Princeton economist Fritz Machlup[26] and substantiated a decade later by the U.S. Department of Commerce.[27] Knowledge and information (which Machlup felt were functionally the same) are rapidly becoming the major economic products of society. Whereas in an earlier age goods were viewed as the ultimate product, today services, and increasingly experiences, are the products of choice.[28] Even goods, such as computers and pizza, are economically viable to the extent that they are marketed and delivered in a personal and information-rich manner—the computer, custom-built or in designer colors; the pizza, delivered to your home or presented in a faux-Italian restaurant, complete with Italian music, tablecloths, and even Italian-language tapes playing in the rest rooms.[29]

The engine that is driving this new transformation may be economics, but the fuel that it runs on is learning. Around the same time that futurists were beginning to herald the coming of the knowledge economy, a number of forward-thinking educators were talking about the transition of America into a Learning Society.[30] If America was to transition fully into a knowledge-based economy, an economy where information and ideas were paramount, then learning across the life span would need to become central to the society as never before. Implicit in these notions was an appreciation of the limitations of the traditional formal education system and a growing awareness of the importance of other, nonschool sources of information and education.[31]

It has often been said that people commonly perceive their times to be filled with more rapid change than usual and to assume that the pace of change is quickening. At least from the days of the sixteenth-century English Puritans, there has been a pervasive assumption that one's parents' lives were different and that one's children will have a still more uncertain and challenging time of it.[32] These ideas seem to be fundamental to American culture, as is the long-held belief in the importance of educating children. Education, it was believed, not only helped one to "make something of oneself" but also taught flexibility, adaptability, and how to survive and even prosper in a chancy world.[33] Similarly, there is a long-standing perception and reality in America that knowledge is available from many, many sources—what educational historian Lawrence Cremin called the "configurations of education."[34] Over the years, Americans have sought and received information from a wide range of both school and nonschool sources. For example, in the early nineteenth century, Americans relied upon such diverse resources as farming almanacs for tips on agriculture and the Evangelical movement for early versions of "self-help" courses.[35] By the early twentieth century, Americans could turn to a wealth of resources to gain more and better knowledge; daily newspapers were abundant, as were periodicals on everything from advertising to plumbing. Libraries, museums, and the increasingly popular encyclopedias were also available.[36] However, all of this notwithstanding, clearly something profound and different is occurring as the twenty-first century begins. The need to learn seems to be taking on a greater importance, a greater urgency, than ever before in our society. The informed citizen, not to be confused with the learned citizen, will be the archetype of the twenty-first century.

America is evolving into a Learning Society because the knowledge economy is being built upon ideas, and developing, let alone keeping up with, new ideas requires learning. It takes information and experience to generate good ideas. The best route to new information, more refined knowledge, and relevant experience is learning. Messing about with ideas above all requires openness to new information and a commitment to learning all the time. Cradle-to-grave learning has long been a goal of our society, but it is increasingly becoming both a necessity and a way of life. As our society is increasingly inundated with information, each individual needs to learn qualitatively and quantitatively better strategies for dealing with information.[37] In the twenty-first century, the learning strategy of choice for most people, most of the time, will be free-choice learning.

Free-choice learning—learning that is intrinsically motivated—is not something new; humans have always done it. However, in the new Learning Society, free-choice learning will consume more of our time and be elevated to a higher status and importance. Free-choice learning is reflective of the learning individuals do because they want to rather than because they have to. It includes watching the news on television, reading an arts magazine, surfing the Internet to find out about a health-related concern, touring a historic site while on vacation, and visiting a natural history museum to see a new exhibition on dinosaurs. All of these experiences are motivated by a desire to find out more about the world, to gain information, to enhance understanding. Whereas as recently as a generation ago, learning was perceived as a necessary but painful process that one "graduated" from sometime in adolescence, by the end of the next generation, learning will be accepted as something that everyone needs to do all the time.[38] And not only will learning be something that everyone needs to do all the time, it will be something that everyone will consciously want to do all the time.

These changes are already apparent. A Canadian research institute has been polling the public for more than a quarter-century about how Canadians spend their leisure time. The most recent survey showed that, on average, Canadians spend about eighteen hours each week engaged in some type of structured learning activity. This represented a 50 percent increase in time spent on such learning when compared with similar data collected in the 1970s. The vast majority of this learning time, nearly 95 percent, was what we are calling free-choice learning, and nearly 85 percent occurred in some kind of informal, nonschool context. Adults in the survey spent their free time learning everything from computer skills for the workplace to home renovation ideas, virtually all of it as part of some type of facilitated, nonschool learning experience.[39]

As demand for free-choice learning increases, so also do efforts to satisfy that demand. The fastest-growing segment of the leisure market is what is known as value-added tourism—ecotourism and cultural tourism.[40] Large toy companies are buying up small educational toy and software companies because, as David Miller, president of the Toy Manufacturers of America was quoted in 1998 as saying, "family entertainment and education is where the business is."[41] The newest approach in marketing major motion pictures is to develop tie-ins between the film and other information-oriented experiences—for example, the television documentary showing how the film was made or exhibitions that extend the movie-going experience. *Lost World: Jurassic Park, Star Wars, Amistad, Star Trek,* and *Titanic* are notable examples of this approach. Many of the newest shopping malls either include space for interactive learning centers or other educational experiences or are built with these as the central attraction. It is widely felt in the shopping mall industry that such additions will be critical to a mall's ability to attract and hold the customers of the future.[42] It is no coincidence that museums figure prominently in all of these scenarios. Museum exhibitions and programming are a proven way to deliver quality learning experiences to a large, diverse public.

Clearly, significant social, political, and economic forces are changing the lives of Americans. The current transformation of American society into a Learning Society is a major reason, if not the major reason, why museums are enjoying unprecedented popularity. Americans in ever growing numbers are seeking out learning-rich leisure experiences, and museums are widely perceived as places to go to satisfy this need; museums provide a good mix of enjoyment and learning.

THE LEARNING HAVES AND HAVE-NOTS

All of this seems very positive, for society and for museums. But there is also a downside. Yes, the world is dramatically changing and the United States is being transformed into a Learning Society, but not all citizens are being equally "transformed." Not everyone in the society is actively seeking free-choice learning experiences, nor are all citizens benefiting equally from the proliferation of free-choice learning resources that promise to bring increased personal freedom and financial betterment. There is a growing gap between the learning "haves" and "have-nots," a gap that ultimately affects all, including the museum community.

This gap is well illustrated by a quote from former Smithsonian Institution secretary S. Dillon Ripley. In his book, *The Sacred Grove,* Ripley describes how his philosophy of museums was established when, at the age of ten, he spent a winter in Paris:

> One of the advantages of playing in the Tuileries Gardens as a child was that at any moment one could be riding the carousel, hoping against hope to catch the ring. The next instant one might be off wandering the paths among the chestnuts and the plane trees, looking for the old woman who sold gaufres, those wonderful hot wafer-thin, wafflelike creations dusted over with powdered sugar. A third instant in time, and there was the Punch and Judy show, mirror of life, now comic, now sad. Another moment and one could wander into one of the galleries of the Louvre. . . . Then out to the garden again where there was a patch of sand in a corner to build sand castles. Then back to the Louvre to wander through the Grand Gallery.[43]

From this experience Ripley derived the philosophy that the learning environment of the museum and the world of fun and games should be seamless, that the individual should be able to move freely and naturally between the two. However, as museum social observer Tony Bennett notes, this was no doubt true for a privileged individual like Ripley, as it is for the millions of others today who enjoy the benefits offered by the Learning Society. But for Bennett himself as a child and many others today, these possibilities do not apply equally.[44]

Speaking directly to this point, museum educator David Anderson states in the United Kingdom's recent museum policy book, *A Common Wealth: Museums in the Learning Age:*

> In 1944, Beveridge identified five great evils—the giants of want, idleness, ignorance, squalor and disease—that society must overcome. Today we might add a sixth, cultural exclusion, which existed fifty years ago, and which continues to deprive many people of the opportunity to participate actively and creatively in their communities. Our society, while generally more affluent, has also become more atomised and more sharply divided. The last two decades have seen the emergence of a 'second nation', a substantial minority which includes a disproportionate number of young people and adults whose lives are blighted by recurrent unemployment, poor housing, poor health and drug-related crime. One in three children now lives in

poverty and in consequence suffers a significant educational disadvantage from birth. These divisions are reflected in museum audiences.[45]

Anderson goes on to say that fifty years ago cultural exclusion may not have been perceived by policymakers as problematic, but today it is a serious societal ill. The chasm between the learning/cultural haves and have-nots appears to be growing daily and rapidly. The causes of this division are self-perpetuating and fed by a positive feedback loop—well-informed and knowledgeable individuals actively seek out more information and resources and become even more well informed and knowledgeable, while the less well informed and knowledgeable individuals opt not to inform themselves and fall further behind. The time to reverse this trend is now. Museums can and should work proactively on the problem, and many already are doing so. But efforts to focus on the have-nots are challenging and time consuming, draining resources from efforts to attract and maintain current audience levels.

Museums are increasingly faced with the challenge of simultaneously competing for the time and attention of two very different communities of learners. They are competing for the learning-oriented leisure time and attention of the haves, individuals with money, commitment, and a long history of supporting museums. These are individuals who are being driven to divide their limited leisure time among an increasingly crowded and competitive field of players. At the same time, museums are working to generate demand for learning among a large, disenfranchised, often cynical have-not community. This is a community that generally has little disposable income, relatively little commitment to what museums traditionally offer, and little or no history of supporting museums. The needs and strategies to compete for these two groups grow increasingly disparate, and the museum's time and resources grow increasingly fragmented. There is no easy way out of this bind; both groups are essential to the long-term survival of the museum community; each requires and deserves ever more attention and commitment. The only solace we can offer is that a better understanding of the nature of how and why people choose to learn or not to learn in museums will be helpful as museums continue to transform themselves in the twenty-first century.

KEY POINTS

- The explosive growth in museum visitation cannot be explained merely by changes in museum practice. The reasons for this growth can be largely attributed to fundamental changes in the leisure behavior patterns of Americans, to changes in the very essence of what it means to be a citizen in the twenty-first century, and to changes in the role museums play in American society as a whole.

- Leisure has become a central part of our culture, considered a necessary and fundamental aspect of life. Increasingly, though, leisure has become dominated by issues of time. Time is replacing money as the most valued leisure resource—the one for which demand has increased the most relative to supply. Museum-going has always been about time rather than money.

- Society is in the midst of changes as great as any in history, changes that are directly influencing museums. As the economy shifts from one that is industrially based to one that is information and knowledge based, America and the rest of the world are transitioning into a Learning Society. Learning across the life span, in particular free-choice learning, is becoming fundamental as never before.

- Americans now spend more time and money on leisure and recreation than they do on food or housing. The fastest-growing segment of the leisure market is what is known as value-added tourism—ecotourism and cultural tourism—a niche into which museums fit. Museums are currently riding a crest of unprecedented popularity driven by the new Learning Society. Americans in ever growing numbers are seeking out museums because they are widely perceived to be good places to go to satisfy the desire for high-quality, enjoyable learning experiences.

- As society is transformed into the Learning Society, not all citizens are equally benefiting. There is a growing gap between the learning "haves" and "have-nots," a gap that ultimately affects all in society, including the museum community.

NOTES

1. Trescott 1998; Lusaka and Strand 1998; Lowry 1999.
2. Roberts 1997; Pitman 1999.
3. Foucault 1970; Bennett 1995; Karp and Levine 1991.
4. Hooper-Greenhill 1994, 3.
5. Schwarzer 1999.
6. Godbey in press; Gershuny 1992.
7. Godbey in press.
8. Godbey in press.

9. Linder 1969.
10. Schwarzer 1999.
11. Godbey 1989, in press.
12. Schwarzer 1999.
13. See, e.g., President's Commission on Americans Outdoors 1986.
14. Szalai 1972.
15. Godbey in press.
16. Falk 1983.
17. Robinson and Godbey 1997.
18. Larson 1997.
19. Graburn 1977.
20. MacCannell 1976, 7.
21. MacCannell 1976, 7.
22. MacCannell 1976.
23. Graburn 1977, 10.
24. Falk 1998, 1999b.
25. Dizard 1982.
26. Machlup 1962.
27. U.S. Department of Commerce 1977.
28. Pine and Gilmore 1999.
29. Pine and Gilmore 1999.
30. E.g., Christoffel 1978; Sakata 1975.
31. Cf. Hilton 1981.
32. Clifford 1981.
33. Clifford 1981.
34. Cremin 1980.
35. Cremin 1980.
36. Harris 1979.
37. Shenk 1997.
38. Long 1983.
39. Lewington 1998.
40. Tribe 1995; Robinson and Godbey 1997; Minic 1997.
41. Leibovich and Stoughton 1998, D1.
42. Haggerty 1997; Milner 1997.
43. Ripley 1978, 140.
44. Bennett 1995.
45. Anderson 1999, 13.

12

The Future of Museums

Prevent trouble before it arises.
Put things in order before they exist.
The giant pine tree grows from a tiny sprout.
The journey of a thousand miles starts from beneath your feet.
—Lao-tzu, *Tao Te Ching*

As mentioned earlier, both the number of visits to museums and the number of visitors have grown tremendously in the past twenty to thirty years. It is unlikely that these trends will reverse anytime soon. We have argued that this change suggests a fundamental shift in the values and priorities of the public relative to museums, a shift in the public's perceptions of the role museums can play in their lives. This shift is part of the transition of the United States and other parts of the world into a Learning Society. The museum community as a whole, some sectors willingly and others grudgingly, has responded to this shift in public perception and currently justifies and boldly promotes itself as a bedrock member of the learning community.[1] This book is also a response to this movement. We have attempted to describe how people learn in museums, why people learn in museums, where and with whom people learn in museums, and ultimately, what people learn in museums. Finally, we need to look at the present, suggest where to go from here, and analyze what lies ahead for a museum community focused upon learning. Borrowing a term from the business community, this chapter can be viewed as a SWOT analysis (strengths, weaknesses, opportunities, and threats). Some of what we'll present here has already been discussed in other parts of this book but warrants repeating.

STRENGTHS

Currently museums are popular, respected, and well loved. There are few institutions in America that enjoy such highly favorable ratings.[2] Museums, as a whole, are experiencing unprecedented rates of visitation and now rank as one of the most popular out-of-home leisure destinations.[3] At present, museums are benefiting from what systems thinkers call a positive feedback cycle—popularity results in good press and positive word of mouth, which results in greater popularity, which results in more good press and positive word-of-mouth, which results in greater popularity, and so on. Each year the cycle reinforces itself; the result is ever larger audiences and ever larger receipts from the gate.

Donors and sponsors like this popularity. Everyone likes to back a winner. Not only are museums enjoying record attendance, they are also growing. They are growing in number: in the decade from 1980 to 1990, the number of museums nearly doubled.[4] In addition, existing museums are expanding at unprecedented rates.[5] It seems that nearly every museum in the country recently had, currently has, or is presently planning a capital campaign. And amazingly enough, most have had relatively little difficulty attracting the funds to fulfill these campaigns. Overwhelmingly, these funds are being used to build new exhibition galleries, auditoriums, theaters, and classroom space. The demands of an ever expanding public have required constant upgrading of exhibitions, more and better programming, and the development of outreach efforts such as web sites, brochures, videos, and even museum-related merchandise. The free-choice learning business is going very well for museums. And like any successful enterprise, the museum community has responded by investing in both infrastructure and product.

Once, a hundred or so years ago, museums were major landmarks, proud symbols of a community's affluence and culture. For many years, though, few new museums were built, and those that were often got shoehorned into whatever existing building was available. Today, museums again are the pride of the community.[6] The new J. Paul Getty Center for the Arts and the California Science Center in Los Angeles; the Rock and Roll Hall of Fame and the Great Lakes Science Center in Cleveland; the National Aquarium, the Maryland Science Center, and Port Discovery Children's Museum in Baltimore are just a few examples of key architectural developments in cities seeking to make both a cultural and economic statement.

Tourism is the number one industry in the world, and cultural and ecological tourism are the fastest-growing segments of this vast market.[7]

Museums, nature preserves, zoos, aquariums, and all the permutations of the industry are the cornerstone of these new value-added tourist efforts.[8] Cities and towns have come to appreciate that a thriving museum community translates into real dollars for the rest of the local economy. Museums are enjoying the support of the political and business communities in ways that were only dreamed about twenty years ago. Whereas museums have always been considered important parts of the community, today they are considered to be vital parts of the community.[9]

As well they should be, given that (a) free-choice learning is hot, and (b) museums have been specializing in this type of learning for a long time, over a century or more. In the public's mind, museums are synonymous with leisure-oriented learning. Museums not only do it, by and large they do it well. Museums have the real objects, the stories behind the objects, and the means to deliver meaningful and authentic experiences to a large audience, in many cases facilitating inquiry through direct, hands-on experiences. The basic tools of museums, exhibitions and programming, have proven to be successful educational strategies, and they continue to be both enjoyable and engaging devices for presenting experiences. Supplemented by web sites, print, and film, museums have proven capable of delivering what the public wants in a form the public finds desirable. As the public's thirst for knowledge has grown, museums have responded by developing more and better methods for delivering the information and experiences people desire.

Not only have exhibitions increased in number, arguably they have increased in quality as well. In part owing to the constantly improving technology and art of exhibition development, and in part owing to a greater focus on the visitor and the utilization of various evaluation procedures, exhibitions and other programs more and more are meeting the needs of a larger, more diverse public. The collective wisdom of the museum community is being shared through publications and meetings, with the result that improvements in exhibition and program design spread quickly and efficiently through the community. By and large, museums are staffed by bright, energetic, and committed staff.

The community is also striving to become more professional. Memberships in all professional organizations are rising, including, for example, the American Association of Museums, the Association of Science-Technology Centers, the American Association of State and Local History, the Association of Zoos and Aquariums, and the American Association of Botanical Gardens and Arboretums.[10] Meetings are larger and better attended.[11] Exhibition halls are larger and have more vendors.[12] Publications have expanded and enjoy greater readership.[13] All of these

are indications of a growth industry. Also positive is the growing awareness that the different types of institutions represented by these organizations have more in common than not. It was not too many years ago
that these organizations saw each other as unrelated or at best vaguely
related. Increasingly, they see each other as part of a larger whole and
thus are opening the door to serious collaboration and cooperation.

A spirit of collaboration is sweeping the museum community, and a
growing number of museums find themselves involved with partnerships
with other cultural and educational institutions, particularly the schools.[14]
All but a very few museums today have developed some kind of partnership with their local schools.[15] In some cases, museums have totally
taken over the responsibility for public education by forming charter
schools or by creating museum schools. The Henry Ford Museum and
Greenfield Village in Michigan administers a charter high school, as does
the Museum of Northern Arizona, while the St. Louis Science Center, the
San Diego Children's Museum, and the Carter House Natural Science
Museum in Redding, California, administer charter elementary schools. A
coalition of New York City museums, in collaboration with the New York
City schools, runs the New York City Museum School for children in
grades 6 through 10. In each case the lead institution is a museum (or consortium of museums), and in each case hands-on, object-based, inquiry
learning is at the heart of the curriculum. Other institutions have taken a
different tack and have become fundamentally involved in statewide
school-reform efforts; notable examples include the Pacific Science Center
in Washington, the Exploratorium in California, the Franklin Institute Science Museum in Philadelphia, and the Fort Worth Museum of Science
and History in Texas.[16]

Partnerships have not been limited to schools. Museums and libraries
across the country are also forming partnerships; notable examples include
a Brooklyn, New York, web site collaboration between the Brooklyn Children's Museum, the Brooklyn Museum of Art, and the Brooklyn Public
Library; in collaboration with the Houston Public Library, the Children's
Museum of Houston has opened the Library for Early Childhood at its
facility; and libraries and museums across five western states have entered
into a collaboration, the Five State American Indian Project, that brings
together into a single network the resources of archives, libraries, and
museums across Colorado, Nevada, Arizona, New Mexico, and Utah so
that Indian tribes can better collaborate and share technical, training, and
funding resources across the region.[17] In addition, museums are forming
collaborations with hospitals, businesses and business associations, and
local government.[18] All of these efforts are indicative of institutions becom-

ing ever more integrated with, and integral to, their communities.

Last, but not least, the core strength of the museum community lies in the knowledge and collections museums possess. In an information age, the holder of the information is an important player. Others, it could be argued, are superior to museums at information delivery, but they depend upon the museum for the raw material, the ultimate authenticity and authority of understanding and knowledge. Collectively, these are significant strengths and provide a solid foundation for the future.

WEAKNESSES

However, not everything is wonderful in museum land. Despite rising popularity overall, not all institutions have enjoyed increasing attendance, and even those who have, have found that it takes more and more effort to maintain, let alone expand, their audience base. Popularity comes at a cost. Once you have tasted success, there is a need and desire to remain successful. For museums that means constant pressure to upgrade, change, and rotate exhibitions. Exhibition development is expensive. State-of-the-art exhibitions, particularly those that include technology, are expensive. Front-end, formative, remedial, and summative evaluation are important parts of the design process these days,[19] but they also add cost. However, if a museum wants to attract new audiences, if it is committed to delivering quality learning experiences, and if it wants to ensure that audiences come back again and again, it must continually invest in new and improved exhibitions and programs. The buzzword of the day is sustainability.

For nonprofit institutions, raising capital is a challenging task. Unlike the for-profit world, for nonprofits it is often difficult to secure bank loans, impossible to raise capital by selling shares of the company, and nearly impossible to generate venture capital. Historically, nonprofits have depended upon either public support or private donations. Public monies in support of museums have been declining, as have monies from private donors, although there are indications that this trend is reversing, in part owing to an expanding economy and a booming stock market. Most museums have turned to earned income from the gate, gift shops, magazines, and large-format films. As audiences have swelled, so has earned income. But it costs money to make money. Generating earned income requires considerable expenditures to produce the items for sale and to market them in an increasingly competitive marketplace. Again, as compared to the corporate world, the capital available to museums to spend on marketing is minuscule. Since the overriding purpose of the museum is not sales, a relatively small percentage of total budget has traditionally been allocated to marketing.

An alternative strategy is to raise money through foundation giving, either private or public, in support of exhibitions and programs. This strategy, too, has significant hidden costs. The first is the infrastructure necessary to compete for these monies in a competitive grant market-place; the other is marketing. Corporate support of exhibitions and programs has increased over the past twenty or so years,[20] but these monies come with significant strings attached, not the least of which is pressure to ensure maximum exposure to the largest possible audience.[21] Even public monies come with a requirement for expanded and broadened audience. Thus, museums find themselves committed to developing ever more costly exhibitions and programs, with the requirement for ever more costly marketing, while investing ever more money in the fund-raising infrastructure necessary to secure these funds, all in an increasingly tight financial market.

One solution to this conundrum has been the creation of traveling exhibitions. These provide built-in marketing opportunities, are easier to attract funding for than permanent exhibitions, and are great at generating and expanding audience. Most museums attempt to bring in at least one and sometimes several traveling exhibitions each year, the more spectacular the better. As a result, many institutions are now on the "blockbuster" treadmill. The museum offers a blockbuster traveling exhibition that brings in large audiences, but then that audience expects another blockbuster or comparable program before it will return.[22] So the museum must offer another blockbuster exhibition to maintain its audience. Each new blockbuster requires greater and greater resources to produce, since the easy ones were created first. Thus, the museum finds itself in a ratcheted situation where there is no going back, only forward.

As the public comes to look more and more to museums to provide quality free-choice learning experiences, it will, inevitably, become more discriminating. In general, the public expects museums to have higher standards than theme parks, to maintain intellectual integrity and accuracy, and to create consistently high-quality learning experiences. The fact that learning is consistently found to occur in and from museums does not mean that museums always maximally facilitate learning. Along with data supporting learning in museums is considerable data showing that the quality and extent of museum learning varies considerably across exhibitions, programs, and institutions.[23] To remain successful in an increasingly competitive marketplace, museums will have to become even better purveyors of free-choice learning. Museums have a tremendous head start in understanding how to provide enjoyable and meaningful learning experiences to the public, but this head start will quickly erode if real progress is not made in perfecting the technology of developing exhibitions and programming.

Understanding learning in general and the learning that occurs from museums in particular will become as fundamental to the long-term survival of museums as it will to all other parts of the educational infrastructure. As the marketplace matures and develops, museums will find it necessary to invest money in learning how to develop and refine the products they offer. Despite a growing number of museum studies programs and the existence of academics and graduate students in other programs interested in museum-based learning, there is not a single U.S. university doctoral-level program dedicated specifically to museum learning and research.[24] By contrast, there are hundreds of doctoral programs for studying learning in laboratory or school settings, and there are even doctoral programs in educational technology and media. The lack of such an infrastructure for museum learning—not just academic programs, but publications, investigators, and financial support as well—at present is a significant weakness. It is in the vested interest of the entire museum community to pool resources and prestige to foster such a research and development effort since no institution is likely to be able to afford to do so singlehandedly; nor will a single institution be able to support the infrastructure necessary to do it effectively. Given the lag time required in converting R&D efforts into useful products, the time to begin this process is clearly now.

In the absence of a deep and widely shared understanding of how people learn from museums, museums are left on their own to figure out how and what to present to the public. As the preceding chapters have attempted to demonstrate, a narrowly focused and limited view of the visitor learning experience has historically constrained documentation of the learning that occurs in museums. This limited view also has affected efforts to raise support for museums and, ultimately, has limited the impact that museums as institutions have had upon the larger society.[25] Museums need to be understood and promoted as integral parts of a society-wide learning infrastructure. Just as the economic health of a nation depends on the strength of its physical infrastructure, so too does the scientific and educational literacy of the nation depend on its educational infrastructure.[26] This infrastructure should be viewed as an interwoven network of educational, social, and cultural resources, of which museums are a vital component.

The public regularly and systematically derives its understanding of the world from many sources that work synergistically to affect what the public does and does not know. Consequently, museum professionals, be they administrators, curators, educators, designers, or evaluators, need to stop treating the museum experience as if it were some kind of isolated, singular event. The learning landscape is becoming increasingly complex and interdependent, but the actions of many in the museum community would suggest that they have neither an appreciation for this complexity nor strategies for accommodating it. The fact that most museum administrators, practitioners, and evaluators continue to limit their view of, and concerns about, learning to what transpires within the four walls of their institution is a significant weakness.

OPPORTUNITIES

The crisis in public education presents museums with an opportunity to take a leadership role in affecting quality learning practices. As mentioned, most American museums have already forged some kind of collaboration with schools, particularly at the precollege level, but in many cases at the postsecondary level as well. But unlike previously, when museums could only hope to be seen as amusing diversions for children, a place to give them a break from the day-to-day routine, museums can and should now demand to be equal partners with schools in the educational enterprise. Already many museums—science, art, and history—run extensive teacher education programs, particularly in inquiry, object-based, and hands-on learning.[27] Despite a drop-off during the 1980s due to the combination of the high cost of buses and the "back to basics" movement in the schools, school field trips are again becoming popular. More and more, museums are developing multiple-visit programs to ensure greater educational impact and to build longer-term relationships with both students and teachers. Those in formal education are gaining an increased awareness, catalyzed in part by the writings of noted educational psychologist Howard Gardner, of how effective and motivating museum-based learning is.[28] Consequently, the knowledge of how such learning can be facilitated, and hopefully also of why it is so effective, becomes a salable commodity. The educational expertise of the museum community, rather than merely its collections, might yet prove to be a tremendously valuable possession.

In the long run, though, schools may not be the most natural and profitable organizations for museums to partner with, given the very different cultures and realities of free-choice and compulsory learning. In our opinion, the real opportunity for museums lies in capitalizing on the rapidly expanding public demand for quality leisure-time free-choice learning experiences. Collaborations with other organizations working in the free-choice learning domain may prove increasingly beneficial for museums, for political, economic, and educational reasons. The public already utilizes the print and broadcast media, community-based organizations, libraries, and the Internet as natural extensions of museum learning. The converse is also true; people use museums to extend and reinforce information learned from other sources. Building educational networks and bridges between these various outlets would do much to extend and reinforce them individually and collectively.

Beyond the educational realm, there are political and economic reasons for forging such collaborations. Although it can be argued that most people learn most of what they know outside school, most of the public money for education goes to the schools. By building a coalition of free-choice learning organizations that includes museums, libraries, print and broadcast media, the Internet, and community-based organizations, a powerful lobbying force for redistributing public education monies could be created. Individually, these organizations have had little ability to compete with the powerful school education lobby; collectively they would have a much a greater chance of success.

In terms of the specific delivery of information, museums have unprecedented opportunities afforded by distance learning technologies, particularly video conferencing and the Internet via the World Wide Web. Because of their collections and their inherent immobility, museums have been severely limited geographically. Located primarily in city centers, physical museums have been left behind as the American population increasingly shifts to the suburbs. However, new distance learning technologies provide an opportunity for museums to reach, not just the suburbanites surrounding their urban cores, but new audiences locally, regionally, nationally, and worldwide. Several museums have been actively exploring video conferencing. Notable examples include the Exploratorium, the Liberty Science Center, the California Science Center, Colonial Williamsburg, the Louisville Science Center, the Children's Museum of Indianapolis, and the Smithsonian Institution's National Museum of American History and National Museum of Natural History. With the exception of the Exploratorium, which has been using video conferencing as a way to expand "casual" visitor populations,[29] virtually all video conferencing efforts to date have been focused on creating virtual field trips for school groups, but the potential of the technology lies beyond the classroom. Although only a relatively few institutions have experimented with video conferencing, virtually every major museum, as well as most smaller institutions, has taken the plunge into the World Wide Web. This technology has the potential to bring a museum's collections and accompanying stories to orders of magnitude larger audiences over the entire globe. Both of these technologies are still in their infancy, but both promise to revolutionize museum practice and priorities.

The diversification of knowledge and collections to be more culturally inclusive also represents a tremendous opportunity for museums. Over the past generation, museums have made considerable efforts to broaden their intellectual and material cultural base to include the contributions of historically underrepresented populations. Efforts have been made to understand the art, history, and culture of African Americans, Asians, Native Americans, Hispanics, and other minority racial/ethnic populations; also included have been the contributions of women, the working class, the poor, and other traditionally disenfranchised populations. In addition, important strides have been made to ensure that those who work within the museum community reflect the cultural and ethnic diversity of the broader society. The result is not only a deeper and richer intellectual understanding of all peoples and their contributions to the society's economic, political, social, and intellectual development but also a significant broadening of opportunities to be truly inclusive of the communities that museums strive to serve. This significant shift in intellectual and cultural priorities opens the door to meaningful dialogue and partnership with all audiences and organizations in the community, many of which were historically uninvolved and largely uninterested in the future of the museum community.

In a similar vein, the aging of America represents another opportunity. Currently, museums serve relatively small numbers of seniors.[30] Over the next couple of decades, older adults will become a greater percentage of the population,[31] but they will not be like past generations of older adults.[32] The aging baby boomers will be better educated, healthier, more affluent, and more adventuresome than their predecessors.[33] Collectively, this population will represent an important, and as yet underexploited, audience for museums.

THREATS

As is often the case, the events that create opportunities are also the events that create threats. The world of education is rapidly changing. Notions of where, when, and from whom to receive one's learning are changing in profound ways. Once the answer to all of the above questions was simple, it was school, but not so today. The historical boundaries and definitions that separated "formal" from "informal" educational settings are becoming increasingly blurred and counterproductive; this is true both for the practitioners who work in these settings and for the learners who use them. Learning in the twenty-first century will be too fundamental to society to narrowly pigeonhole where and when it should occur and who should be responsible for ensuring that it happens. In the twenty-first century, learning will become truly lifelong and increasingly dominated by free-choice, as opposed to compulsory, experiences. Accordingly, the settings for that learning will become more and more multifarious. Museums will not be alone in aggressively seeking to serve a larger share of the learning needs of the public, because it is not only the boundaries between formal and informal that are blurring but also the boundaries between education and entertainment.[34]

As these traditional boundaries disintegrate, there will be more and more competitors vying to provide learning services. Educational offerings will become big business. Take, for example, the infamous tycoon Michael Milken's recently formed company, Knowledge Universe. Knowledge Universe, with over a billion dollars in revenues after only a year or two of existence, is a for-profit education business that is involved in everything from preschools to CD-ROM tutorials to executive training and continuing education for retirees.[35] Learning, broadly defined, will become the major product of the twenty-first century. In order for museums to remain important players in the Learning Society marketplace, they, like schools, libraries, and other established educational institutions, will have to get even better at facilitating learning, or some enterprising, likely for-profit alternative such as Milken's will replace them.

What has historically been the realm of the nonprofit world will increasingly become the realm of free enterprise. Already, Disney offers seminars and weekend learning excursions. Disney is building children's museums not just for others but also for themselves. And Disney's latest major theme park, Animal Kingdom, is by any definition a zoo. Like Marine World, Sesame Street Place, and Discovery Zone before it, Animal Kingdom is just the beginning of a trend to capitalize on a proven revenue generator, free-choice learning.[36] Competing with the capital (which includes the funds to buy collections) and marketing clout of the likes of a Disney or Discovery will present major challenges to the traditionally nonprofit museum community.

Similarly, many museums, particularly science museums, have invested heavily in large-format theaters such as IMAX as a device to bring in audience and generate revenue. For more than a decade, the museum community has had a virtual monopoly on this technology, and it has proven extremely profitable. However, the migration of large-format theaters into shopping malls and other for-profit venues is already beginning. How will the museum community compete against these venues? Will the market become glutted, from the standpoint both of the number of screens and of film quality?

Speaking of shopping malls, if Pine and Gilmore's prognostication is correct, shopping malls and other similar venues will become more and more museum-like.[37] In the Experience Economy they prophesy, shopping malls and even hotels will incorporate experience-based museums. Will the public be capable of, or even interested in, discriminating between a "real" museum and the new breed of "commercial" museums that will spring up? These establishments will not only proliferate but also will charge considerably more for admission, perhaps an order of magnitude more, than museums currently charge.

Threats will come not only from the for-profit sector. Other nonprofit organizations will also be competing for a piece of the public education pie. Schools, for example, may not always be staggering as they are now. Schools, both public and private, remain the financial giants in the education world. As the experience of General Motors, Xerox, AT&T, and IBM in the business world suggests, it is not wise to rule out a giant in the future, even though it may seem on the verge of collapse now. If, and probably more accurately when, schools finally accept the inevitable and reform their practices, they will be a force to be reckoned with. They will greedily snap up any and every good idea they can find, including the museum concept. Don't be surprised to see future public schools built around museums—museums owned and run by the school system, not some independent museum nonprofit. Other nonprofits also will come to more closely resemble museums. More and more libraries are mounting exhibitions and even opening gift shops. Public television stations have stores and, increasingly, exhibition efforts as well. Soon, it might be hard to figure out what exactly distinguishes a museum from any other educational organization.

Even other museums potentially pose a threat. Large, well-financed museums like the Smithsonian Institution and the Exploratorium are experimenting with creating "franchise-like" spin-off institutions in other cities. Simultaneously, the 1980s Wall Street mania of mergers and acquisitions is beginning to hit the museum community. The Boston-based

Computer Museum was recently acquired by the Museum of Science, Boston, and the financially ailing Baltimore City Life Museums were acquired by the Maryland Historical Society. Will this be the wave of the future? Will smaller organizations be able to survive increasing competition from bigger organizations? Will bigger organizations begin systematically acquiring smaller organizations in the name of efficiency?

Soon distinguishing itself from its imitators may be the least of a museum's problems. The museum's objects themselves may become so widely available that no one will bother to visit a museum, real or otherwise. The explosion of the virtual world, particularly the World Wide Web, has many in the museum community anxious, if not downright spooked. What will happen to museums if anyone, anywhere, can access a museum's collections? If someone can visit a virtual museum exhibition, will anyone come to see a real one? Although these are legitimate questions, and, for some, the answer may be that the virtual world will suffice, the best guess at the moment—and it can only be that—is that virtuality will never replace reality. In other words, although people might be thrilled to visit a museum web site and view objects through the electronic medium, our guess, as well as that of others more informed than us, is that if given the opportunity, most people will readily choose the real experience every time.[38] The future lies in the blending, not the separation, of the virtual and the real world.

CONCLUSIONS

The next several decades will be exciting times for all involved in the educational enterprise, particularly in the area of free-choice learning. Currently, museums are riding high on the swelling wave of public interest in, and commitment to, free-choice learning. Museums' ability to sustain and build upon their current popularity will depend on their ability to define their niche and capitalize on the public's shifting values, preferences, needs, and priorities relative to learning. The future of museums promises to be bright, but how bright depends upon the willingness of the museum community to fully embrace and proactively respond to the profound changes occurring in the larger society.

As a community, museums need to take full advantage of their individual and collective strengths. The museum community has a head start on many of its potential competitors in the free-choice learning arena. They presently enjoy a high degree of public esteem and clearly possess expertise in presenting often-complex ideas enjoyably and successfully to the public. But as is the case for any founding industry, complacency is a recipe for obsolescence. The museum community needs to build on its current knowledge base by investing in research and development to improve and refine its current educational expertise. It needs to lobby for, and help to support, a research and development infrastructure. This infrastructure is essential to the long-term health of the community, for from it will come the future leaders in the field, as well as the future breakthroughs that will help the community remain on the cutting edge of free-choice learning.

The museum community must also recognize its place in the larger educational infrastructure. Museums will need to identify and perfect their niche. They will need to continue to build partnerships and coalitions among all the members of the infrastructure. Particularly, though, museums should form alliances with other constituents of the free-choice learning community. These alliances are essential if museums are to help effect a shift in the political definition of learning, which in turn should lead to significant increases in public and private support for museums.

Museums also need to embrace and shape new technologies to their particular requirements and values. Fear of technology will not make it go away. Besides, the best guess is that the new virtual reality is unlikely to replace good old-fashioned reality anytime soon.

Finally, the challenges presented by the increasing commoditization of learning and the breakdown of traditional boundaries between education and entertainment and between the for-profit and the nonprofit world seem daunting. Still, the museum community has resources that the competition does not—authority, authenticity, and the ability to create lasting, transformational experiences. Museums' major weapons, besides history and current popularity, are their long-standing authority as honest, neutral, and informed experts and the possession of real things presented in real ways. The quickest way museums can undermine these advantages is by trying to out-Disney Disney. This approach will not succeed. It is not that museums should not be entertaining and fun, quite the contrary. Quality learning experiences that are transformational are enjoyable. Rather, museums should never compromise on authenticity, and they should never do anything that compromises their standing as neutral and knowledgeable experts. Exploring partnerships may be one avenue. The new Smithsonian Entertainment Division is working with mainstream Hollywood film studios to produce historically accurate feature films. By continuing to push the envelope in contextualizing objects, by developing new and innovative ways to present information that enable learners to readily grasp important ideas within a leisure setting, and by leading the way in the emergence of the new Transformational Economy, museums will be able to maintain their edge as premier free-choice learning venues. With hard work and a little good fortune, museums should be capable of building upon their long-term position as important educational institutions. By forging strategic partnerships with other free-choice learning institutions and by understanding their unique place within their individual community's and the nation's educational infrastructures, museums have the ability to emerge as key players in the coming Learning Society.

KEY POINTS

Strengths

- Museums are popular, respected, and well-loved.

- Museums are enjoying unprecedented financial and community support.

- Museums know how to present real objects and authoritative knowledge in enjoyable and compelling ways.

- Museums employ dedicated, collaborative, and increasingly professional staff.

- Museums' core strengths are the knowledge and collections they possess.

Weaknesses

- Museums are faced with a growing, and seemingly insatiable, demand for funds.

- Funding museums is becoming ever more challenging owing to their nonprofit nature and a growing and increasingly competitive funding marketplace.

- Museums currently lack deep and widely shared understanding of how people learn from museums.

- Museums generally suffer from a parochial and narrow view of their place within the educational infrastructure.

Opportunities

- The crisis in education created by the public's perception of the inadequacies of formal schooling creates a vacuum that museums can partially fill.

- Museums stand to benefit politically and economically by forging partnerships with other free-choice learning institutions.

- Broadening collections, expanding audiences, reaching out to historically underserved communities are great opportunities for museums.

Threats

- The rapidly changing educational-leisure world could overwhelm museums, burying institutions under a wave of competition and change.

- The nonprofit sector faces significant challenges from for-profit corporations; museums could be replaced by for-profit (and nonprofit) lookalikes.

- The rapid spread of virtual experiences, virtual collections, and virtual museums could undermine the need for real experiences, real collections, and real museums.

NOTES

1. American Association of Museums 1992.
2. Miller and Pifer 1996.
3. Lusaka and Strand 1998.
4. American Association of Museums, personal communication, September 1999.
5. Lusaka and Strand 1998.
6. Graubard 1999.
7. Tribe 1995; Robinson and Godbey 1997.
8. Larson 1997.
9. Langston 1997; Phelps 1997; Gelfeld 1997; Said 1999.
10. American Association of Museums, personal communications; Association of Science-Technology Centers, personal communications; American Association of State and Local History, personal communications; Association of Zoos and Aquariums, personal communications; American Association of Botanical Gardens and Arboretums, personal communications, September 1999.
11. American Association of Museums, personal communications; Association

of Science-Technology Centers, personal communications; American Association of State and Local History, personal communications; Association of Zoos and Aquariums, personal communications; American Association of Botanical Gardens and Arboretums, personal communications, September 1999.

12. American Association of Museums, personal communications; Association of Science-Technology Centers, personal communications; American Association of State and Local History, personal communications; Association of Zoos and Aquariums, personal communications; American Association of Botanical Gardens and Arboretums, personal communications, September 1999.

13. American Association of Museums, personal communications; Association of Science-Technology Centers, personal communications, September 1999.

14. Chesebrough 1997.

15. Chesebrough 1997.

16. Schatz and Dierking 1999.

17. Bartholow 1999.

18. Langston 1997; Phelps 1997; Gelfeld 1997.

19. Screven 1990; Crane et al. 1994.

20. Lusaka and Strand 1998.

21. Mintz 1994.

22. Mintz 1994.

23. Cf. Bitgood, Serrell, and Thompson 1994; Dierking and Falk 1994.

24. Friedman 1995; Silverman et al. 1996.

25. Muscat in press.

26. St. John and Perry 1993.

27. St. John 1991; Inverness Research Associates 1996; Schatz and Dierking 1998; Middlebrooks 1999.

28. Cf. Gardner 1991.

29. Semper 1997.

30. Doering and Bickford 1994, 1996; Falk 1998.

31. U.S. Department of Commerce 1996.

32. Foot and Stoffman 1996.

33. Krugman 1996; Foot and Stoffman 1996.

34. Mintz 1994.

35. Martin 1998.

36. Mintz 1994.

37. Pine and Gilmore 1999.

38. Anderson 1994, 1999; Ferren 1997.

References

Abrams, C., and J. H. Falk. 1995. *Art Around the Corner evaluation pilot testing.* Technical Report. Annapolis, Md.: Science Learning.

——. 1996. *Art Around the Corner: Year 2 evaluation report.* Technical report. Annapolis, Md.: Science Learning.

Abrams, C., J. H. Falk, and M. Adams. 1997. *Art Around the Corner: Year 3 evaluation report.* Technical report. Annapolis, Md.: Science Learning.

Abrams, C., D. R. Jones, and J. H. Falk. 1997. *Summative evaluation of "Points in Time" at the Senator John Heinz Pittsburgh Regional History Center.* Annapolis, Md.: Institute for Learning Innovation.

Achenbach, J. 1999. The too-much-information age. *Washington Post,* March 12. A1, A22.

Adams, G. D. 1989. The process and effects of word-of-mouth communication at a history museum. Master's thesis, Boston University.

Aggleton, J. P., ed. 1992. *The amygdala: Neurological aspects of emotion, memory, and mental dysfunction.* New York: Wiley-Liss.

Ahrentzen, S. G., M. Jue, A. Skorpanich, and G. W. Evans. 1982. School environments and stress. In *Environmental stress,* edited by G. W. Evans, 224–55. New York: Cambridge University Press.

Albjerg Graham, P. 1998. Educational dilemmas for Americans. *Daedalus* 127 (1): 233–47.

Allen, S. 2000. Froggy talk: Lenses on conversations. Paper presented as part of a paper set, Museum Learning Collaborative: Studies of Learning from Museums, at the annual meeting of the American Educational Research Association, New Orleans.

Amabile, T. M. 1983. *The social psychology of creativity.* New York: Springer-Verlag.

——. 1985. Motivation and creativity: Effects of motivational orientation on creative writers. *Journal of Personality and Social Psychology* 48: 393–97.

American Association of Museums. 1992. *Excellence and equity: Education and the public dimension of museums.* Washington, D.C.: American Association of Museums.

Amin, R., and J. H. Falk. 1998. The *World of Life* exhibition: Summative evaluation. Unpublished technical report. Annapolis, Md.: Institute for Learning Innovation.

Anderson, D. 1999. *A common wealth: Museums in the learning age.* London: Department for Culture, Media and Sport.

Anderson, D. 1999. Understanding the impact of post-visit activities on students' knowledge construction of electricity and magnetism as a result of a visit to an interactive science centre. Ph.D. diss., Queensland University of Technology. Brisbane, Australia.

Anderson, D., and K. B. Lucas. 1997. The effectiveness of orienting students to the physical features of a science museum prior to visitation. *Research in Science Education* 27(4): 485–94.

Anderson, D., K. B. Lucas, I. Ginns, and L. Dierking. In press. Development of knowledge about electricity and magnetism during a visit to a science museum and related post-visit activities. *Science Education.*

Anderson, M. L. 1994. Perils and pleasures of the virtual museum. *Museum News* 736: 37–38, 64.

———. 1999. Museums of the future: The impact of technology on museum practices. *Daedalus* 128 (3): 129–62.

Anderson, P. 1993. *The museum impact and evaluation study: Roles of affect in the museum visit and ways of assessing them.* Chicago: Museum of Science and Industry.

Anzai, Y., and T. Yokohama. 1984. Internal models in physics problem solving. *Cognition and Instruction* 1: 397–450.

Aprison, B. 1993. The National AIDS Exhibit Consortium. *Curator* 362: 88–93.

Ash, D. 2000. Life science conversations: Families building thematic understanding. Paper presented as part of a paper set, Museum Learning Collaborative: Studies of Learning from Museums, at the annual meeting of the American Educational Research Association, New Orleans.

Asher, S. R., S. L. Odden, and J. M. Gottman. 1976. *Children's friendships in school settings.* Vol. 1 of *Current topics in early childhood education,* edited by L. G. Katz, 33–61. New York: Erlbaum.

Association of Science-Technology Centers. 1998. *The 1998 yearbook of science center statistics.* Washington, D.C.: Association of Science-Technology Centers.

Ausubel, D. P., J. D. Novak, and H. Hanesian. 1978. *Educational psychology: A cognitive view.* New York: Holt, Rinehart & Winston.

Azmitia, M. 1996. Peer interactive minds: Developmental, theoretical, and methodological issues. In *Interactive minds: Life-span perspectives on the social foundation of cognition,* edited by P. Baltes and U. Staudinger. Cambridge: Cambridge University Press.

Baddeley, A. 1994. *Human memory: Theory and practice.* Hillsdale, N.J.: Erlbaum.

Balling, J. D., and E. A. Cornell. 1985. Family visitors to science-technology centers: Motivations and demographics. Grant no. SED-8112927. Washington, D.C.: National Science Foundation.

Balling, J. D., J. H. Falk, and R. A. Aronson. 1980. Pretrip orientations: An exploration of their effects on learning from a single visit field trip to a zoological park. Final report, National Science Foundation, Grant no. SED77-18913.

Bandura, A. 1964. Behavior modification through modeling procedure. In *Research in behavior modification,* edited by L. Krasner and L. Ullman. New York: Holt, Rinehart & Winston.

———. 1967. Behavioral psychotherapy. *Scientific American* 216 (9): 78–86.

———. 1977. *Social learning.* Englewood Cliffs, N.J.: Prentice Hall.

Bandura, A., and R. Walters. 1963. *Social learning and personality development.* New York: Holt, Rinehart & Winston.

Barclay, C. R. 1988. Truth and accuracy in autobiographical memory. In *Practical aspects of memory: Current research and issues,* edited by M. Greenberg, P. Morris, and R. Sykes, 1: 289–94. Chichester: John Wiley.

Barker, R. G. 1968. *Ecological psychology.* Palo Alto, Calif.: Stanford University Press.

Barker, R. G., and H. F. Wright. 1955. *Midwest and its children.* New York: Harper & Row.

Barkow, J., L. Cosmides, and J. Tooby. 1992. *The adapted mind: Evolutionary psychology and the generation of culture.* New York: Oxford University Press.

Bartholow, C. 1999. Linking up: Museums and libraries. *Museum News* 78 (2): 36–39, 58–59.

Baum, L., G. Hein, and M. Solvay. n.d. In their own words: Teen voices from YouthALIVE! Typescript.

Baum, L., and C. Hughes. 1999. Evaluating theatre programs at the Boston Museum of Science. Paper presented at the annual meeting of the Association of Science-Technology Centers, October 2–5, Tampa, Fla.

Bayley, N. 1970. Development of mental abilities. In vol. 1 of *Carmichael's manual of child psychology,* edited by P. H. Mussen, 1163–1209. New York: Wiley.

BBC Research and Consulting. 1997. New audiences/Dynamic experience research. Technical report. Denver Museum of Natural History.

Beck, G., E. L. Cooper, G. S. Habicht, and J. J. Marchalonis. 1994. Primordial immunity: Foundations for the vertebrate immune system. *Annals of the New York Academy of Sciences* 109: 712–32.

Beck, G., and G. S. Habicht. 1991. Primitive cystokines: Harbingers of vertebrate defense. *Immunology Today* 12 (3): 180–83.

———. 1996. Immunity and the invertebrates. *Scientific American* 275 (5): 60–66.

Belcher, M. 1991. *Exhibitions in museums.* Washington, D.C.: Smithsonian Institution Press.

Bennett, T. 1995. *The birth of the museum.* London: Routledge.

Benton, D. P. 1979. Intergenerational interaction in museums. Ed.D. diss., Columbia Teachers College, 1979. Abstract in *Dissertation Abstracts* 40 (4A): 2289.

Berk, L. E. 1986. Private speech: Learning out loud. *Psychology Today,* May, 34–42.

———. 1989. *Child development.* Boston: Allyn & Bacon.

Berlin, B., and P. Kay. 1969. *Basic color terms.* Berkeley and Los Angeles: University of California Press.

Berlyne, D. E. 1950. Novelty and curiosity as determinants of exploratory behaviour. *British Journal of Psychology* 41: 79–88.

Berry, J. W. 1983. Textured contexts: Systems and situations in cross-cultural psychology. In *Human assessment and cultural factors,* edited by S. H. Irvine and J. W. Berry, 117–25. Amsterdam: North Holland Press.

Bettelheim, B. 1980. Curiosity—Its applicability in a museum setting. In *Proceedings of the Children in Museums international symposium,* edited by Office of Museum Programs, 22–31. Washington, D.C.: Smithsonian Institution.

Bevlin, M. E. 1977. *Design through discovery.* 3d ed. New York: Holt, Rinehart & Winston.

Bexton, W. H., W. Heron, and T. H. Scott. 1954. Effects of decreased variation in the sensory environment. *Canadian Journal of Psychology* 8: 70–76.

Bielick, S., and D. Karns. 1998. *Still thinking about thinking: A 1997 telephone follow-up study of visitors to the Think Tank exhibition at the National Zoological Park.* Washington, D.C.: Smithsonian Institution, Institutional Studies Office.

Birney, B. 1986. A comparative study of children's perceptions and knowledge of wildlife and conservation as they relate to field trip experiences at the Los Angeles County Museum of Natural History and the Los Angeles Zoo. Ph.D. diss., University of California at Los Angeles.

Birney, R. 1982. An evaluation of visitors' experiences at the Governor's Palace, Colonial Williamsburg, Va. *Academic Psychology Bulletin* 4: 135–41.

Bitgood, S., and D. Patterson. 1993. The effects of gallery changes on visitor reading and object viewing time. *Environment and Behavior* 25 (6): 761–81.

———. 1995. Principles of exhibit design. *Visitor Behavior* 2 (1): 4–6.

Bitgood, S., and K. Richardson. 1987. Wayfinding at the Birmingham Zoo. *Visitor Behavior* 1 (4): 9.

Bitgood, S., B. Serrell, and D. Thompson. 1994. The impact of informal education on visitors to museums. In *Informal Science Learning,* edited by V. Crane et al. Dedham, Mass.: Research Communications.

Bonner, J. T. 1980. *The evolution of culture in animals.* Princeton, N.J.: Princeton University Press.

Borun, M., M. B. Chambers, and A. Cleghorn. 1996. Families are learning in science museums. *Curator* 39 (2): 123–38.

Borun, M., M. B. Chambers, J. Dritsas, and J. I. Johnson. 1997. Enhancing family learning through exhibits. *Curator* 40 (4): 279–95.

Borun, M., A. Cleghorn, and C. Garfield. 1995. Family learning in museums: A bibliographic review. *Curator* 38 (4): 262–70.

Borun, M., and J. Dritsas. 1997. Developing family-friendly exhibits. *Curator* 40 (3): 178–96.

Borun, M., J. Dritsas, J. I. Johnson, N. Peter, K. Wagner, K. Fadigan, A. Jangaard, E. Stroup, and A. Wenger. 1998. *Family learning in museums: The PISEC perspective.* Philadelphia,: Franklin Institute.

Borun, M., C. Massey, and T. Lutter. 1993. Naïve knowledge and the design of science exhibitions. *Curator* 36 (3): 201–19.

Bransford, J. 1979. *Human cognition: Learning, understanding, and remembering.* Belmont, Calif.: Wadsworth.

Brett, G. S. 1928. *Psychology ancient and modern.* London: Longmans.

Broudy, H. S. 1987. *The role of imagery in learning.* Los Angeles: Getty Center for Education in the Arts.

Brown, J. S., A. Collins, and P. Duguid. 1989. Situated cognition and the culture of learning. *Educational Researcher* 18 (1): 32–42.

Bruner, J. 1990. *Acts of meaning.* Cambridge: Harvard University Press.

———. 1996. *The culture of education.* Cambridge: Harvard University Press.

Bryan, J. H. and P. London. 1970. Altruistic behavior by children. *Psychological Bulletin* 73: 200–211.

Caine, R., and G. Caine. 1994. *Making connections: Teaching and the human brain.* Alexandria, Va.: Association for Supervision and Curriculum Development.

Calvin, W. H. 1997. *How brains think.* New York: Basic Books.

Canale, J. R. 1977. The effect of modeling and length of ownership on sharing behavior of children. *Social Behavior and Personality* 5: 187–91.

Carey, S. 1985. *Conceptual change in childhood.* Cambridge: MIT Press.

Cashdan, E. 1989. Hunters and gatherers: Economic behavior in bands. In *Economic anthropology,* edited by S. Plattner, 21–48. Stanford, Calif.: Stanford University Press.

Ceci, S. J., and M. Leichtman. 1992. Memory cognition. In *Handbook of neuropsychology,* edited by S. Segalowitz and I. Rapin, 223–49. Amsterdam: Elsevier.

Ceci, S. J., and A. Roazzi. 1994. The effects of context on cognition: Postcards from Brazil. In *Mind in context,* edited by R. J. Sternberg and R. K. Wagner, 74–101. Cambridge: Cambridge University Press.

Chadwick, J. 1998. Public utilization of museum-based WorldWideWeb sites. Ph.D. diss., University of New Mexico.

Charlesworth, W. 1979. An ethological approach to studying intelligence. *Human Development* 22: 212–16.

Chase, R. A. 1975. Museums as learning environments. *Museum News* 5: 36–43.

Cheney, D. L., and R. M. Seyfarth. 1990. *How monkeys see the world: Inside the mind of another species.* Chicago: University of Chicago Press.

Chesebrough, D. 1997. A survey of characteristics, factors, and conditions of museum partnerships. Ph.D. diss., Duquesne University.

Chi, M. T. H., N. deLeeuw, and C. LaVancher. 1994. Eliciting self-explanations improves understanding. *Cognitive Science* 18 (5): 439–77.

Chi, M. T. H., P. J. Feltovich, and R. Glaser. 1980. Categorization and representation of physics problems by novices and experts. *Cognitive Science* 5: 121–52.

Christoffel, P. 1978. *Toward a learning society: Future federal funding of learning.* Princeton, N.J.: College Board.

Churchland, P. S. 1986. *Neurophilosophy: Toward a unified science of mind-brain.* Cambridge: MIT Press.

Clifford, G. 1981. The past is prologue. In *The future of education: Policy issues and challenges,* edited by K. Cirincione-Coles. Beverly Hills, Calif.: Sage.

Coe, J. 1985. Design and perception: Making the zoo experience real. *Zoo Biology* 4: 197–208.

Cohen, R., B. Eylon, and U. Ganeil. 1983. Potential differences and current in simple electric circuits: A study of students' concepts. *American Journal of Physics* 51: 407–12.

Cohen, Y. A. 1971. The shaping of men's minds: Adaptations to the imperatives of culture. In *Anthropological perspectives on education,* edited by M. L. Wax, S. Diamond, and F. O. Gearing, 19–50. New York: Basic Books.

Cohen, M., G. Winkel, R. Olsen, and F. Wheeler. 1977. Board maps and directions signs. *Curator* 20 (2): 85–97.

Cole, M. 1975. An ethnographic psychology of cognition. In *Cross-cultural perspectives on learning*, edited by R. W. Brislin, S. Bochner, and W. J. Lonner. New York: Wiley.

Cole, M., and S. Scribner. 1974. *Culture and thought: A psychological introduction.* New York: Wiley.

Comte, A. 1855. *The positive philosophy of Auguste Comte.* Translated by Harriet Martineau. New York: Calvin Blanchard.

Confrey, J. 1990. A review of the research on student conceptions in mathematics, science, and programming. *Review of Research in Education* 16: 3–56.

Cooley, C. H. 1902. *Human nature and the social order.* New York: Scribner.

Cortazzi, M. 1993. *Narrative analysis.* Washington, D.C.: Falmer Press.

Cosmos Corp. 1998. *Learnings from the YouthALIVE! Initiative from the year 2 evaluation.* Bethesda, Md.: Cosmos Corp.

Covington, M. V. 1992. *Making the grade: A self-worth perspective on motivation and school reform.* Cambridge: Cambridge University Press.

Crane, V., H. Nicholson, M. Chen, and S. Bitgood. 1994. *Informal science learning: What the research says about television, science museums, and community-based projects.* Dedham, Mass.: Research Communications.

Cremin, L. 1980. *American education: The national experience.* New York: Harper & Row.

Crowley, K., and M. Callanan. 1998. Describing and supporting collaborative scientific thinking in parent–child interactions. *Journal of Museum Education* 23 (1): 12–17.

Crowley, K., M. Callanan, J. L. Lipson, J. Galco, K. Topping, and J. Shrager. In review. Shared scientific thinking in everyday parent–child activity.

Crowley, K., J. Galco, M. Jacobs, and S. R. Russo. 2000. Explanatoids, fossils, and family conversations. Paper presented as part of a paper set, Museum Learning Collaborative: Studies of Learning from Museums, at the annual meeting of the American Educational Research Association, New Orleans.

Crowley, K., and R. S. Siegler. In review. Explanation and generalization in young children's strategy learning.

Csikszentmihalyi, M. 1975. *Beyond boredom and anxiety.* San Francisco: Josy-Bass.

———. 1990a. *Flow: The psychology of optimal experience.* New York: HarperCollins.

———. 1990b. Literacy and intrinsic motivation. *Daedalus* 119 (2): 115–40.

———. 1993. *The evolving self.* New York: HarperCollins

———. 1995. Education for the twenty-first century. *Daedalus* 124 (4): 115–40.

Csikszentmihalyi, M., and K. Hermanson. 1995. Intrinsic motivation in museums: Why does one want to learn? In *Public institutions for personal learning,* edited by J. H. Falk and L. Dierking. Washington, D.C.: American Association of Museums.

Csikszentmihalyi, M., and J. Nakamura. 1989. The dynamics of intrinsic motivation: A study of adolescents. In *Research on motivation in education*, vol. 3, *Goals and cognitions.* New York: Academic Press.

Csikszentmihalyi, M., K. Rathunde, and S. Whalen. 1993. *Talented teenagers: The roots of success and failure.* New York: Cambridge University Press.

Damasio, A. R. 1994. *Descartes' error: Emotion, reasons, and the human brain.* New York: Avon Books.

Davis, E. M. 1997. Making history: An inquiry into how children construct the past. Ph.D. diss., University of North Carolina, Chapel Hill.

deCharms, R. 1968. *Personal causation: The internal affective determinants of behavior.* New York: Academic Press.

Deci, E. L. 1971. Effects of externally mediated rewards on intrinsic motivation. *Journal of Personality and Social Psychology* 18: 105–15.

———. 1972. Intrinsic motivation, extrinsic reinforcement, and inequity. *Journal of Personality and Social Psychology* 22: 113–20.

———. 1992. The relation of interest to the motivation of behavior: A self-determination theory perspective. In *The role of interest in learning and development,* edited by K. A. Renninger, S. Hidi, and A. Krapp. Hillsdale, N.J.: Erlbaum.

Deci, E. L., and R. M. Ryan. 1985. *Intrinsic motivation and self-determination in human behavior.* New York: Plenum.

Deci, E. L., A. J. Schwartz, L. Sheinman, and R. M. Ryan. 1981. An instrument to assess adults' orientations toward control vesus autonomy with children: Reflections on intrinsic motivation and perceived competence. *Journal of Educational Psychology* 73: 642–50.

DeLoache, J. S., and A. L. Brown. 1979. Looking for Big Bird: Studies of memory in very young children. *Quarterly Newsletter of the Laboratory of Comparative Human Cognition* 1: 53–57.

de Waal, F. B. M. 1982. *Chimpanzee politics: Power and sex among apes.* New York: Harper & Row.

de Waal, F. B. M., and L. M. Lutrell. 1988. Mechanisms of social reciprocity in three primate species: Symmetrical relationship characteristics or cognition? *Ethology and Sociobiology* 9: 101–18.

Dewey, J. 1913. *Interest and effort in education.* Boston: Riverside Press.

———. 1938. *Experience and education.* New York: Macmillan.

Diamond, J. 1980. The ethology of teaching: A perspective from the observations of families in science centers. Ph.D. diss., University of California, Berkeley, 1980. Abstract in *Dissertation Abstracts International* 40: 3510A.

———. 1986. The behavior of family groups in science museums. *Curator* 29 (2): 139–54.

———. 1999. *Practical evaluation guide: Tools for museums and other informal educational settings.* Walnut Creek, Calif.: AltaMira.

Diener, C. I., and C. S. Dweck. 1980. An analysis of learned helplessness: The process of success. *Journal of Personality and Social Psychology* 31: 674–85.

Dierking, L. D. 1987. Parent–child interactions in a free choice learning setting: An examination of attention-directing behaviors. Ph.D. diss., University of Florida.

———. 1989. What research says to museum educators about the family museum experience. *Journal of Museum Education* 14 (2): 9–11.

———. 1990. *Evaluation of the Super Week program.* Final report. Annapolis, Md.: Science Learning.

———. 1998. Interpretation as a social experience. In *Contemporary issues in heritage and environmental interpretation*, edited by K. A. Renninger, S. Hidi, and A. Krapp. London: Stationery Office.

———. 1999. *Summative evaluation of "Aliens": Pacific Science Center*. Annapolis, Md.: Institute for Learning Innovation.

Dierking, L. D., and M. Adams. 1996. *"Spirit of the Motherland" exhibition: Summative evaluation*. Annapolis, Md.: Science Learning.

Dierking, L. D., and J. H. Falk. 1994. Family behavior and learning in informal science settings: A review of the research. *Science Education* 78 (1): 57–72.

———. 1998. Audience and accessibility. In *The virtual and the real*, edited by K. A. Renninger, S. Hidi, and A. Krapp, 57–70. Washington, D.C.: American Association of Museums.

Dierking, L. D., and D. G. Holland. 1994. Getting inside visitors' heads: Utilizing interpretive carts as a mechanism for analyzing visitor conversations. In *Proceedings of the 1994 Annual Visitors Studies Conference*, edited by S. Bitgood. Jacksonville, Ala.: Center for Social Design.

Dierking, L. D., and L. M. W. Martin, eds. 1997. Special issue of *Science Education* 81 (6).

Dierking, L. D., and W. Pollock. 1998. *Questioning assumptions: An introduction to front-end studies*. Washington, D.C.: Association of Science-Technology Centers.

Dizard, W. P. 1982. *The coming information age*. New York: Longman.

Doering, Z. D., and A. Bickford. 1994. *Visits and visitors to the Smithsonian Institution: A summary of studies*. Institutional Studies Report no. 94-1. Washington, D.C.: Smithsonian Institution.

———. 1996. Visits and visitors to the Smithsonian. In *Visitor studies: Theory, research, and practice*, vol. 9, edited by M. Wells and R. Loomis. Jacksonville, Ala.: Center for Social Design.

Doering, Z. D., and A. J. Pekakirk. 1996. Questioning the entrance narrative. *Journal of Museum Education* 21 (3): 20–22.

Draper, L. 1984. Friendship and the museum experience: The interrelationship of social ties and learning. Ph.D. diss., University of California, Berkeley.

Durkheim, E. [1895] 1938. *The rules of sociological method*. Translated by F. Alcan. Reprint, New York: Free Press.

Dweck, C. S. 1986. Motivational processes affecting learning. *American Psychologist* 41: 1040–48.

Dweck, C. S., and E. S. Elliott. 1983. Achievement motivation. In *Handbook of child psychology*, vol. 4, *Socialization, personality, and social development*, edited by E. M. Hetherington, 643–91. 4th ed. New York: Wiley.

Dweck, C. S., and P. Leggett. 1988. A social-cognitive approach to motivation and personality. *Psychological Review* 95: 256–73.

Edelman, G. 1985. Neural Darwinism: Population thinking and higher brain function. In *How we know: The inner frontiers of cognitive science*, edited by M. Wells and R. Loomis, 1–30. Proceedings of Nobel Conference 20. San Francisco: Harper & Row.

———. 1987. *Neural Darwinism: The theory of group selection*. New York: Basic Books.

Egan, K. 1989. Accumulating history. *History and Theory* 22: 66–80.

Ellenbogen, K. 2000. They bump into information there: A museum-going family. Paper presented as part of a paper set, Museum Learning Collaborative: Studies of Learning from Museums, at the annual meeting of the American Educational Research Association, New Orleans.

Elliot, R., and R. Vasta. 1970. The modeling of sharing: Effects associated with vicarious reinforcement, symbolization, age, and generalization. *Journal of Experimental Child Psychology* 10: 8–15.

Epstein, J. E. 1995. School/family/community partnerships: Caring for the children we share. *Phi Delta Kappan:* 701–11.

Epstein, S. 1973. The self-concept revisited, or a theory of a theory. *American Psychologist* 28: 405–16.

Evans, G. 1980. Environment and cognition. *Psychological Bulletin* 88: 259–87.

———. 1995. Learning and the physical environment. In *Public institutions for personal learning,* edited by J. H. Falk and L. Dierking, 119–26. Washington, D.C.: American Association of Museums.

Eylon, B., and M. C. Linn. 1988. Learning and instruction: An examination of four research perspectives in science education. *Review of Educational Research* 58 (3): 251–301.

Eysenck, H. J. 1986. The theory of intelligence and the psychophysiology of cognition. In *Advances in the psychology of human intelligence,* edited by R. J. Sternberg, 3:1–34. Hillsdale, N.J.: Erlbaum.

Falk, J. H. 1976. Outdoor education: A technique for assessing student behaviors. *School Science and Mathematics* 75: 226–30.

———. 1983. The use of time as a measure of visitor behavior and exhibit effectiveness. *Roundtable Reports* 7 (4): 10–13.

———. 1988. Museum recollections. In *Visitor studies: Theory, research, and practice,* edited by S. Bitgood et al., 1: 60–65. Jacksonville, Ala.: Center for Social Design.

———. 1991. *Front-end evaluation: HIV/AIDS.* Annapolis, Md.: Science Learning.

———. 1993. *Leisure decisions influencing African American use of museums.* Washington, D.C.: American Association of Museums.

———. 1997a. Testing a museum exhibition design assumption: Effect of explicit labeling of exhibit clusters on visitor concept development. *Science Education* 81 (6): 679–88.

———. 1997b. Pushing the boundaries: Strategies for assessing long-term learning in museums. *Current Trends* (American Association of Museums) 12: 17–23.

———. 1998. Visitors: Who does, who doesn't, and why. *Museum News* 77 (2): 38–43.

———. 1999a. Museums as institutions for personal learning. *Daedalus* 128 (3): 259–75.

———. 1999b. Assessing learning in a learning society. *Informal Learning Review* no. 38: 12–15.

———. In press. Free-choice science learning: Framing the issues. In *Free-choice learning: Building the informal science education infrastructure,* edited by J. H. Falk. New York: Teachers College Press.

Falk, J. H., and R. Amin. 1998. *"World of Life": Summative evaluation for the California Science Center.* Report. Annapolis, Md.: Institute for Learning Innovation.

———. 1999. *The California Science Center whole museum study.* Technical report. Annapolis, Md.: Institute for Learning Innovation.

Falk, J. H., and J. D. Balling. 1982. The field trip milieu: Learning and behavior as a function of contextual events. *Journal of Educational Research* 76 (1): 22–28.

Falk, J. H., J. D. Balling, and J. Liversidge. 1985. *Information and agenda: Strategies for enhancing the educational value of family visits to a zoological park.* Interim Report, Scholarly Studies no. 1231S4-01. Washington, D.C.: Smithsonian Institution.

Falk, J. H., P. Brooks, and R. Amin. 1998. The Los Angeles Science Education Research Project: Quarterly report (March). Technical report, Institute for Learning Innovation, Annapolis, Md.

———. In press. The role of free-choice learning on public understanding of science: California Science Center LASER Project. In *Free-choice learning: Building the informal science education infrastructure,* edited by J. H. Falk. New York: Teachers College Press.

Falk, J. H., and L. D. Dierking. 1990. The effect of visitation frequency on long-term recollections. In *Proceedings of the Third Annual Visitor Studies Conference,* edited by S. Bitgood, 94–104. Jacksonville, Ala.: Center for Social Design.

———. 1992. *The museum experience.* Washington, D.C.: Whalesback Books.

———. 1995. *Public institutions for personal learning: Establishing a research agenda.* Washington, D.C.: American Association of Museums.

———. 1997. School field trips: Assessing their long-term impact. *Curator* 40 (3): 211–18.

———. n.d. The long-term recollections of museum professionals. Typescript.

Falk, J. H., L. D. Dierking, and D. G. Holland, 1995. "Establishing a long-term learning research agendas for museums." In *Public Institutions for Personal Learning,* edited by J. H. Falk and L. D. Dierking, 31–34. Washington, D.C.: American Association of Museums.

Falk, J. H., and D. G. Holland. 1991. *Summative evaluation of "Circa 1492: Art in the Age of Discovery" National Gallery of Art.* Annapolis, Md.: Science Learning.

———. 1993. *"What About AIDS?" traveling exhibition: Remedial evaluation.* Annapolis, Md.: Science Learning.

———. 1994. *Summative evaluation results: Visitors' use of the "American Encounters" exhibition at the National Museum of American History.* Annapolis, Md.: Science Learning.

———. 1996. Self: A pilot study in free-choice learning. Science Learning, Annapolis, Md. Typescript.

Falk, J. H., D. G. Holland, C. Abrams, and L. D. Dierking. n.d. A longitudinal study of visitor learning. Science Learning, Annapolis, Md. Typescript.

Falk, J. H., D. G. Holland, and L. D. Dierking. 1992. A study of visitor expectations and their effect on visitation, Mystic Seaport Museum. Annapolis, Md.: Museum Experience Associates.

Falk, J. H., J. J. Koran Jr., L. D. Dierking, and L. Dreblow. 1985. Predicting visitor behavior. *Curator* 28: 249–57.

Falk, J. H., J. Luke, and C. Abrams. 1996 . Woman's health: Formative evaluation as the Maryland Science Center. Report. Science Learning, Annapolis, Md.

Falk, J. H., and J. F. Lynch. 1981. The evolution of self. Typescript.

Falk, J. H., W. W. Martin, and J. D. Balling. 1978. The novel field trip phenomenon: Adjustment to novel settings interferes with task learning. *Journal of Research in Science Teaching* 15: 127–34.

Falk, J. H., T. Moussouri, and D. Coulson. 1998. The effect of visitors' agendas on museum learning. *Curator* 41(2), 106–20.

Falk, J. H., K. Phillips, and J. Boxer Johnson. 1993. Utilizing formative evaluation as a tool in facilitating public understanding of science: The *Electricity and Magnetism* exhibit as case study. In *Visitor studies: Theory, research, and practice*, vol. 6, edited by S. Bitgood. Jacksonville, Ala.: Center for Social Design.

Feher, E. 1993. Learning science with interactive exhibits. *Curator* 36 (4): 246–47.

Feher, E., and K. Rice. 1988. Shadows and anti-images: Children's conceptions of light and vision, 2. *Science Education* 72 (5): 637–49.

Feher, E., and K. Rice Meyer. 1992. Children's conceptions of color. *Journal of Research in Science Teaching* 29 (5): 505–20.

Feinberg, J., and M. Abu-Shumays. 2000. Looking through the glass: Tracing identity strands through a history museum exhibit. Paper presented as part of a paper set, Museum Learning Collaborative: Studies of Learning from Museums, at the annual meeting of the American Educational Research Association, New Orleans.

Feldman, C., J. Bruner, D. Kalmar, and B. Renderer. 1995. Plot, plight, and dramatism: Interpretation at three ages. *Human Development* 36 (6): 327–42.

Ferren, B. 1997. The future of museums: Asking the right questions. *Journal of Museum Education* 22 (1): 3–7.

Fishbein, H. D. 1976. *Evolution, development, and children's learning*. Pacific Palisades, Calif.: Goodyear.

Fishman, J. A. 1964. A systematization of the Whorfian hypothesis. In *Approaches, contexts, and problems of social psychology*, edited by G. G. Sampson, 27–43. Englewood Cliffs, N.J.: Prentice-Hall.

Fivush, R., J. Hudson, and K. Nelson. 1984. Children's long-term memory for a novel event: An exploratory study. *Merrill-Palmer Quarterly* 30 (3): 303–17.

Flavell, J. H. 1981. Monitoring social cognitive enterprises: Some thing else that may develop in the area of social cognition. In *Social cognitive development: Frontiers and possible futures*, edited by J. H. Flavell and L. Ross, 272–87. New York: Cambridge University Press.

———. 1985. *Cognitive development*. 2d ed. Englewood Cliffs, N.J.: Prentice-Hall.

Foot, D. K., and D. Stoffman. 1996. *Boom, bust, and echo: How to profit from the coming demographic shift*. Toronto: Macfarlane, Walter & Ross.

Forman, E. A., and J. Larreamendy-Joerns. 1995. Learning in the context of peer collaboration: A pluralistic perspective on goals and expertise. *Cognition and Instruction* 13: 549–64.

Foucault, M. 1970. *The order of things: An archaeology of the human sciences*. London: Tavistock.

Freeberg, D. 1989. *The power of images*. Chicago: University of Chicago Press.

Friedman, A. 1995. Creating an academic home for informal science education. *Curator* 38 (4): 214–20.

Freud, S. 1959. Inhibitions, symptoms, and anxiety. In vol. 20 of *The standard edition of the complete psychological works of Sigmund Freud.* London: Hogarth Press and Institute of Psychoanalysis.

Gallagher, W. 1993. *The power of place: How our surroundings shape our thoughts, emotions, and actions.* New York: Poseidon.

Gardner, H. 1983. *Frames of mind: The theory of multiple intelligences.* New York: Basic Books.

———. 1991. *The unschooled mind: How children think and how schools should teach.* New York: Basic Books.

Garro, L. 1986. Language, memory, and focality: A reexamination. *American Anthropologist* 88: 128–36.

Gelfeld, B. 1997. Museums building partnerships: Denver Museum of Natural History. *Museum News* 76 (3): 45–46, 67.

Gelman, R. 1978. Cognitive development. *Annual Review of Psychology* 29: 297–332.

Gentner, D., and D. R. Gentner. 1983. Flowing waters or teeming crowds: Mental models of electricity. In *Mental models,* edited by D. Gentner and A. L. Stevens, 99–129. Hillsdale, N.J.: Erlbaum.

Gerber, E. 1975. The cultural patterning of emotion in Samoa. Ph.D. diss., University of California, San Diego.

———. 1985. Rage and obligation: Samoan emotion in conflict. In *Person, self, and experience,* edited by G. White and J. Kirkpatrick. Berkeley and Los Angeles: University of California Press.

Gershuny, J. 1992. Are we running out of time? *Futures,* January/February, 1–18.

Giusti, E. 1996. *Infectious disease: Front-end study.* New York: American Museum of Natural History.

Gladwin, T. 1970. *East is a big bird.* Cambridge: Harvard University Press.

Gleason, J. B. 1973. Code switching in children's language. In *Cognitive development and the development of language,* edited by T. E. Moore. New York: Academic Press.

Godbey, G. C. 1989. Anti-leisure and public recreation policy. In *Freedom and constraint:The paradoxes of leisure,* edited by Fred Coalter. London: Routledge.

———. In press. The use of time and space in assessing the potential of free-choice learning. In *Free-choice science learning: Defining and building an infrastructure,* edited by J. H. Falk. New York: Teachers College Press.

Gore, L., M. Mahnken, J. Norstrom, and D. Walls. 1980. A profile of the visitors: The Dallas Museum of Natural History. University of Dallas. Typescript.

Gottfried, A. 1985. Academic intrinsic motivation in elementary and junior high school students. *Journal of Educational Psychology* 77: 631–45.

Graburn, N. H. 1977. The museum and the visitor experience. In *The visitor and the museum,* 5–32. Prepared for the Seventy-second Annual Conference of the American Association of Museums, Seattle.

Graubard, S. R. 1999. Preface to the issue America's Museums. *Daedalus,* 1283, v–xiv.

Gray, R., and M. Piro. 1984. The effects of prosocial modeling on young children's nurturing of a "sick" child. *Psychology and Human Development* 1: 41–46.

Greenberg, J. B. 1989. Funds of knowledge: Historical constitution, social distribution, and transmission. Paper presented at the annual meeting of the Society for Applied Anthropology, Santa Fe, N.M.

Gregg, M., and G. Leinhardt. 2000. Finding identity through the past: Student teachers at the Birmingham Civil Rights Institute. Paper presented as part of a paper set, Museum Learning Collaborative: Studies of Learning from Museums, at the annual meeting of the American Educational Research Association, New Orleans.

Griffin, J. 1998. School-museum integrated learning experiences in science: A learning journey. Ph.D. diss., University of Technology, Sydney.

Griffin, J., and L. D. Dierking. 1999. Perceptions of learning and enjoyment in informal settings. Typescript.

Griffin, J., and D. Symington. 1997. Moving from task-oriented to learning-oriented strategies on school excursions to museums. *Science Education* 816: 763–80.

Griffiths, P. E. 1997. *What emotions really are.* Chicago: Chicago University Press.

Gross, L. 1997. The impact of television on modern life and attitudes. Paper presented at the 1997 International Conference on the Public Understanding of Science and Technology, Chicago.

Guberman, S. R., K. Emo, S. Simmons, J. Taylor, and G. Sullivan. 1999. Parent–child conversations in a natural history museum. Paper presented at the annual meeting of the American Educational Research Association, Montreal.

Hagen, S. 1997. *Buddhism plain and simple.* Boston: Charles E. Tuttle.

Haggerty, M. 1997. Developers offer plans for Tariff Building: Housing, stores, museum among proposed uses. *Washington Post,* September 2, Business, p. D9.

Hall, E. T. 1969. *The hidden dimension.* Garden City, N.Y.: Doubleday.

Hansen, J. F. 1979. *Sociocultural perspectives on human learning: An introduction to educational anthropology.* Englewood Cliffs, N.J.: Prentice-Hall.

Harlow, H. F. 1954. Motivational forces underlying behavior. In *Kentucky symposium: Learning theory and clinical research,* 36–53. New York: Wiley.

Harris, N. 1979. The lamp of learning: Popular lights and shadows. In *The organization of knowledge in modern America, 1860–1920,* edited by A. Oleson and J. Voss. Baltimore: Johns Hopkins University Press.

Harter, S. 1981. A new self-report scale of intrinsic versus extrinsic orientation in the classroom: Motivational and informational components. *Developmental Psychology* 17: 300–312.

———. 1983. Developmental perspectives on the self-system. In *Handbook of child psychology,* vol. 4, *Socialization, personality and social development,* edited by E. M. Hetherington, 275–385. 4th ed. New York: Wiley.

Hayward, D. G., and M. Brydon-Miller. 1984. Spatial and conceptual aspects of orientation: Visitor experiences at an outdoor history museum. *Journal of Environmental Systems* 13 (4): 317–32.

Hedge, A. 1995. Human-factor considerations in the design of museums to optimize their impact on learning. In *Public Institutions for Personal Learning,* edited by J. H. Falk and L. D. Dierking, 105–18. Washington, D.C.: American Association of Museums.

Heider, E. 1972. Universals in color naming and memory. *Journal of Experimental Psychology* 93: 10–20.

Hein, G. E. 1998. *Learning in the museum.* London: Routledge.

Hein, G. E., and M. Alexander. 1998. *Museums, places of learning.* Washington, D.C.: American Association of Museums, Education Committee.

Henderlong, J., and S. G. Paris. 1996. Children's motivation to explore partially completed exhibits in hands-on musuems. *Contemporary Educational Psychology* 21: 111–28.

Hensel, K. 1987. Families in a museum: Interactions and conversations at displays. Ph.D. diss., Columbia University Teachers College.

Herbart, J. F. [1806] 1965. Umriss pedagogischer vorlesungen [Lectures on pedagogy]. In *Pedagogische schriften,* edited by J. F. Herbart, 2: 9–155. Düsseldorf: Kupper.

Heyman, G. D., and C. S. Dweck. 1992. Achievement goals and intrinsic motivation: Their relation and their role in adaptive motivation. *Motivation and Emotion* 16 (3): 231–47.

Hidi, S. 1990. Interest and its contribution as a mental resource for learning. *Review of Educational Research* 60: 549–71.

Hilke, D. D. 1989. The family as a learning system: An observational study of families in museums. In *Museum visits and activities for family life enrichment,* edited by B. H. Butler and M. B. Sussman. *Marriage and Family Review,* vol. 13. New York: Haworth Publishing.

Hilke, D. D., and J. D. Balling. 1985. *The family as a learning system: An observational study of family behavior in an information rich environment.* Final report. Grant no. SED-812927. Washington, D.C.: National Science Foundation.

Hilton, W. J. 1981. Lifelong learning. In *The future of education: Policy issues and challenges,* edited by K. Cirincione-Coles. Beverly Hills, Calif.: Sage.

Hilts, P. J. 1995. *Memory's ghost: The strange tale of Mr. M. and the nature of memory.* New York: Simon & Schuster.

Hiss, T. 1990. *The experience of place.* New York: Knopf.

Hobson, J. A. 1989. *Sleep.* New York: Scientific American Library; distributed by W. H. Freeman.

Hofer, M. A. 1987. Early social relationships: A psychobiologist's view. *Child Development* 58: 633–47.

Hoffman, M. L. 1981. Perspectives on the difference between understanding people and understanding things: The role of affect. In *Social cognitive development: Frontiers and possible futures,* edited by J. H. Flavell and L. Ross, 67–81. New York: Cambridge University Press.

Holland, D. G., and J. H. Falk. 1994. *"What About AIDS?" traveling exhibition: Summative evaluation.* Annapolis, Md.: Science Learning.

Hood, M. 1983. Staying away: Why people choose not to visit museums. *Museum News* 61 (4): 50–57.

Hooper-Greenhill, E. 1994. *Museums and their visitors.* London: Routledge.

Horn, A., and J. Finney. 1994. *Bay Area research report: A multi-cultural audience survey for Bay Area museums.* San Francisco: Museum Management Consultants.

Hudson, J., and K. Nelson. 1983. Effects of script structure on children's story recall. *Developmental Psychology* 19: 525–635.

Hughes, C. 1988. *Museum theatre: Communicating with visitors through drama.* Portsmouth, N.H.: Heinemann.

Inverness Research Associates. 1995. *Youth ALIVE!: A review of the program's first three years.* New York: DeWitt Wallace Reader's Digest Fund.

———. 1996. *An invisible infrastructure: Institutions of informal science education.* Vol. 1. Washington, D.C.: Association of Science-Technology Centers.

Irvine, S.H. and J. W. Berry. 1988. The abilities of mankind: A reevaluation. In *Human abilities in cultural context,* edited by R. J. Sternberg, 3–59. New York: Cambridge University Press.

Isen, A. M., K. Daubman, and J. Gorgoglione. 1987. The influence of positive affect on cognitive organization: Implications for education. In *Aptitude, learning, and instruction,* vol. 3, *Conative and affective processes,* 143–64. Hillsdale, N.J.: Erlbaum.

Iser, W. 1978. *The act of reading: A theory of aesthetic response.* Baltimore: Johns Hopkins University Press.

Jackson, G. B. 1998. *YouthALIVE! Workskills development: Making it work.* Washington, D.C.: George Washington University.

Jackson, M., and L. McClelland. 1979. Processing determinants of reading speed. *Journal of Experimental Psychology: General* 108: 151–81.

James, W. [1890] 1950. *Principles of psychology.* 2 vols. Reprint, New York: Dover.

Jensen, N. 1994. Children's perceptions of their museum experiences: A contextual perspective. *Children's Environments* 11 (4): 300–324.

Kaplan, S. 1977. Participation in the design process: A cognitive approach. In *Perspectives on environment and behavior: Theory, research, and application,* edited by D. Stokols, 221–44. New York: Plenum.

Kaplan, S., L. D. Gruppen, L. M. Leventhal, and F. Board. 1989. *The components of expertise: A cross-disciplinary review.* Technical Report 89-Nov-01. Bowling Green, Ohio: Department of Computer Science, Bowling Green State University.

Kaplan, S., and R. Kaplan. 1982. *Cognition and environment.* New York: Praeger.

Karp, I., and D. Levine. 1991. *Exhibiting cultures: The poetics and politics of museum display.* Washington, D.C.: Smithsonian Institution Press.

Katz, E., and T. Liebes. 1986. Mutual aid in the decoding of *Dallas*: Preliminary notes from a cross-cultural study. In *Television in transition,* edited by P. Drummond and R. Patterson, 187–98. London: British Film Institute.

Kay, P., and W. Kempton. 1984. What is the Sapir-Whorf hypothesis? *American Anthropologist* 86: 65–79.

Keil, F. C. 1979. *Semantic and conceptual development: An ontological perspective.* Cambridge: Harvard University Press.

Kelley, H. H. 1973. The processes of causal attribution. *American Psychologist* 28: 107–28.

Kimche, L. 1978. Science centers: A potential for learning. *Science* 199 (20): 270–73.

Koran, J. J., Jr., M. L. Koran, L. D. Dierking, and J. Foster. 1988. Using modeling to direct attention in a natural history museum. *Curator* 31 (1): 36–42.

Korn, R. 1992. *Electric space: Space Science Institute.* Alexandria, Va.: Randi Korn & Associates.

Krakauer, T. It's fun, but can it really be science? *Scientific American Explorations,* Winter, 7.

Kropf, M. B. 1989. Family visits to museums: The experience as described in the research. *Journal of Museum Education* (Spring/Summer).

Krugman, P. 1996. The aging of America. *N.Y. Times Book Review,* October 20.

Kubota, C. A., and R. G. Otstad. 1991. Effects of novelty-reducing preparation on exploratory behavior and cognitive learning in a science museum setting. *Journal of Research in Science Teaching* 28 (3): 225–34.

Labov, W. 1970. The logic of non-standard English. In *Language and poverty,* edited by F. Williams. Chicago: Markham.

Lakota, R. A. 1975. The National Museum of Natural History as a behavioral environment. Smithsonian Institution, Washington, D.C. Typescript.

Langston, B. 1997. Museums building partnerships: Bowers Museum of Cultural Art. *Museum News* 76 (3): 39–41.

Lao-tzu. 1988. *Tao te ching.* Translated by S. Mitchell. New York: Harper & Row.

Larkin, J. H. 1983. The role of problem representation in physics. In*Mental models,* edited by D. Gentner and A. L. Stevens, 75–98. Hillsdale, N.J.: Erlbaum.

Larkin, J. H., J. McDermott, D. P. Simon, and H. Simon. 1980. Expert and novice performance in solving physics problems. *Science* 208: 1335–42.

Larson, G. O. 1997. *American canvas: An arts legacy for communities.* Washington, D.C.: National Endowment for the Arts.

Lave, J. 1990. The culture of acquisition and the practice of understanding. In *Cultural psychology: Essays on comparative human development,* edited by J. W. Stigler, R. A. Shweder, and G. Herdt, 309–27. Cambridge: Cambridge University Press.

———. 1991. Situating learning in communities of practice. In *Socially shared cognition,* edited by L. B. Resnick, J. M. Levine, and S. D. Teasley, 63–82. Washington, D.C.: American Psychological Association.

Lave, J., and E. Wenger. 1991. *Situated learning: Legitimate peripheral participation.* Cambridge: Cambridge University Press.

Lebeau, R. B., P. Gyamfi, K. Wizevich, and E. Koster. In press. Supporting and documenting free-choice in informal science learning environments. In *Free-choice learning: Building the informal science education infrastructure,* edited by J. H. Falk. New York: Teachers College Press.

Lee, R., and I. Devore, eds. 1968. *Man the hunter.* Chicago: Aldine.

Leibovich, M., and S. Stoughton. 1998. When keeping up isn't child's play. *Washington Post,* December 15, Business, p. D1.

Leinhardt, G. 2000. Museum Learning Collaborative: Studies of learning from museums. Paper set presented at the annual meeting of the American Educational Research Association, New Orleans.

Leinhardt, G., and C. Tittle. 2000. Talking to oneself: Diary studies of museum experiences. Paper presented as part of a paper set, Museum Learning Collaborative: Studies of Learning from Museums, at the annual meeting of the American Educational Research Association, New Orleans.

Lepper, M. R., and D. I. Cordova. 1992. A desire to be taught: Instructional consequences of intrinsic motivation. *Motivation and Emotion* 16 (3): 187–208.

Lepper, M. R., and D. Greene. 1978. *The hidden costs of reward: New perspectives on the psychology of human motivation.* Hillsdale, N.J.: Erlbaum.

Leshowitz, B. 1989. It is time we did something about scientific illiteracy. *American Psychologist* 44: 1159–60.

Levy, R. L. 1973. *Tahitians: Mind and experience in Society Islands.* Chicago: University of Chicago Press.

———. 1985. Emotion, knowing, and culture. In *Culture theory: Essays on mind, self, and emotion,* edited by R. Shweder and R. LeVine. Cambridge: Cambridge University Press.

Lewin, K. 1951. *Field theory in social science.* Edited by D. Cartwright. New York: Harper.

Lewington, J. 1998. More Canadians pursuing informal learning, survey reveals. *Globe and Mail,* November 11, A13.

Lewis, E. L. 1991. The process of scientific knowledge acquistion of middle school students learning thermodynamics. Ph.D. diss., University of California, Berkeley.

Linder, S. 1969. *The harried leisure class.* New York: Columbia University Press.

Loftus, E. F. 1979. *Eyewitness testimony.* Cambridge: Harvard University Press.

Loftus, E. F., and W. Marburger. 1983. Since the eruption of Mount St. Helens, has anyone beaten you up? Improving the accuracy of retrospective reports with landmark events. *Memory and Cognition* 11: 114–20.

Long, H. B. 1983. *Adult and continuing education: Responding to change.* New York: Teachers College Press.

Loomis, R. J. 1987. *Museum visitor evaluation: New tool for museum management.* Nashville, Tenn.: American Association for State and Local History.

Lowry, G. D. 1999. The state of the art museum, ever changing. *New York Times,* January 10, Arts and Leisure, 1.

Lucy, J., and R. Shweder. 1979. Whorf and his critics: Linguistic and non-linguistic influences on color memory. *American Anthropologist* 81: 581–615.

Luke, J., M. Adams, C. Abrams, and J. H. Falk. 1998. *Art Around the Corner: Longitudinal evaluation report.* Annapolis, Md.: Institute for Learning Innovation.

Luke, J., K. Buchner, L. D. Dierking, and B. O'Ryan. 1999. *Creative world summative evaluation: California Science Center.* Annapolis, Md.: Institute for Learning Innovation.

Luria, A. R. 1982. *Language and cognition.* New York: Wiley.

Lusaka, J., and J. Strand. 1998. The boom—and what to do about it. *Museum News* 77 (6): 54–60.

Lutz, C. 1982. The domain of emotion words on Ifaluk. *American Ethnologist* 9: 113–28.

———. 1985. Ethnopsychology compared to what: Explaining behavior and consciousness among the Ifaluk. In *Person, self, and experience,* edited by G. White and J. Kirkpatrick. Berkeley and Los Angeles: University of California Press.

————. 1986. Emotion, thought, and estrangement: Emotion as a cultural category. *Cultural Anthropology* 1: 287–309.

MacCannell, D. 1976. *The tourist: A new theory of the leisure class.* New York: Schocken.

Macdonald, S., 1993. *Museum visiting: A science exhibition showcase.* Sociology and Social Anthropology Working Papers, no 1. Keele, Germany: Keele University.

Machlup, F. 1962. *The production and distribution of knowledge in the U.S.* Princeton, N.J.: Princeton University Press.

Maehr, M. L. 1984. Meaning and motivation: Toward a theory of personal investment. In *Research on motivation in education,* vol. 1, *Student motivation.* New York: Academic Press.

Maloney, L., and C. Hughes, eds. 1999. *Case studies in museum, zoo, and aquarium theater.* Washington, D.C.: American Association of Museums.

Mandler, J. M., M. De Forest, S. Scribner, and M. Cole. 1980. Cross-cultural invariance in story recall. *Child Development* 51: 19–26.

Mandler, J., and M. Goodman. 1982. Remembrance of things parsed: Story structure and recall. *Cognitive Psychology* 9 (1): 111–51.

Marsh, H. W., I. D. Smith, and J. Barnes. 1985. Multidimensional self-concepts: Relations with sex and academic achievement. *Journal of Educational Psychology* 77: 581–96.

Martin, J. 1998. Lifelong learning spells earnings. *Fortune,* July 6, 33–38, 78.

Martin, L. M. W., and R. F. Leary. 1996. Using narrative to introduce science concepts to diverse audiences in a science center. Paper presented at the Second Conference for Socio-Cultural Research, Geneva, Switzerland.

————. 1997. Does narrative belong in a science center? Paper presented at the annual meeting of the National Association for Research in Science Teaching. Chicago.

Martin, L. M. W., and R. Toon. In review. Narratives in a science center: Forms of interpretation and people's identities as learners.

Martin, W. W., J. H. Falk, and J. D. Balling. 1981. Environmental effects on learning: The outdoor field trip. *Science Education* 65: 301–9.

Maslow, A. 1954. *Motivation and personality.* New York: Harper & Row.

Matusov, E., and B. Rogoff. 1995. Evidence of development from people's participation in communities of learners. In *Public institutions for personal learning,* edited by J. H. Falk and L. D. Dierking, 97–104. Washington, D.C.: American Association of Museums.

McClelland, J. L., and D. E. Rumelhart, eds. 1987. *Parallel distributed processing: Explorations in the microstructure of cognition,* vol. 2. Cambridge: MIT Press.

McCombs, B. L. 1991. Motivation and lifelong learning. *Educational Psychologist* 26 (2): 117–27.

McCoy, N. 1993. Getting in touch with history. *Grapevine* (Material Culture Newsletter, Smithsonian Institution), April, 3.

McDermott, L. C. 1984. Research on conceptual understanding in mechanics. *Physics Today* 37: 24–32.

McGraw, K. O. 1978. The detrimental effects of reward on performance: A literature review and prediction model. In *The hidden costs of rewards,* edited by M. R. Lepper and D. Greene,. 33–60. Hillsdale, N.J.: Erlbaum.

McKelvey, L., J. H. Falk, A. Schreier, H. O'Mara, and J. De Prizio. 1999. *Conservation impacts study: National Aquarium in Baltimore.* Annapolis, Md.: Institute for Learning Innovation.

McLean, K. 1993. *Planning for people in museum exhibitions.* Washington, D.C.: Association of Science-Technology Centers.

McManus, P. 1987. It's the company you keep: The social determination of learning-related behavior in a science museum. *International Journal of Museum Management and Curatorship* 53: 43–50.

———. 1989. Oh yes they do: How museum visitors read labels and interact with exhibit text. *Curator* 32 (3): 174–80.

———. 1992. Topics in museums and science education. *Studies in Science Education* 20: 157–82.

———. 1993. Memories as indicators of the impact of museum visits. *Museum Management and Curatorship* 12: 367–80.

Mead, G. H. 1924/25. The genesis of the self and social control. *International Journal of Ethnoscience.* 35: 251–77.

———. 1934. *Mind, self, and society from the standpoint of a social behaviorist.* Chicago: University of Chicago Press.

Medved, M. I. 1998. Remembering exhibits at museums of art, science, and sport. Ph.D. diss., University of Toronto.

Medved, M. I., and K. Oatley. In press. Memory and science literacy: Remembering exhibits from a science centre. *International Journal of Science Education.*

Melton, A. 1972. Visitor behavior in museums: Some early research in environmental design. *Human Factors* 14 (5): 393–403.

Merriman, N. 1991. *Beyond the glass case.* Leicester, England: Leicester University Press.

Middlebrooks, S. 1999. *Preparing tomorrow's teachers: Preservice partnerships between science museums and colleges.* Washington, D.C.: Association of Science-Technology Centers.

Miles, R. S. 1986. Museum audiences. *International Journal of Museum Management and Curatorship* 5: 73–80.

Miller, G. A. 1956. The magical number seven, plus or minus two: Some limits on our capacity for processing information. *Psychological Review* 63: 81–97.

Miller, J., and L. Pifer. 1996. Science and technology: The public's attitudes and the public's understanding. In *Science and Engineering Indicators,* 7-1–7-21. Washington, D.C.: National Science Board.

Milner, B. 1997. Play centres dress up downtowns. *Globe and Mail* (Toronto), September 15, B1.

Minic, D., ed. 1997. *Tourism Works for America: 1997 report.* Washington, D.C.: Tourism Works for America Council.

Mintz, A. 1994. That's edutainment! *Museum News* 73 (6): 33–36.

Moll, L. C., and J. B. Greenberg. 1990. Creating zones of possibilities: Combining social contexts for instruction. In *Vygotsky and education,* edited by L. Moll, 319–48. Cambridge: Cambridge University Press.

Moussouri, T., 1997. Family agendas and family learning in hands-on museums. Doctoral diss., University of Leicester, Leicester, England.

Muscat, A. In press. Future directions for free-choice learning: A practitioner's view. In *Free-choice learning: Building the informal science education infrastructure,* edited by J. H. Falk. New York: Teachers College Press.

Neisser, U. 1976. *Cognition and reality: Principles and implications of cognitive psychology.* San Francisco: W. H. Freeman.

——, ed. 1982. *Memory observed: Remembering in natural contexts.* San Francisco: W. H. Freeman.

Nelson, K. 1986. *Event knowledge.* Hillsdale, N.J.: Erlbaum.

Nelson, K., and A. L. Brown. 1978. The semantic-episodic distinction in memory development. In *Memory development in children,* edited by P. A. Ornstein, 233–41. Hillsdale, N.J.: Erlbaum.

Nelson, K., and J. Gruendel. 1981. Generalized event representations: Basic building blocks of cognitive development. In *Advances in developmental psychology,* edited by M. Lamb and A. Brown, 1: 131–58. Hillsdale, N.J.: Erlbaum.

Newby, F. 1972. *Environmental impact appraisal of proposed developments in the Harney Peak Area of the Black Hills.* Pacific Southwest Forest and Range Experiment Station. Berkeley, Calif.: USDA Forest Service.

Newman, D. F, F. Griffin, and M. Cole. 1989. *The construction zone: Working for cognitive change in schools.* Cambridge: Cambridge University Press.

Nickerson, R. S., and M. J. Adams. 1979. Long-term memory for a common object. *Cognitive Psychology* 6: 93–107.

Ogbu, J. U. 1995. The influence of culture on learning and behavior. In *Public institutions for personal learning,* edited by J. H. Falk and L. D. Dierking, 79–95. Washington, D.C.: American Association of Museums.

Ogden, J. L., D. G. Lindburg, and T. L. Maple. 1993. The effects of ecologically relevant sounds on zoo visitors. *Curator* 36 (2): 147–56.

O'Keefe, J., and L. Nadel. 1978. *The hippocampus as a cognitive map.* Oxford: Clarendon Press.

Osberg, S. 1998. Shared lessons and self-discoveries: What research has taught Children's Discovery Museum. *Journal of Museum Education* 23 (1): 19–20.

Paris, S. G. 1997. Situated motivation and informal learning. *Journal of Museum Education* 22 (2 and 3): 22–27.

Paris, S. G., and D. R. Cross. 1983. Ordinary learning: Pragmatic connections among children's beliefs, motives, and actions. In *Learning in children,* edited by J. Bisanz, G. Bisanz, and R. Kail, 137–69. New York: Springer-Verlag.

Paris, S. G., and M. Mercer. 2000. Connecting museum objects with personal experiences. Paper presented as part of a paper set, Museum Learning Collaborative: Studies of Learning from Museums, at the annual meeting of the American Educational Research Association, New Orleans.

Passini, R. 1984. *Wayfinding in architecture.* New York: Van Nostrand Reinhold.

Perkins, D. N., and G. Salomon. 1989. Are cognitive skills context-bound? *Educational Researcher* 18 (1): 16–25.

Perry, D. 1989. *The creation and verification of a developmental model for the design of a museum exhibit.* Ph.D. diss., Indiana University.

Phelps, E. 1997. Museums building partnerships: Houston Museum District Association. *Museum News* 76 (3): 42–44.

Piaget, J. [1937] 1954. *The construction of reality in the child.* Reprint, New York: Basic Books.

———. 1981. *Intelligence and affectivity: Their relationship during child development.* Translated and edited by T. A. Brown and C. E. Kaegi. Annual Reviews Monograph. Palo Alto, Calif.: Annual Reviews.

Piaget, J., and B. Inhelder. 1969. *The psychology of the child.* New York: Basic Books.

Pine, B. J., II, and J. H. Gilmore. 1999. *The experience economy: Work is theatre and every business a stage.* Boston: Harvard Business School Press.

Pintrich, P., and E. DeGroot. 1990. Motivational and self-regulated learning components of classroom academic performance. *Journal of Educational Psychology* 82: 33–40.

Pitman, B. 1999. *Presence of mind: Museums and the spirit of learning.* Washington, D.C.: American Association of Museums.

Poole, F. J. P. 1985. Coming into social being: Cultural images of infants in Bimin-Kuskusmin fold psychology. In *Person, self, and experience,* edited by G. White and J. Kirkpatrick. Berkeley and Los Angeles: University of California Press.

Porter, T., and B. Mikellides. 1976. *Colour for architecture.* London: Studio Vista.

Prentice, R., A. Davies, and A. Beeho. 1997. Seeking generic motivations for visiting and not visiting museums and like cultural attractions. *Museum Management and Curatorship* 6 (1): 45–70.

President's Commission on Americans Outdoors. 1986. *Report of the President's Commission on Americans Outdoors.* Washington, D.C.: U.S. Government Printing Office.

Prochaska, J. O., and C. C. DiClemente. 1986. Toward a comprehensive model of change. In *Treating addictive behaviors,* edited by W. R. Miller and N. Heather. Boston: Plenum.

Ramey-Gassert, L., H. J. Walberg III, and H. J. Walberg. 1994. Reexamining connections: Museums as science learning environments. *Science Education* 78 (4): 345–63.

Ravitch, D., and C. Finn Jr. 1987. *What do our seventeen-year-olds know? A report on the first national assessment of history and literature.* New York: Harper & Row.

Rennie, L. J., and T. P. McClafferty. 1995. Using visits to interactive science and technology centers, museums, aquaria, and zoos to promote learning in science. *Journal of Science Teacher Education* 6 (4): 175–85.

Resnick, L. B., and W. W. Ford. 1981. *The psychology of mathematics for instruction.* Hillsdale, N.J.: Erlbaum.

Ripley, D. 1978. *The sacred grove: Essays on museums.* Washington, D.C.: Smithsonian Institution Press.

Roberts, L. 1997. *From knowledge to narrative: Educators and the changing museum.* Washington, D.C.: Smithsonian Institution Press.

Robinson, J., and G. Godbey. 1997. *Time for life: The surprising ways Americans use their time.* University Park: Penn State Press.

Rogoff, B. 1990. *Apprenticeship in thinking: Cognitive development in social context.* New York: Oxford University Press.

———. 1996. Evaluating development in the process of participation: Theory, methods, and practice building on each other. In *Change and development: Issues of theory, application, and method,* edited by E. Amsel and A. Renninger. Hillsdale, N.J.: Erlbaum.

Rogoff, B., and J. Lave, eds. 1984. *Everyday cognition: Its development in social contexts.* Cambridge: Harvard University Press.

Rohrkemper, M., and L. Corno. 1988. Success and failure on classroom tasks: Adaptive learning and classroom teaching. *Elementary School Journal* 88: 297–312.

Roschelle, J. 1995. Learning in interactive environments: Prior knowledge and new experience. In *Public institutions for personal learning,* edited by J. H. Falk and L. D. Dierking, 37–51. Washington, D.C.: American Association of Museums.

Rose, S. 1993. *The making of memory: From molecules to mind.* New York: Anchor Books/Doubleday.

Rosenberg, M. 1979. *Conceiving the self.* New York: Basic Books.

Rosenfeld, S. 1979. The context of informal learning in zoos. *Roundtable Reports* 4 (2): 1–3, 15–16.

———. 1980. Informal education in zoos: Naturalistic studies of family groups. Ph.D. diss., University of California, Berkeley.

Rosenfield, I. 1990. *The invention of memory.* New York: Basic Books.

Rosenzweig, R., and D. Thelen,. 1998. *The presence of the past: Popular uses of history in American life.* New York: Columbia University Press.

Roth, W.-M., and A. Roychoudhury. 1992. The social construction of scientific concepts, or the concept map as conscription device and tool for social thinking in high school science. *Science Education* 65 (5): 531–57.

Rounds, J., ed. 1999. Making meaning in exhibits. *Exhibitionist* (Fall).

Rowe, M. B. 1974a. Wait-time and rewards as instructional variables, their influence on language, logic, and fate control: Part 1. Wait time. *Journal of Research in Science Teaching* 11: 81–94.

———. 1974b. Relation of wait-time and rewards to the development of language, logic, and fate control: Part 2. Rewards. *Journal of Research in Science Teaching* 11: 81–94.

Rubin, K. H. 1980. Fantasy play: Its role in the development of social skills and social cognition. *New Directions in Child Development* 9: 69–84.

Sachatello-Sawyer, B., and R. Fellenz. 1999. A national study of adult museum programs. Study funded by the U.S. Department of Education Field-Initiated Studies Program.

Said, T. 1999. America's promise and a place for museums. *Museum News* 78 (3): 40–45, 56–57.

Sakata, B. 1975 Toward lifelong learning. *Educational Perspectives,* December, 14.

Salmi, H. 1998. Motivation and meaningful science learning in informal settings. Paper presented at the annual meeting of the National Association for Research in Science Teaching, April, San Diego.

Saltz, R., and E. Saltz. 1986. Pretend play training and its outcomes. In *The young child at play: Reviews of research,*edited by G. Fein and M. Rivkin, 4:155–73. Washington, D.C.: National Association for the Education of Young Children.

Scardamalia, M., and C. Bereiter. 1991. Higher levels of agency for children in knowledge building: A challenge for the design of new knowledge media. *Journal of the Learning Sciences* 1: 37–68.

Schank, R. C., and R. P. Abelson. 1977. *Scripts, plans, goals, and understanding*. Hillsdale, N.J.: Erlbaum.

Schatz, D., and L. D. Dierking. 1999. Systemic change in science education reform: Pacific Science Center. *Journal of Museum Education* 23 (2): 22–24.

Schauble, L., and M. Gleason. 2000. What do adults need to effectively assist children's learning? Paper presented as part of a paper set, Museum Learning Collaborative: Studies of Learning from Museums, at the annual meeting of the American Educational Research Association, New Orleans.

Schauble, L., G. Leinhardt, and L. Martin. 1998. A framework for organizing a cumulative research agenda in informal learning contexts. *Journal of Museum Education* 22 (2 and 3): 3–8.

Schiefele, U. 1991. Interest, learning, and motivation. *Educational Psychologist* 26 (3–4): 299–323.

Schwartz, J. 1998. A search for the Net impact on human social life. *Washington Post* September 7, A3.

Schwarzer, M. 1999. Schizophrenic agora: Mission, market, and the multi-tasking museum. *Museum News* 78 (60): 41–47.

Screven, C. 1986. Exhibits and information centers: Some principles and approaches. *Curator* 29 (4): 109–37.

———. 1990. Uses of evaluation before, during, and after exhibit design. *ILVS Review: A Journal of Visitor Behavior* 1 (2): 33–66.

Scribner, S. 1976. Situating the experiment in cross-cultural research. In vol. 1 of *The developing individual in a changing world*, edited by K. F. Riegel and J. A. Meacham. Chicago: Aldine.

——— 1986. Thinking in action: Some characteristics of practical thought. In *Practical intelligence: Nature and origins of competence in the everyday world*, edited by R. J. Sternberg and R. K. Wagner, 13–30. Cambridge: Cambridge University Press.

Semper, R. 1997. Hybrid spaces, networked places: New media and museums. *Journal of Museum Education* 22 (1): 17–18.

Serrell, B. 1996. *Exhibit labels: An interpretive approach*. Walnut Creek, Calif.: AltaMira.

———. 1998. *Paying attention: Visitors and museum exhibitions*. Washington, D.C.: American Association of Museums.

Serrell, B., and Jennings, H. 1985. We are here: Three years of wayfinding studies at the Brookfield Zoo. In *Proceedings of the 1985 American Association of Zoological Parks and Aquariums*. Columbus, Ohio: American Association of Zoological Parks and Aquariums.

Shat, M., and R. Gelman. 1977. Beyond syntax: The influence of conversational constraints on speech modifications. In *Talking to children*, edited by C. E. Snow and C. A. Ferguson. Cambridge: Cambridge University Press.

Shaughnessy, J. M. 1985. Problem solving derailers: The influence of misconceptions on problem solving performance. In *Teaching and learning mathematical problem solving*, edited by E. A. Silver, 399–415. Hillsdale, N.J.: Erlbaum.

Shenk, D. 1997. *Data smog: Surviving the information glut.* New York: Harper-Collins.

Shepard, R. N., and L. A. Cooper. 1982. *Mental images and their transformations.* Cambridge: MIT Press.

Shweder, R. A. 1990. Cultural psychology: What is it? In *Cultural psychology: Essays on comparative human development,* edited by J. W. Stigler, R. A. Shweder, and G. Herdt, 1–43. Cambridge: Cambridge University Press.

Silverman, L. H. 1990. Of us and other "things": The content and function of talk by adult visitor pairs in an art and history museum. Ph.D. diss., University of Pennsylvania.

———. 1995. Visitor meaning-making in museums for a new age. *Curator* 38 (3): 161–70.

———. 1999. Meaning-making matters: Communication, consequences, and exhibit design. *Exhibitionist* 18 (2): 9–14.

Silverman, L. H., L. C. Roberts, D. Perry, and K. Morrissey. 1996. "If we build it . . .": Toward a doctoral program in museology. *Curator* 39 (4): 234–37.

Smith, I. D., and J. Barnes. 1985. Multidimensional self-concepts: Relations with sex and academic achievement. *Journal of Educational Psychology* 77: 581–96.

Smith, J. K., L. F. Wolf, and S. P. Starodubtsev. 1995. Cross-cultural learning in two art museums: The Poushkin and the Metropolitan. *Current Trends in Audience Research and Evaluation* (CARE, American Association of Museums) 8: 75–78.

Snow Dockser, L. 1987a. Parent–child interaction in a children's museum: The inter-related dynamics of the informal learning environment. Paper presented at the Seventeenth Annual Symposium of the Jean Piaget Society.

———. 1987b. Family interviews in a play exhibit. *Journal of Museum Education* 12 (1): 17–18.

———. 1989. Mothers in children's museums: A neglected dynamic. Ph.D. diss., University of Pennsylvania.

Sommer, R., and H. Olsen. 1980. The soft classroom. *Environment and Behavior* 12: 3–16.

Sotto, E. 1994. *When teaching becomes learning: A theory and practice of teaching.* London: Cassell.

Spock, M., and H. J. Leichter. 1999. Learning from ourselves: Pivotal stories of museum professionals. In *Bridges to understanding childrens museums,* edited by N. F. Gibans, 41–82. Cleveland, Ohio: Mandel Center for Nonprofit Organizations, Case Western Reserve University.

Spohrer, J. C., E. Soloway, and E. Pope. 1989. A goal/plan analysis of buggy Pascal prgrams. In *Studying the novice programmer,* edited by E. Soloway and J. C. Spohrer, 355–99. Hillsdale, N.J.: Erlbaum.

St. John, M. 1991. *First-hand learning: Teacher education in science museums.* Washington, D.C.: Association of Science-Technology Centers.

St. John, M., and D. Perry. 1993. A framework for evaluation and research: Science, infrastructure, and relationships. In *Museum visitor studies in the '90s,* edited by S. Bicknell and G. Farmelo, 59–66. London: Science Museum.

Stainton, C. 2000. Voices and images: Connections between identity and art. Paper presented as part of a paper set, Museum Learning Collaborative: Studies of

Learning from Museums, at the annual meeting of the American Educational Research Association, New Orleans.

Stanton, J. C. 1994. Museum exhibitions: The development and application of a cyclic evaluation model. Master's thesis, University of Melbourne.

Sternberg, R. J. 1985. *Beyond IQ: A triarchic theory of human intelligence.* New York: Cambridge University Press.

———. 1990. *Metaphors of mind.* New York: Cambridge University Press.

Sternberg , R. J., and R. K. Wagner, eds. 1986. *Practical intelligence: Nature and origins of competence in the everyday world.* Cambridge: Cambridge University Press.

Stevenson, J. 1991. The long-term impact of interactive exhibits. *International Journal of Science Education* 13 (5): 521–31.

Strike, K. A., and G. J. Posner. 1985. A conceptual change view of learning and understanding. In *Cognitive structure and conceptual change,* edited by L. H. T. West and A. L. Pines. New York: Academic Press.

Suedfeld, P. 1980. *Restricted environmental stimulation.* New York: Wiley.

Sundstrom, E. 1986. *Workplaces.* New York: Cambridge University Press.

Sylwester, R. 1995. *In celebration of neurons.* Alexandria, Va.: Association for Supervision and Curriculum Development.

Szalai, A. 1972. *The use of time.* The Hague, Netherlands: Mouton.

Talbot, J. F., R. Kaplan, F. E. Kuo, and S. Kaplan. 1993. Factors that enhance effectiveness of visitor maps. *Environment and Behavior* 25 (6): 743–60.

Taylor, R. B. 1988. *Cultural ways: A concise introduction to cultural anthropology.* Prospect Heights, Ill.: Waveland Press.

Taylor, S. 1986. Family behavior at the Steinhart Aquarium. Ph.D. diss., University of California, Berkeley.

———, ed. 1991. *Try it! Improving exhibits through formative evaluation.* Washington, D.C.: Association of Science-Technology Centers.

Teversky, A., and D. Kahneman. 1982. Judgement under uncertainty: Heuristics and biases. In *Judgement under uncertainty: Heuristics and biases,* edited by D. Kahneman, P. Slovic, and A. Teversky, 3–20. Cambridge: Cambridge University Press.

Tharp, R. G., and R. Gallimore. 1988. *Rousing minds to life: Teaching, learning, and schooling in social context.* Cambridge: Cambridge University Press.

Thelen, D. 1989. Memory and American history. *Journal of American History* 75 (4): 17–29.

Thorndike, E. L. 1923. The influence of first-year Latin upon the ability to read English. *School Sociology* 17: 165–68.

Thorndike, E. L., and R. S. Woodworth. 1901. The influence of improvement in one mental function upon the efficiency of other functions. *Psychological Review* 8: 247–61.

Tisdal, C., and J. Gang. 1994. *Cosmic carnival: All the wonders of the universe.* St. Louis, Mo.: St. Louis Science Center.

Trescott, J. 1998. Exhibiting a new enthusiasm: Across U.S., museum construction, attendance are on the rise. *Washington Post,* June 21, A1.

Tribe, J. 1995. *The economics of leisure and tourism.* Oxford, England: Butterworth-Heinemann.

Trowbridge, D. E., and L. C. McDermott. 1980. Investigation of student understanding of acceleration in one dimension. *American Journal of Physics* 50: 242–53.

Tuckey, C. J. 1992. Schoolchildren's reactions to an interactive science center. *Curator* 35 (1): 28–38.

Tunnicliffe, S. D. 1995. Talking about animals: Studies of young children visiting zoos, a museum, and a farm. Ph.D. diss., King's College, London.

———. 1996. The relationship between pupil's age and the content of conversations generated at three types of animal exhibits. *Research in Science Education* 26 (4): 461–80.

Tulley, A., and A. M. Lucas. 1991. Interacting with a science museum exhibit: Vicarious and direct experience and subsequent understanding. *International Journal of Science Education* 13: 533–42.

U.S. Bureau of the Census. 1996. *Statistical abstracts of the United States, 1996.* Washington, D.C.: U.S. Government Printing Office.

U.S. Department of Commerce. 1977. *The information economy.* Washington, D.C.: U.S. Government Printing Office.

———. 1996. *Population projections of the U.S. by age, sex, race, and Hispanic origin: 1995 to 2050.* Washington, D.C.: U.S. Government Printing Office.

VanLehn, K. 1989. *Mind bugs: The origins of procedural misconceptions.* Cambridge: MIT Press.

Velez-Ibanez, C. G. 1988. Networks of exchange among Mexicans in the U.S. and Mexico: Local mediating responses to national and international transformations. *Urban Anthropology* 17 (1): 27–51.

Vygotsky, L. S. [1930, 1933, 1935] 1978. *Mind in society: The development of higher mental processes.* Edited by M. Cole, V. John-Steiner, S. Scribner, and E. Souberman. Reprint, Cambridge: Harvard University Press.

———. 1979. Consciousness as a problem in the psychology of behavior. *Soviet Psychology* 17 (4): 3–35.

Wachs, T., and G. Gruen. 1982. *Everyday experience and human development.* New York: Plenum.

Weiner, B., ed. 1974. *Achievement motivation and attribution theory.* Morristown, N.J.: General Learning Press.

———. 1987. *An attributional theory of motivation and emotion.* New York: Springer-Verlag.

Weissner, P. 1982. Risk, reciprocity, and social influences on !Kung San economics. In *Politics and history in band societies,* edited by E. Leacock and R. B. Lee. Cambridge: Cambridge University Press.

Wellman, H. M., and S. C. Somerville. 1980. Quasi-naturalistic tasks in the study of cognition: The memory-related skills of toddlers. *New Directions for Child Development* 49: 1–12.

Wells, G. 1992. The centrality of talk in education. In *Thinking voices: The work of the national oracy project,* edited by K. Norman. London: Hodder & Stoughton.

Wertsch, J. V. 1985. *Vygotsky and the social formation of the mind.* Cambridge: Harvard University Press.

———. 1986. *Mind in context: A Vygotskyian approach.* Paper presented at the American Educational Research Association meeting, San Francisco.

———. 1997. Narrative tools of history and identity. *Culture and Psychology* 3 (1): 5–20.

West, L. H. T., and A. L. Pines, eds. 1985. *Cognitive structure and conceptual change.* New York: Academic Press.

White, R. W. 1959. Motivation reconsidered: The concept of competence. *Psychological Review* 66: 297–333.

Wicker, A. W. 1979. *An introduction to ecological psychology.* Monterey, Calif.: Brooks/Cole.

Wierzbicka, A. 1986. Human emotions: Universal or culture specific? *American Anthropologist* 88: 313–28.

Wiser, M., and S. Carey. 1983. *When heat and temperature were only one.* In *Mental models,* edited by D. Gentner and A. L. Stevens, 267–97. Hillsdale, N.J.: Erlbaum.

Wolf, R., and B. L. Tymitz. 1979. *Do giraffes ever sit? A study of visitor perceptions at the National Zoological Park.* Washington, D.C.: Smithsonian Institution Press.

Wolins, I. S., N. Jensen, and R. Ulzheimer. 1992. Children's memories of museum field trips: A qualitative study. *Journal of Museum Education* 17 (2): 17–27.

Youniss, J. 1975. Another perspective on social cognition. In *Minnesota symposia on child psychology,* edited by A. Pick, 9: 173–93. Minneapolis: University of Minnesota Press.

Zimmer, C. 1995. First cell. *Discover* 16 (11): 70–78.

Index

265

About the Authors

JOHN H. FALK is currently director of the Institute for Learning Innovation, a nonprofit research and development organization in Annapolis, Maryland. Before founding and directing the institute, he worked at the Smithsonian Institution for fourteen years, holding a number of senior positions, including special assistant to the assistant secretary for research; director, Smithsonian Office of Educational Research; and associate director for education, Chesapeake Bay Center for Environmental Studies. He holds a joint doctorate in biology and education from the University of California, Berkeley. He is internationally known for his research on free-choice learning and is the author of more than sixty scholarly articles in the areas of learning, biology, and education, as well as numerous educational materials and books. He is coauthor with Lynn Dierking of *The Museum Experience* (1992) and coeditor with her of *Public Institutions for Personal Learning: Establishing a Research Agenda* (1995). His research priorities include learning in free-choice settings (with particular expertise in museums), the long-term impact of free-choice learning institutions on individuals and communities, and minority attendance trends at cultural institutions and in other leisure activities.

LYNN D. DIERKING is associate director of the Institute for Learning Innovation, Annapolis, Maryland, and has been a faculty member in the University of Maryland's College of Education, an associate in the Smithsonian Office of Educational Research, and a museum educator. She has also coordinated a Maryland-based community partnership program and was director of the *Science in American Life* Curriculum Project, a national middle school curriculum development effort, at the Smithsonian's National Museum of American History. She holds a Ph.D. in science education

271

from the University of Florida, Gainesville. She is internationally recognized for her research on the behavior and learning of children, families, and adults in free-choice learning settings and has published extensively in these areas, including a book, *Questioning Assumptions: An Introduction to Front-End Studies in Museums* (1998), written with Wendy Pollock. Her research priorities include learning in diverse settings (with particular emphasis on museums), the long-term impact of free-choice learning experiences on individuals and families, and the development and evaluation of community-based programs.